Identity
CRISIS

JIM HARPER

Identity
CRISIS

How Identification Is Overused
and Misunderstood

CATO
INSTITUTE
WASHINGTON, D.C.

Library of Congress Cataloging-in-Publication Data

Harper, Jim, 1967–
   Identity crisis : how identification is overused and misunderstood / Jim
Harper.
      p. cm.
   Includes bibliographical references and index.
   ISBN 1-930865-84-8 (cloth) — ISBN 1-930865-85-6 (paper)   1. Privacy, Right of—
United States.   2. Identification—United States.   I. Title.

JC596.2.U5H37 2006
323.44'8—dc22   2006040557

Cover design by Jon Meyers.
Printed in the United States of America.

CATO INSTITUTE
1000 Massachusetts Ave., N.W.
Washington, D.C. 20001
www.cato.org

Contents

CONTENTS

1. Introduction

Take a moment to appreciate the air. So good is the air around us. It holds the oxygen we carry into our lungs. It disperses the carbon dioxide we produce. When we vibrate the air just so, the vibrations reach other people's ears as sounds, and they can hear us. Common, ordinary air has so many ingenious uses.

All is not sweetness and light with air, of course. It transports smoke and bad smells sometimes. Some pollutants in air can do us harm. Scientists are studying these things and, as sure as the passage of time, we will know more about what is good to have in air, what is bad, and what are matters of indifference.

Now consider something just as essential for living as air, and nearly as ubiquitous. It is something you use every day, many times a day, for your good purposes. The people you see use it for theirs. You probably think no more of it than you think of breathing most of the time, but if you stopped you would die just as certainly as if you stopped inhaling sweet, sustaining air.

Air is a tangible thing. This is not a thing like air, though. This is a process. It is the process of identification.

We all know that air is made of constituent gases like nitrogen, oxygen, and carbon dioxide. Do we know what identification is made of?

We have a pretty good idea of the difference between good air and bad air. Usually, we can tell the difference by smell. Where our senses fail us, science, again, is constantly studying the health effects of the things we might breathe.

Is similar work being done to figure out when identification is good or bad for us? Not very much. To the extent there is debate about identification, it tends to operate on gut instinct and slogan: "No to national ID!" "Identification is essential in this age of terrorism." We can do better.

The identification policies of the past are being tested by the dawning of the Information Age. If you are unsure of what the

1

"identification policies of the past" have been, that is for good reason. Identification has rarely been a subject of articulated policy or policies. It has just happened. This essential economic and social process, a key part of human development through the millennia, is something not many people have thought much about.

We are at the dawn of the Information Age, and life is changing. Identification is changing. Advances in communications over the last few decades, and the rise of large institutions in the last few centuries, mean that different actors are identifying one another for new and different reasons. They are doing so in new and different ways, with new and different consequences.

Yet identification policies to meet those challenges have been developed strictly ad hoc. Each new challenge in identification— each new method and each new reason for identifying people—has been just tacked onto past practice, unconsidered. This is the policy-development equivalent of auto repair by electrical tape and baling wire. Now is the time for some discussion of identification policy as policy, instead of something we all just do and have done to us.

The starting point is identification theory. Despite its importance, there is a dearth of theoretical explanation for identification: what it is and how it works. Ask yourself the next time you see a friend or loved one: How do I know who this is? Identification theory provides the answers. Four categories of identifiers help us sort among one another and organize the mental "files" we all keep on one another. Individuals and institutions use different kinds and qualities of identifiers that vary with the myriad purposes of identification.

Considering how readily we use it, identification is an extremely complex process. If often unconsciously, verifiers use sophisticated risk management techniques to identify people efficiently, demanding just enough identity information—and no more than is necessary—for each transaction. Identification systems ride on top of one another to further increase the efficiency with which people are identified.

It is only half the battle to know what identification is. The purposes of identification—its role in transactions and its effects on people—are just as important. Like identification processes, the consequences of identification have gone largely unconsidered. Few people know what identification does and what it does not do. Few

2

people know when it works and when it fails. This lack of knowledge hinders our ability to use it wisely and to set the most appropriate identification policies.

Identification is a sort of economic and social glue. It is there at the start of every relationship—between individuals, among businesses and people, between governments and subjects—and it is there at the continuation of every such relationship. Just as it brings people together for good purposes, identification holds people together when things go badly. Identification ensures that the right person— the right physical body—is held accountable for bad acts.

Identification is almost always conjoined with record keeping of some sort. Records organized by identity allow information to be used in deciding whether a person is pleasant company, financially sound, wanted by law enforcement, permitted to enter a building, or whatever the case may be.

All organized record-keeping systems amount to surveillance systems of one kind or another. They can be used for good or for bad. Surveillance allows companies to provide consumers better service and lower prices—or to harass them with junk communications. Surveillance puts government agents in a position to capture terrorists—or to intimidate dissenters.

Whatever the use, it is important to know that most formal demands for identification are either the front end of a surveillance system or the groundwork for the surveillance system that will be needed to make that identification requirement serve a purpose.

For good reasons, our culture and laws protect and prize anonymity—the withholding of identity information. When anonymity is the default rule, it puts individuals in a position to structure their relationships and lives as they wish, rather than having attachments imposed on them. Anonymity protects particular prized behaviors like free speech, dissent, and nonconformity.

Identification cards sit at the "top of the heap" of identification processes and at the center of identification policy debates. An identification card is best conceived as a communications device that carries information from a person, through a card-issuing intermediary, to a verifier. It allows a person to be treated as "known" on a first encounter.

Identification cards are at once ingenious and quite fallible. This communication chain contains many weaknesses; and a raft of recent public policy changes aims to shore up government-issued identification cards.

Some policymakers are laying heavy bets on identification. The REAL ID Act, passed by the U.S. Congress in 2005, is a clear example. These bets will deeply influence our social system and our personal and national security. The proponents of uniform identification systems and national identification are betting in our names (literally) that they can solve complex social, economic, and security problems with this tool. Don't be too sure.

Life is changing on Planet Earth. Because of the rapid growth of digital communications, computing, and data storage technologies, the dominant motif of the modern era is the decline of practical obscurity. For millennia, most information about people has been hard to come by. In 1950, you would have had a hard time knowing where you had lunch on November 7 of the previous year. Imagine trying in 1850 to retrieve the text of a letter you had written and sent in 1849. Today, your calendar and e-mails from last year are close at hand. Information like this is not just available to you, but to many others as well.

Indeed, more information about people is more available and useful to more people and institutions than ever. And the trend is continuing. It is easy to overhype the decline of practical obscurity as a pure negative. It is not. Along with concerns and harms, declining obscurity comes with many benefits. But it is a big change in the context of our lives and the structure of society that we must carefully consider and control. Identification policy is central to doing that.

Modern identification systems and techniques are naturally expanding the use of surveillance and increasing the use of dossiers. That use benefits us in many ways, but it also threatens a society in which the request for "your papers, please"—even if in digital form—is a dominant theme.

In very recent history, authoritarian governments in many countries have used identification systems to administer sometimes horrific programs. Uniform identification systems permitted totalitarian governments like the Soviet Union and Nazi Germany to administer their monstrosities very efficiently.

The costs of too uniform identification systems are not just paid by historical victims of collectivism, war, and strife. Residents of peaceful and stable countries like the present-day United States pay a price as well: identity fraudsters ply their trade using the essentially insecure identification policies and systems that we have backed into, without reflection, during the last 70 years.

A diverse identification system would at once protect against identity fraud, give people more autonomy and liberty, and act as a fail-safe against broken democracy. Rather than a uniform government-created and -mandated identification system, different organizations and institutions should offer identification and credentialing services using a wide variety of techniques and methods, each suited to a particular purpose.

The way forward for identification policy is not easy, but the policies to pursue are essentially these: Identification should be used less, by businesses and governments alike. It has fewer benefits than we often assume and higher costs with each passing year. Nonidentifying authorization should be preferred when it can be used—and this is often the case. Finally, we should recognize that identification and credentialing are a valuable economic process, just like communications, payments, and credit reporting. A diverse, competitive identification and credentialing industry would be far better, and far more protective of liberty, than the uniform, government-monopolized identification system on the advance today.

As we explore these topics, we will venture into many current controversies, such as the United States' national identification system, as extended by the REAL ID Act. Congress passed the act as a nominal response to the terror attacks of September 11, 2001, prompted by the 2004 report of the National Commission on Terrorist Attacks Upon the United States. The law federalized the rules for state-issued identification cards. Under REAL ID, any state-issued identification card that does not comply with the act cannot be used to access federal facilities, to board commercial aircraft, to enter nuclear power plants, or for any other purposes that the secretary of homeland security determines. Though issued by states, the REAL ID is a national identification system that, as a practical matter, is required for all Americans.

We will examine the modern crime of identity fraud and its roots in identification policy. Identity fraud is the use of another person's identity to defraud people and institutions out of money, goods, and services. Police agencies have been lackadaisical about pursuing this crime, and the U.S. Congress has sown confusion about it. In the Identity Theft and Assumption Deterrence Act, Congress branded it

5

with its popular but inaccurate name, "identity theft," and defined the crime so broadly that all kinds of different frauds are captured within one definition. With the limited set of identifiers used in the financial services system, U.S. identification processes are economically efficient but insecure for individuals. Identity fraud is one of the results.

A solution often put forward is to regulate the use of the Social Security number. Because the U.S. government assigns them, many people are urging the government to prevent certain otherwise lawful uses of Social Security numbers. But the Social Security number is most people's financial name. Regulation of entire identifiers is a strange exercise of government authority that could have unusual and unpleasant consequences. And, of course, it would be obeyed only by the lawful—not by the lawbreakers that commit identity fraud. Better for the government to lead the way: stop using the Social Security number as a uniform identifier itself. The deft solution is to get governments at all levels to take their thumbs off the uniform-identification side of the scale.

We will come to better understand surveillance—in both its acceptable and unacceptable forms. In its nonpejorative sense, "surveillance" is just "watching over." When we watch one another, and record and share our observations, we make and mold the society we live in. When businesses know what people are like, what they want, and when they want it, this surveillance puts them in a position to serve people in the best ways they can find. But many people dislike corporate surveillance. Even more do they dislike government surveillance of the kind that would have been needed for the Defense Department's ill-fated Total Information Awareness program. Identification is, at its heart, a surveillance tool.

And we will study terrorism. We will examine again what happened on 9/11, with a special focus on the role of identification. We will look at the Oklahoma City bombing of 1995. Identification was involved in both of those horrible attacks—as it is everywhere—but, contrary to popular belief, false identification had no central role in those terror attacks on U.S. soil.

We will examine risk management and apply it to the terrorism context. We will learn more about what it takes to prevent terror attacks or control their consequences.

6

Our exploration of the world of identification will take us on travels through history, literature, TV, and the movies. Hopefully, this will make a more engaging book.

Some may find this book quite basic. It spends more time on identification theory and principles than on cutting-edge technologies and this year's policy fights. Others may find it weighted down with identification jargon. This is unfortunate, but perhaps it goes with the territory. We have not yet a settled language that we use to talk about all the different concepts: identification, authorization, "verifiers," and so on. In short, this book sits uncomfortably between futuristic "digital identity management" and the basic introduction to identification theory and policy that many people need.

Identification is an area of information policy that deserves a great deal more attention from social scientists, anthropologists, risk managers, policymakers, and others. Currently, we understand it about as well as the alchemists of long ago understood the air. By examining it more closely, like scientists study the constituent gases all around us, we can understand how facts combine to make identities. Like the oxygen in air combines with fuel and heat to make fire, we must learn how to capture identification and use its power without getting burned.

This book is a snapshot. The theory and concept of identification are only on their first baby steps. Many of the stories are contemporary, and they will grow stale. Many of the policies discussed here are recent, and they will change. Nothing would be more gratifying than to pick up this book in 20 years to find that the ideas and challenges in it are dated, obvious, and quaint. The alternative is a world where, even more than today, identification is overused and misunderstood.

PART I

IDENTIFICATION

2. Understanding Identification

Think about the last time you saw your next-door neighbor. It might have been in front of your house or apartment, or maybe at the local store. Did you stop to talk? Did you want to? Did you mean it when you said, "Good to see you again"? How did you know it was your neighbor?

Most of these questions are easy to answer. Perhaps a little tougher to answer honestly. . . . But that last question—How did you know it was your neighbor?—is an odd one. You could answer any number of ways: "I just knew," or "I recognized her," or "I'm the head of the community association." These are all decent answers, but they are incomplete.

How do people know other people? What allows us to connect memories and information, good feelings or bad ones, to other people? How do we know enough about other people to call them friends? How do other people know us? How do banks know enough about us to loan us money?

A big part of the answer is *identification*.

Identification is so embedded in our daily interactions that people rarely give it much thought, but it is an essential social and economic process. Identification is a part of nearly every meaningful encounter among people. It is a part of every sophisticated commercial and legal transaction. It is part of most every contact between a government and citizens. It is even an essential part of encounters among animals.

Imagine for a moment a world without identification, a world in which you could not recognize people and they could not recognize you. It would take extraordinary effort to meet our human needs, both physical and emotional.

Organized production would break down. Each day would be a sort of Groundhog Day for workers who did not recognize one another. They would all feel like it was the first day on the job as they searched for "new" collaborators on projects.

Home life and social life would be alien and bizarre. People would have to introduce themselves to new "friends" and family members each time they saw one another. Love relationships would range from short and shallow to nonexistent. People would occupy all of their time with getting acquainted rather than creating deep and lasting bonds. Life would be insecure because every person met on the street or entering the home would be a stranger—perhaps a serial killer, perhaps a sibling.

This silly mind game illustrates how integral identification is to our lives and livelihoods. It is a natural and necessary process for all kinds of social interactions, for productive enterprise, and for personal security.

From before the time of the first human family and clan, people have needed to know with whom they are interacting. Without identification, primordial humans would not have known how to distinguish friends and family members from outside raiders and cannibals. In modern times, identification helps people and institutions find each other, communicate with each other, transact, and hold each other accountable.

Although identification is deeply innate and incredibly important, it is by no means simple. In fact, identification is a very complex process. By parsing identification and looking at all its components, we can better understand how our society and economy work. We can understand more fully the consequences of identification. We can determine when it is good to be identified and when it might be bad. We can better determine what public policies surrounding identification promote the interests we most want to protect.

The words that describe the complex process of identification can be quite confusing. For example, the words "identifier," "identity," and "identification" all sound similar, and they share the same Latin root, but each has a distinct meaning in identification theory. It is important to distinguish among them and to use them carefully.

Identifiers

The building blocks of identification are "identifiers." Identifiers are facts that distinguish people and entities from one another. What we often call a "characteristic" or an "attribute" becomes an identifier when it is used for sorting and organizing people and institutions in our thoughts and records.

For example, an attribute of a person named Thomas is the fact that his name is "Thomas." Thomas may have other characteristics or attributes, such as his owning a T-shirt, but his name will be more commonly used as an identifier. Indeed, names exist to be identifiers.

A T-shirt is unlikely to be used as an identifier very often, though it can be. In a remote village of sub-Saharan Africa or high in the Himalayas, for example, ownership of a T-shirt may be a distinguishing characteristic and thus a useful identifier. People might call Thomas "the guy with the T-shirt." Wearing a bright blue ascot in such a place might be an extremely distinct attribute and thus a worthy identifier. Perhaps there, as in most places, it would earn the effete Thomas a punch in the stomach.

So identifiers are facts used to sort and categorize people and entities from one another. Although there are many different kinds, identifiers have traditionally been grouped into three categories: something you are, something you know, and something you have.[1] An additional category—something you are assigned—is sufficiently distinct from the others to be treated separately. These categories are not hermetically sealed from one another, but they are a helpful way of organizing the world of identifiers. Each of the next four chapters examines these categories of identifiers more carefully.

"Something-you-are" identifiers are characteristics that are inherent in a person or attached to his or her physical body. They include hair color, fingerprints, DNA, voice, signature, and other biometrics.

"Something-you-are-assigned" identifiers include names, titles, numbers, and addresses. These identifiers are socially defined. That is, they exist because of traditions in human societies that define and organize people, places, statuses, times, and so on. These identifiers are associated with people but not inherent or attached.

"Something you know" is the characteristic of having some distinct knowledge—usually knowledge that few others have. Common examples of something-you-know identifiers include knowledge of passwords and mothers' maiden names.

Finally, a "something-you-have" identifier is the characteristic of possessing some distinct item. Identification cards are the most common example. Something-you-have identifiers are often called "tokens" because there are many examples beyond cards. In the future, something-you-have identifiers may take many forms and use many different technologies.

Different identifiers have different qualities. Some identifiers are fixed to a person—or at least they are likely to stay fixed—for life, such as the fingerprint or mother's maiden name. Others are transient and exist only for a few moments, such as "bending over tying his shoe." Some identifiers are unique to each individual (DNA), whereas others are quite commonplace (brown hair). Of course, rare and unique identifiers are more powerful, more consequential, and more interesting. The quality of identifiers along the vectors of fixity, distinctiveness, and permanence helps determine how they are best used and how useful they are.

On "Identity"

GEORGE: *Ah you have no idea of the magnitude of this thing. If she is allowed to infiltrate this world, then George Costanza as you know him, ceases to exist! You see, right now, I have Relationship George, but there is also Independent George. That's the George you know, the George you grew up with—Movie George, Coffee Shop George, Liar George, Bawdy George.*

JERRY: *I, I love that George.*

GEORGE: *Me too! And he's dying, Jerry! If Relationship George walks through this door, he will kill Independent George! A George divided against itself cannot stand!*

— George Costanza, on the budding friendship between his friends and his fiancée. *Seinfeld* episode 118, "The Pool Boy" (first aired November 16, 1995).

Most people think their "identity" and their personality are pretty much the same, and most people think it is normal to have just one. Having multiple personalities may be a psychological disorder, but it is not at all unusual to have multiple identities.

Your parents know one of your identities. It started with your appearance at birth and continued with the name they

(continued next page)

(continued)

gave you, the nickname they called you by, the sound of your voice, the way you walk, and thousands of other things.

Your insurance company knows quite a different identity of yours. It knows you by your last name, (comma), first name, and middle initial; by your address; by your phone number; by your Social Security number; and so on.

Your "identities," it turns out, are collections of information that other people and institutions have about you, collections that they use to distinguish you from other people in their minds or records. People have financial identities, online identities, relationship identities, work identities, and nightlife identities.

Using multiple identities, we help control who knows what about us and how they know it. Having multiple identities is part of having a single, whole, healthy personality. As we learned from *Seinfeld*'s George Costanza, losing control of one's separate identities can be very disconcerting.

Identification and Authentication

"Identification" occurs when one person or entity compares the identifiers of another with a set of identifiers that he or she has previously recorded and finds a match between the two. The person making the identification, called the "verifier," can then summon information and memories about the identified party. Identification allows a relationship to pick up where it previously left off—with anything from a conversation about last weekend's symphony performance, to a transfer of millions of dollars, to interrogation or arrest.

Identification happens so automatically among people that we rarely think of it, but when we walk down the street, we quickly and automatically scan the characteristics (identifiers) of people we see and check them against the identifiers of people we know. The result is that we recognize our friends and pick them out to say hi to.

It is a bit pedantic to parse interpersonal identification so carefully, of course. But these same processes are performed by large institutions, which cannot see or hear, and by people who are interacting remotely. They also cannot see or hear one another in the ways they are used to. In these instances, identification is not nearly as innate and natural. We can learn from natural identification how designed identification processes should work.

Modern times are changing identification. The growth in size and complexity of institutions, such as governments and corporations, presents new challenges for identification. In the past, local government officials and sales clerks may have known most local residents and customers. Today, an impersonal institution cannot eyeball you and know who you are. To know you, if they must, they have to get a little bit "personal."

Likewise, the growth of remote communications—the Internet, in particular—has changed the way people identify one another. We cannot see each other when we interact online and e-merchants cannot see us. False identification and authorization are substantial and growing criminal tools. The wonderful economic and social benefits of remote communication and commerce come with serious challenges for identification compared with the natural, instinctual methods of identification used in the past.

A discrete step in many online transactions is often called "authentication." An example of authentication is the use of a pass code in a username–pass code combination: The username identifies and the pass code authenticates. Although the use of the word "authentication" makes the process sound new, it is just a distinct part of a new way of identification.

A semantic difference between the words "identification" and "authentication" reveals an important point, however: Identification connotes a personal transaction in which there is nearly perfect accuracy. When was the last time you didn't recognize your sister? Authentication, on the other hand, admits to a risk that a comparison might be inaccurate. When we check to see if something is "authentic," we review its provenance, like an old painting, doing our best to ensure it is what it is claimed to be. We can never be certain because hundreds of years have elapsed since the painter's hand touched the canvas. No one alive can bear witness to the painting's authorship. But we are sure enough to go forward.

When people are in the same room, absolute identification is automatic, cheap, and easy, but identification remains very inconvenient and expensive in remote and institutional transactions. Institutional and remote identification work within reasonable tolerances to be "sure enough" that someone or something is what it claims to be. When organizations choose sets of identifiers, they do so to minimize the risk of inauthenticity—not to achieve absolutely perfect identification. In that sense, they "authenticate" rather than identify, but we will use the terms "identify" and "identification" in this book, exploring the integrity of identification processes in chapter 8.

Authorization

Individuals and institutions are constantly deciding whether transactions or interactions will go forward. They decide whether to take phone calls, for example, whether other people can enter their buildings, whether a person gets a handshake or a kiss, whether to accept a check, a credit card, or insist on cash. They base these decisions on the characteristics of the other party. Is the person's credit good? Is the person attractive? Does the person have a lawful purpose? Is it a salesperson or a spouse? "Authorization" is what we will call it when someone decides that a transaction or interaction can go forward.

Many people probably assume that automated teller machines (ATMs) use identification. After all, they dispense money from real people's checking accounts, and it is pretty important to give money to the right person. But most of today's ATMs, which use cards and pass codes (often wrongly called PINs or personal identification numbers), are actually using nonidentifying authorization. Anyone who has a properly issued ATM card and who knows the associated pass code is authorized by the bank's system to withdraw money and perform other transactions—regardless of his or her identity. Of course, the user of a card and pass code is usually the person to whom it was issued, but an ATM user does not prove his or her identity to take out money. This is based on intelligent and efficient balancing of the costs of identifying ATM users against the risks of fraud, topics covered in later chapters.

Often, though, identity is the factor on which authorization hinges. A family gives unrestricted access to their home only to particular people. Only certain corporate officers may sign checks over $10,000. In these cases, benefits or powers are available only to particular individuals. Their identity determines whether a transaction can go forward. Identity is the key characteristic in many authorizations, but not all of them. Identification is a tool often used in authorization but authorization can occur without identification. We will return to this point several times in this book.

Piggybacking

A common technique that brings tremendous efficiency to identification processes is "piggybacking." Identification systems commonly ride on top of one another: a person's having been identified by one person or institution is accepted as suitable identification by another person or institution. The second institution may then assign an identifier that is accepted by successors as sufficient identification, and so on.

At a party, for example, a person might introduce his friend Morgan to another friend and point out that Morgan is an economist. After talking for a while, Morgan's new acquaintance might introduce her to a third person, calling her "Morgan, the economist." This latter introduction has piggybacked on the prior one and created a new moniker (identifier) for the increasingly popular Morgan.

The next day, when Morgan's two new acquaintances meet for breakfast, they might identify her as "Morgan, the economist." They will have adopted this identifier for Morgan relying entirely on the knowledge of Morgan that came from her friend, who has not yet shown up for breakfast.

Piggybacking is natural and necessary, obviously, and it has only good consequences in a simple social environment like a party. However, piggybacking is regularly and increasingly exploited for fraudulent purposes. A fraudster may procure one false identification card, use it to get another one, use that to get a third, and then open financial accounts under this entirely manufactured identity, using highly credible identification documents.

Banks, credit card issuers, and other financial services providers are deeply engaged in solving the challenge of manufactured or fraudulently used identification. The solutions are not easy. Chapter 22 discusses one root of the problem in uniform financial identification systems. An important solution is to use diverse identification systems, as discussed in chapter 25.

Multifactor Identification

Institutions use a number of techniques to lower the risk of dealing with the wrong person. One such technique is "multifactor" identification or authorization. This is the use of identifiers from more than one category.

A simple walk through the probabilities shows why multifactor identification makes sense. If you are looking in a packed football stadium for someone and know only that the person has brown eyes (something you are), the chance of finding the wrong person is fairly high. If, in addition, you know that the person is carrying a book (something you have), the chance of misidentification drops pretty sharply. If you look further for someone who can recite a secret code (something you know), your chance of a correct identification is almost ensured. Multifactor identification reduces the risk of error and misidentification.

Identification Cards

Identification cards, documents, or tokens are the most sophisticated identification tools, sweeping in all of the most interesting processes and challenges of identification. They are a something-you-have identifier, obviously. But by embedding information about the bearer (something you are) or secret code information (something you know) for comparison, they become multifactor identification tools.

When they work, identification cards or tokens provide one-stop, instant identification, which is very useful, efficient, and necessary in some cases. They allow people to be treated as "known" even at a first encounter. Putting aside for now when identification is actually needed, a key question is what makes an identification card work and what allows it to fail.

An identification card or token is probably best considered a communication device. It communicates identity information through the medium of some trusted third party. This communication chain has three steps, each of which can be breached. The three steps in the identification card communication chain are subject-to-issuer, issuer-to-verifier, and verifier check:

- First, the subject of the identification document communicates information about him- or herself to the issuer and, the issuer puts this information on the card or token (subject-to-issuer).
- Second, the card or token communicates information about the person to the verifier (issuer-to-verifier).

- Third, the verifier checks the identifiers on the card or token against the subject, verifying that the identifiers embedded in the document match the identifiers of the person presenting it (verifier check).

Each step is a point of weakness in the communication chain. In the first step, the subject may provide false information and the issuer may not check its veracity. In the second step, the document or token may be modified or forged so that the information it conveys is false. In the third step, the verifier may not carefully compare the identifiers embedded in the document with the person presenting it, meaning that the information, although accurate, is not about the person presenting the card.

Many efforts are under way to improve the reliability of identification cards and tokens and to make them higher-quality communication devices. Not all of these improvements should be accepted uncritically, for reasons discussed later in this book. Given the susceptibility of identification cards, though, the relatively low levels of fraud we experience are a testament to the honesty and good character of the vast majority of people.

This majority—the honest people—are the ones on whose behalf policies about identification should be designed. They should be protected from fraud but they should not be forced to use identification systems that compromise key interests, such as civil liberties, privacy, autonomy, and obscurity, just to get at the few wrongdoers.

Identification theory and identification cards are tough sledding. These topics involve a lot of unfamiliar concepts, difficult terms, and complex ideas about how our society and economy works. This chapter has probably been the worst of it; the chapters that follow go through each of the many concepts introduced here with the aim of demystifying them and making them familiar and workable.

Ultimately, understanding how identification works and what it does will put you in a position to decide what you think of it. Identification and authorization processes are appearing in new places and taking on new forms and roles. These changes have consequences.

3. Something You Are

BrownHorizonsArt.com is a small online store typical of the hundreds of thousands of small business websites put online by people around the world. Dedicated to African-American art and home décor, the site has a workmanlike design, with links to merchandise, featured items, and information about delivery options. The items on display represent an attractive cross section of reasonably priced African-American art pieces.

One of the items for sale on BrownHorizonsArt.com is a small statuette called *Bond Between Mother and Child*. In sleek dark porcelain, it depicts a mother sitting on the ground holding her child. Her legs together in front of her are bent at the knees, providing a seat for her baby whom she holds before her with outstretched arms. Mother and child both lean forward, so close that their foreheads are touching. Their eyes are fixed on one another and they seem to drink each other in.

The smoothed, generic lines of the figurine dispense with details about time and place, fashion and country. Rather, the piece focuses on a powerful and familiar thing: relationship.

Bond Between Mother and Child illustrates the beauty of a scene that has played itself out again and again for thousands of years, in every generation, and in every culture. This familiar image is a reminder of all people's essential kinship, of hope, and of the importance of remembering our humanity.

But why is this scene so familiar? Do we really understand what it depicts?

We all know the importance of the relationship between parents and children, but we also know very little about it. Much of the bonding process is instinctive, buried in hormonal and chemical responses that science is only beginning to unveil. The workings of parental and romantic love are objects of fascinating scientific study, just as they are objects of intense and enjoyable art.

One thing that happens as a relationship forms between a parent and child is that the two learn to identify each other very well. When

21

Figure
BOND BETWEEN MOTHER AND CHILD

a mother and child stare into each other's eyes, touch each other's hands and faces, watch each other's movements, and listen to each other's voices, they instinctively record their observations and collect them. They use these observations later, also innately and instinctively, to recognize each other.

Because they recognize and associate memories and feelings with each other, parents and children develop continuous, deep, and flowing relationships. Parents of young children do observe that little ones' young brains will drop association with a parent who has been absent at length—traveling on business or stationed overseas, for example. But, in general, thanks to recognizing each other, there is no need to begin a new relationship each time two people encounter each other. This observation is both obvious and essential.

But how does this recognition process work?

Science has not revealed the precise steps that the brain takes, but we can describe the way the mind organizes identifying information in familiar terms: Each fact we observe or learn about another person is a characteristic. Certain characteristics are distinctive. That is, they differ from the characteristics of other people.

Consider the features of the face. Distinctive characteristics include the spacing, shape, and color of the eyes, the shape of the mouth and lips, the color of the skin, the shape of the head, the framing created by hair, the distance among different features, and many other things. Neural science is only beginning to discover the processes that the human brain uses to identify people through fixed aspects of the face and to communicate through facial movements.[1] Needless to say, most people are expert interpreters and processors of the facial elements and facial cues.

Identifiers

Some of these distinctive characteristics are used as index cards of a sort. The ones we use consciously when we describe people are such things as hair color, eye color, height, weight, and skin color.

When we see people again, our senses and brains instantaneously observe their characteristics and correlate them with the characteristics we have seen before. If there is a match between the "index card" characteristics we have seen previously and the characteristics we are observing, we have identified a person. Facts and feelings linked to that person in our memories come forth seamlessly.

Anyone who has recognized the sound of a loved one's footsteps or who has been reassured by the sound of another's breathing can understand how we also use audible characteristics to recognize others. To varying degrees, we also use the rest of our senses— smell, touch, and probably even taste—to pick up index card characteristics.

These index card characteristics—the facts about people that distinguish them from one another—are "identifiers." Any characteristic becomes an identifier when it is used for sorting and organizing people in our thoughts and records.

Of course, the elements of the face and body are but a few of the hundreds of different identifiers out there in constant use. There are many more identifiers, and many other kinds. Different identifiers work differently, and many of them are less innate than the sensory identifiers, but they are common constituents of identification just the same.

The identifiers we have discussed here, facial features, the sounds people make, and their smells, fall into just one of the categories of identifiers commonly used in identification theory: the category of "something you are." These identifiers are facts about people, physically connected to them, that can be observed by others and used to make that connection or recognition that is identification.

Biometrics

In the *Bond Between Mother and Child* statuette, mother and child are collecting from each other a type of identifier that is unique and powerful. Each is taking the measure of the other's body and bodily characteristics. Though it may spoil the intimacy and beauty of the figurine to say it, they are using "biometrics."

When we recognize each other—when we see a friend walking down the street or hear a spouse sneezing in the kitchen—we note and compare the physical identifiers found on and about each other's bodies with identifier information we have collected before. Our observations are not denominated in millimeters, degrees, or wavelengths, of course—the process is a natural one performed in the brain—but we are just as surely measuring each other's physical characteristics.

This process is biometrics. Students of etymology know that the term is formed from two Greek roots: *bios* (life) and *metron* (measure or degree). Biometrics is simply the measurement of living things. Biometric identification is the measurement of identifiers from living (and formerly living) things to distinguish them from one another.

Biometrics is widely spoken of as an emerging, high-tech field, but it has been practiced since before recorded history—by humans, animals, and even plants. The "new" field of biometrics refers to the use of machines and computers in biometric identification, an important development that has distinct consequences.

There are two major categories of biometrics: physiological and behavioral.

Physiological biometrics measures the distinct traits that people have on their bodies. Examples of physiological biometrics are all the things we think of most commonly as physical identifiers—hair color, eye color, sex, skin color, height, weight, and so on. It also includes many more identifiers that will come into use with the advance of technology: retina and iris scans, facial geometry analysis, and fingerprint scanning. There are many more examples.

The second category, behavioral biometrics, measures the distinct actions that humans take, which are generally very hard to copy from one person to another. Behavioral biometrics includes voice printing and gait analysis, which measure the sound created by the human speaker's voice box or the distinct movements of a person walking. Analyzing voices and movements is easily done by humans, less easily done by machines today, but the technologies that read behavioral biometrics are ceaselessly improving.

One commonly used and well-recognized behavioral biometric is the handwritten signature, used daily by people to sign checks, letters, notes, and contracts. The name "behavioral biometric" may be intimidating, but the signature is an entirely familiar identifier that we are accustomed to using all the time. When a notary public attests to a document, having watched a person sign it and checked an identification document, his or her observation of the signing is a use of behavioral biometrics to prove identity.

Most biometrics—and the most dependable—rely on identifiers that are somewhat or largely dictated by genetics. That is, the identifiers used are controlled by the sequences of chromosomes that we inherited from our biological parents.

A basis in genetics does not necessarily make a biometric identifier permanently fixed or easy to measure, however. Hair dyes, contact lenses, surgeries, skin bleaches, facial hair, and makeup all change or obscure the gifts we have been given in our genes. Although DNA analysis is viewed as highly reliable today, gene therapies of the future might allow a person to alter the "signal" genes in DNA analysis. Presently, 13 DNA regions are compared in DNA analysis to make an identification.[2]

Many biometric techniques are based on nongenetic identifiers, or mixed—genetic and nongenetic—identifiers. Such identifiers reflect a mix of genetics and life experience that has left relatively permanent evidence on the body. Nongenetic or partially genetic physiological biometric identifiers include weight, tattoos, dental records, birthmarks, and photographs.

Yes, common photography is a physiological biometric tool. In the early days, photographers used chemicals to record and reproduce the photons of light that bounced off a human face and other scenery, reproducing eye and hair color, facial shape, distinct features, unique sets of features, and so on. Modern photography captures photons digitally, to be displayed as pixels, or dots, on a fine grid. Either way, the stored image is a collection of identifiers that we humans are highly trained to distinguish.

These identifiers are augmented by life experience, of course. Pictures of the same person at a young and old age can be quite different. Nonetheless, pictures are regularly compared with other pictures or with people presenting themselves for identification. The familiar technology of photography is a biometric technology, if a clumsy one compared with the emerging, machine-readable techniques.

The "quality" of biometric identifiers is important to consider. Many of them are both fixed to a person and highly distinct. That makes them extremely powerful.

There are also important consequences when biometric identifiers are scanned by machines rather than people. But we should not get ahead of ourselves and get into identification's consequences or appropriate identification policies before we have captured all of identification theory.

Using the *Bond Between Mother and Child* statuette as a starting point for studying identification theory may tend to spoil the intimate feeling of the piece. But nothing shows better the importance of identification or how it operates in human environments. Instinctively, people measure each other and record their observations, an exercise in natural biometrics. They use some of these observations as index cards to sort among one another. These index card characteristics are identifiers.

Biometrics are some of the most important identifiers because of their unique characteristics, but they are only a starting point for understanding identification. Something you are is only one category of identifiers. The second one is something you are assigned. As we will see in the next chapter, assigned identifiers have a substantial role in organizing societies, proving who people are, and determining what they are entitled to do or have.

4. Something You Are Assigned

In the early 16th century during the reign of Henry VIII, a Welsh-man was called before an English judge. When the judge asked his name, he replied a bit grandiosely, "Thomas Ap [son of] William, Ap Thomas, Ap Richard, Ap Hoel, Ap Evan Vaughan."

This was how the Welshman would have identified himself on any formal occasion in his village, and he was undoubtedly proud of the lineage it represented. But this was not his village. The judge snapped at him to "leave the old manor [sic]" of speaking and use his real name. Embarrassed, he thereafter called himself Thomas "Moston," using the name of his principal house for his last name.[1]

This was one small episode in the long history of how formalized last names came into being. The Western tradition of passing the father's last name down through generations was originally applied and enforced by government officials, mostly for the purposes of taxing, raising armies, performing censuses, and other things that increased the knowledge and power of the state.

Before efforts to regularize names, early societies used vernacular naming conventions that do not suit modern, welfare-state gover-nance or, of course, a modern society. Most people in the United States are familiar with vernacular naming thanks to the continent's history with Native Americans. Although their practices ranged widely over the vast expanse of the North American continent, many Native Americans used locally relevant descriptive names until the European-origin settlers brought about higher levels of administra-tive order. A Native American girl might have been called "Runs-from-the-Bear" because of a childhood incident. She might have been renamed "Rides-the-Tall-Horse" thanks to relatively greater bravery demonstrated in later life. Neither name—and certainly not the abrupt name change—works well in a phone book or on a tax collector's rolls.

History is rife with examples of governments promoting naming systems for their purposes. The Dawes Act of 1887, also known as

27

the General Allotment Act, authorized the president of the United States to give 160 acres to the head of each Native American family. This was intended to convert tribes from their communal ways and make landowning subjects of the native population. To administer this transition, they needed appropriate, government-recognized names. Federal authorities fanned out to convert names like "Standing Bull" to "Charles Stanbull."

While the U.S. government was interested in confining and regimenting Native Americans in the 1890s, in the next century the Canadian government wanted to supply its indigenous population with pensions, family allowances, schooling, and medical services. A system was devised in the mid-1930s to replace the otherwise obscure Inuit naming system with disks with codes on them, such as "E-6-2155," standing for "East Zone, District 6, individual 2155." This code would be the basis for record keeping on the government's new wards. The Inuit were expected to wear these disks like dog tags around their necks. They did not cooperate and the disk system was abandoned in 1969.

Centuries earlier, Europeans too resisted government-enforced naming. A census taken in Florence, Italy, in 1427 attempted to capture the names, wealth, residences, landholdings, and ages of all local inhabitants. Foot-dragging among the populace, who were aware of its purpose, saw to it that the survey experienced little success. But this effort and others across history have wedged populations into naming conventions that are useful and effective for monitoring and tracking.

Naming and other organizing systems have not only served governments and administrators, of course. Landed elites have historically adopted last names that reinforced their claims to property. It could be useful politically to have one's last name, which came from one's father, match up with the name of the local manor, especially when one's land grants were in doubt. Many Norman invaders of Britain took the names of the lands they conquered as their surnames.

Names are the most familiar examples of socially constructed identifiers. That is, they are something that a person is assigned by the state, by other people, or by custom. These identifiers include personal names like "John Smith" and numbers like the Social Security number. They also include addresses, affiliations, and descriptions like "cheerful." These things place people in context for the variety of social and economic roles they play. Rather than something physically connected to a person or uniquely produced by their bodies, these identifiers are something that society has assigned.

Nearly anything can serve as an identifier. If a person tells a new acquaintance "I will meet you at Fifth and Main at 5:00," the fact that a person stands at Fifth and Main at the appropriate time plays a key role in allowing the acquaintance to identify him or her. Location is a social construction, as is time. They are both useful identifiers for the single interaction of meeting up at Fifth and Main.

Assigned Identifiers in Advancing Societies

Assigned identifiers did not get their start with administrative government, of course. In chapter 2, we briefly imagined how a primordial clan needed to identify its members so it could distinguish friends and family from marauders or cannibals. Now let us imagine that the clan has advanced socially and grown in size. It has begun to use language and to have more complex interactions both among a larger family and with some outsiders. What kinds of social tools did it develop to smooth interactions within the clan and with strangers?

That is where vernacular naming undoubtedly got its start. The name is one of the most familiar identifiers that is "assigned." Primordial people may have used grunts and gestures to refer to individuals. Those signals undoubtedly grew more distinct as language skills evolved.

For fun, let's say that one member of this family came to be called "Bodo," a simple, two-syllable utterance that requires little lingual development to pronounce. When the family affixed this name to one of their own, they had developed a remarkable way of distinguishing among one another in the abstract, a vast expansion beyond their ability to distinguish only among those immediately present.

The convention of using a surname that passed through the father's line of descent evolved only relatively recently, in historical terms, for most of the population. Many people in the world do not use this convention and some in the West have altered or abandoned it because of its symbolism with regard to gender equity.

In small, agrarian, and largely immobile societies, people's names joined to loose descriptors sufficed quite well to distinguish them from all others in the territory. In England around the turn of the

18th century, it is estimated that eight given names accounted for nearly 90 percent of the total male population (John, Edward, William, Henry, Charles, James, Richard, and Robert). To avoid confusion, locals merely appended descriptive second names to the first, names that connoted relationships, employment, locations, or other characteristics. Examples include William's John (later to become John Williamson), John the Miller (John Miller), John by the Brook (John Brooks), or John-Who-Does-Little (you figure it out). There were relatively fewer people and most did not travel or move outside the regions in which they were born. Local people had a local solution for the confusion that could arise from identical given names.

As discussed above, the growth of acquisitive, conscripting, and administrative government saw to it that patronymic last names were adopted and used, at least in the West. Now that the convention is widely accepted, Westerners typically use the combination of a given name and surname to distinguish people from one another. This combination places a person in context, first as a member of a family and then as a distinct member of that family.

Naming does more than identify people, of course. Parents spend hours poring over baby-name books and consulting family members about the right name to give their new children. The choice of a name may suggest character traits parents would like to see in a baby, or it may honor older family members, living or dead.

Over the last century, though, changing circumstances have begun to make names obsolete as distinctive identifiers. First of all, there are more people, which increases the chance that two people in the same place will have the same name. And names are rarely unique over a broad area. Even unusual names may be repeated several times in a country with millions of inhabitants. Our society is a great deal more mobile than any previous society has been; people may pull up stakes and move vast distances several times in a life. And the growth in size, scope, and complexity of institutions and organizations has increased the chance that they will encounter duplications among names.

Names are also subject to change, through marriage, divorce, and adoption, for example. Some people are known by different names in different social settings, such as itinerants, writers and performers who use pseudonyms, and married women who use a hyphenated name or a maiden name professionally and a married name personally.

In short, names do not sort among people in the modern world very well. Because of their social meaning, the idea of naming people is obviously not disappearing any time soon, but the utility of naming does not meet the demands of our modern economy and society.

Uniform Identifiers to Replace Names

Uniform identifiers have arisen as the response to weakness in the quality of names as identifiers. A uniform identifier is a number or other string of characters that is unique to each individual, often designed and assigned precisely for the purpose of identification.

Uniform identifiers are particularly useful in institutions that must sort among hundreds of thousands or millions of customers or citizens. They provide the indexing system in the institutional "mind" that links people to information about them so that their access to privileges, entitlements, conveniences, or physical spaces can be determined.

The Social Security number is the premier uniform identifier in the United States. The Social Security number was adopted to administer one federal program, of course, and the policy of having a national uniform identifier was not considered at the time. Rather, widespread use of the Social Security number was backed into by a series of government policies. The obvious economic utility of a uniform identifier drove its adoption in the private sector during the 1970s, particularly in the credit-reporting industry, which was consolidating at the time.

We will return to the Social Security number and the consequences of uniform identification systems in chapter 22. Suffice it to say here that uniform identifiers provide a good deal of efficiency—to both institutions and wrongdoers. As we will discuss in later chapters, excess efficiency in the hands of identity fraudsters, governments, or even corporations threatens important interests of consumers and citizens such as personal security, liberty, and privacy.

Any uniform numbering system can be used as a uniform identifier. It does not have to be assigned for the purpose of identifying people. Internet Protocol addresses, for example, are unique numbers that distinguish each computer or other device connected to the Internet. If a person uses the same computer with a static (unchanging) IP address, that number may serve as a distinct identifier of that person to someone wanting to track him or her.

In early 1999, computer chip maker Intel announced that all chips of one series it built would include a unique identifier, called the processor serial number.[2] This could be used as a uniform identifier for the people that used each computer. Strenuous objections to the practice caused Intel to discontinue it. Particularly in computing environments, uniform identifiers can have considerable power, which makes them important to understand and control.

Other Assigned Identifiers

The variety of something-you-are-assigned identifiers is limited only by the imagination. Earlier, we spoke of a meeting between two new friends that would take place at 5:00 on the corner of Fifth and Main. This example uses two social constructions, time and location, as identifiers that whittle away the chance of misidentification. If two sets of people happen to have decided on a meeting at Fifth and Main at that particular time, this bad luck will create a 50 percent chance of error. But usually, such identifiers will lead to an easy, accurate identification.

Communications devices and accounts—phone numbers, e-mail addresses, and instant-messaging handles—are exceedingly common identifiers that are assigned by telecommunications companies and Internet service providers. Obviously, people lock their landline phones inside their houses and offices, they carry their cell phones on their persons, and they access e-mail and instant messaging with usernames and passwords. This means that a call or message from a familiar phone number, e-mail address, or instant-messaging handle is likely to be from that actual person. Fraud in these systems occurs but, as a proportion of all transactions, it remains relatively rare.

A good rule of thumb for suppressing fraud is not to give someone account numbers or other information over the phone or a website unless you made the call or typed the URL into your browser. The reason is that phone numbers and Web addresses serve pretty well as something-you-are-assigned identifiers. Dialing a financial institution's phone number makes it nearly 100 percent likely that a person within the actual institution will be reached. People use phone numbers as identifiers all the time—in this case, individuals use them to identify institutions.

Arguably, identifiers such as e-mail addresses shade into the something-you-know category because e-mail accounts ride atop passwords, which allow people access based on something known. This method of identification (and authorization) is discussed in the next chapter. Using someone's e-mail address to identify them is also an example of how some identification systems "piggyback" on other identification systems. Piggybacking is discussed in chapter 9.

Names, addresses, times, locations, and descriptions are just a few of the particulars we use to tell people from one another. They are all details that are culturally and socially assigned. They are used constantly for identification, even if we rarely articulate that fact to ourselves.

Civilization has advanced and changed in myriad ways in the last hundred years or so. Institutions are larger and have larger scope. People move more often and are more abundant. These changes have weakened the usefulness of socially assigned identifiers such as the given name and surname.

The rise of uniform identifiers like Social Security numbers, account numbers, and other codes and character strings comes as a response, but it has never been considered as a discrete policy. The Social Security number in the United States has become a uniform— and usually distinct—financial "name." Although it has had substantial economic benefits for businesses and consumers, it has had substantial negative consequences too, and those may increase in the future. These issues are discussed in the chapters that follow this survey of identification theory. But in the next chapter, we examine the third category of identifier: something you know.

5. Something You Know

Odysseus shot an arrow through Antinous's throat and, with another arrow, ripped a hole in Eurymachus's chest and liver. Arriving home after 20 years, he was pretty ticked off by what he found.

His victims were the worst of a hundred or so suitors who, taking advantage of customary Greek hospitality, had occupied his estate during his long absence and epic journey. With the others, Antinous and Eurymachus were pursuing the hand of Odysseus's wife Penelope and plotting to kill his son. The successful suitor would have had the edge on replacing Odysseus as king of Ithaca.

Recall that Odysseus had gone off to fight the Trojan War. He had come up with the idea for the Trojan horse: a successful plan to fill a giant wooden horse with troops and give it to the Trojans, thereby gaining entrance to their city.

After the war, his trip home took a few wrong turns. Exploring the land of the Cyclopes, Odysseus got a little too close to one of the beasts and had to blind it to escape. Unfortunately, his victim was Polyphemus, a son of Poseidon. Angering the god of the sea is rarely a good idea for an oceangoing traveler.

Odysseus almost fell prey to the Sirens' song. He lashed himself to the mast to prevent himself from steering his ship onto the rocks. He dodged between Scylla, a six-headed monster, and Charybdis, a nasty whirlpool, but his men feasted on the cattle of Zeus at his next stop. Naturally, the sun god was outraged and destroyed his ship.

Odysseus washed ashore on Calypso's island where he stayed as the lover of this lustful goddess-nymph for the next seven years. But he did not want immortality and eternal nooky. He wanted to be with Penelope in his land of Ithaca. So with the help of the Phæacians, he returned home.

After all this, Odysseus deserved a break, a simple reunion with his faithful and patient wife. But it was not to be. His house was overrun with suitors. A band of men were eating his food and drinking his wine, hitting on his maidservants, courting his wife, and plotting against his son.

Biding his time, Odysseus entered the house disguised as a beggar. The years had taken their toll, so he was recognized only by the small number of faithful servants who saw a characteristic scar on his knee—something you are—and by his son (who got help identifying him from the goddess Athena). He commanded their silence as to his identity.

Penelope had a sense that this beggar might be Odysseus, but wanted to be sure. So she organized a contest where suitors would string and fire Odysseus's bow.

No one could even come close until Odysseus the beggar gave it a shot. He strung the bow and fired it through a straight row of 12 axes. Odysseus then took a few moments to slaughter the houseful of suitors, starting with Antinous and Eurymachus. For good measure, he dispatched a decent number of misbehaved servants as well.

But Penelope was a cautious woman who would not swoon for just any archer who could cause an epic bloodbath. She wanted to be absolutely sure of Odysseus's identity. After the bodies and gore were cleaned up, Penelope loudly asked her nurse to move the bedstead out of the couple's chamber and spread blankets on it.

Odysseus hit the roof. He had built their bed himself, shaping it from a living olive tree. A master carpenter, Odysseus had constructed the bedroom around the permanently fixed bed. He knew that the bed could not be moved and he was outraged that the bed he had built with his own hands, for his loving wife and himself, might have been destroyed.

When Penelope saw his reaction, she was entirely assured that the man before her was her husband Odysseus. The two were reunited at last. For the first time in 20 years, they had a night together in that bed. Athena delayed the dawn to give the two a little more time.

Today, we might characterize Odysseus's wholesale slaughter of the interlopers as a slight overreaction, but this story is not recounted to illustrate proportionality in vengeance or criminal sentencing. (Remember, Odysseus was king.) Rather, the sweet reunion of Odysseus and Penelope shows the role that knowledge plays in identification. The ultimate proof of Odysseus's identity was something he knew.

Something you know is the second major category of identifiers. The possession of special knowledge—facts, lore, histories, codes, passwords, and the like—is a distinct type of identifier.

Like biometric identification, "epistemetric"[1] identification compares the contents of an individual's mind with what he or she should know given other elements of his or her potential, alleged, or claimed identity. A match strengthens the identification of the person. Using knowledge as an identifier adds to our ability to identify others and it extends that ability to higher-order interactions.

Innate Fact Checking

Identifying someone by what he or she knows may seem less intuitive than things like visual identification, which we discussed in chapter 3. As with the biometrics we use to make in-person identification, few people think about the checking processes we innately use in our conversations. But as the story of Odysseus shows, something-you-know identifiers are very useful and common.

They are not always used to consciously "test" others as Penelope did with Odysseus. Rather, identification using this category of identifier is highly ingrained in human relationships and interactions. Everyone knows about the skill levels different people bring to the effort: People who do poorly at checking others' statements against background knowledge or logic are called "gullible." But nearly everyone, to a greater or lesser degree, observes the coherence and consistency of one another's statements and assertions.

Imagine having a police officer on foot patrol in your town or city ask you for directions to a major thoroughfare, park, or building. Consider a violin teacher giving a lesson without noticing that her student's violin was wildly out of tune. What would you think if you asked a postal worker the price of a first-class stamp and he did not know it, but sat on your front stoop reading your mail?

These are all examples of people's claimed roles not matching up with the knowledge we would expect them to have. Police officers almost always know the way around their beats. Violin teachers notice when instruments are out of tune. And postal workers are likely to know the price of a first-class stamp, as well as the rules against reading customers' mail.

Fact Checking in Paradise

On State Street in beautiful Santa Barbara, California, shops, restaurants, and bars line block after touristy block of Spanish-style construction. On weekend nights, many students from the nearby university come downtown to carouse. One such student in the late 1980s was named Bob. Many weekends, he and his roommates and friends would go downtown for the nightlife.

Bob enjoyed playing practical jokes. Because his ancestry was Asian and Portuguese, he had black hair and dark tan skin. Many mistook him for a Filipino or other Pacific Islander. Bob had been to Hawaii and learned a small amount of local Hawaiian dialect, or pidgin.

So Bob would walk up to tourists in Hawaiian shirts on State Street and ask in his best pidgin, "Ay, braddah, you fra' d'islands or wha'?" Their confused responses were always amusing for Bob's titillated pals because they illustrated how *un*-Hawaiian—and thus uncool—were the people wearing Hawaiian shirts. It was all good fun. Bob even printed up mock business cards to show his buddies, cards which named him, "Yufa D'Ilenz."

Then the day came when Bob plied his prank against some actual Hawaiians. Daringly, as usual, Bob walked up to the two men and asked his patented question. One of them answered, in perfect pidgin, "Yeah, brah. Wea you fra'?"

Pausing a just-noticeable instant, Bob replied, ". . . North Shore!"

A local Hawaiian would not name "North Shore" as his residence and the two real Hawaiians knew it. They could not square Bob's claim of being from Hawaii with how he named "North Shore" as his home. They knew that he was lying.

Bob also knew that they were onto him. He did not press his case any longer and got away from the befuddled Hawaiians, who were much bigger than he was. That, of course, was the last time Bob approached a tourist in a Hawaiian shirt to ask if he was "fra' d'Islans."

Granted, the lack of knowledge in each of these cases may only reveal profound incompetence. But to different degrees, these scenarios would put many people on notice that something is wrong. We are natural fact checkers, and most people would be inclined to inquire further about the bona fides of the lost police officer, the tone-deaf violin teacher, or the ignorant, nosy letter carrier.

As a percentage of total communications, people probably try to deceive one another fairly rarely. Most commonly, we use knowledge to quickly and subtly confirm the accuracy of other people's stated identities and authorities. People are constantly reassured of other people's identities and roles because actions and words meet up with expectations. We all understand and expect that a person having a certain identity or position will know certain things, be they family history, special technical skills, training in arts or sciences, and so on.

The most interesting examples, of course, are people's feigning or gaining knowledge to establish false identities. One legendary imposter was Frank Abagnale, who posed as an airline pilot, an attorney, a college professor, and a pediatrician during a years-long crime spree that was memorialized in the book and movie *Catch Me If You Can*.[2]

Ferdinand Waldo Demara Jr. impersonated a doctor of zoology, a law student, a cancer researcher, a hospital orderly, a deputy sheriff, and a teacher during his criminal career. He is most famous for adopting the identity of Dr. Joseph Cyr and managing numerous successful surgeries, including the removal of a bullet from a man's chest.[3]

These are two examples of extremely bright people who have either acquired or faked knowledge to create a false identity and to perpetuate fraud. The failure of fact checking in these cases shows how important it is.

Most people are honest and few are good enough to fake knowledge very long, so imposter fraud is relatively rare—though perhaps not rare enough. In the vast majority of cases, "something you know" effectively validates people's claimed identities.

Your Mother's Maiden Name

Perhaps some bloodshed could have been avoided if Penelope had just asked Odysseus for his mother's maiden name. That is, of course, the quintessential something-you-know identifier. Just about everyone who has interacted over the telephone with a financial services provider in recent years has been asked for this information to confirm his or her identity.

Because of its common usage, the quality of the mother's maiden name as an identifier has dropped. Everyone who wants to commit financial fraud knows that this piece of information will be requested, and it is not hard to learn.

So wise institutions are diversifying the something-you-know identifiers they use. Some are shifting to other, similar facts, such as father's middle name. Some are offering consumers a choice of knowledge-based identifiers, such as city of birth, name of a favorite pet, and so on.

Institutions that have a good deal of information about individuals may use it to create knowledge-based identifiers on the fly. Credit card issuers sometimes ask customers to confirm their identities by naming a recent purchase, or by picking a very recent or very large transaction from a purchase "lineup." Some credit bureaus are doing the same with information such as former addresses, using their deep knowledge of consumers to create identifiers that are easy for the real consumer to answer but very hard for an impostor to predict and research ahead of time.

These techniques raise the quality of something-you-know identifiers. We will return to the relative quality of identifiers in chapter 7.

Higher-Order Transactions

Notice that the mother's maiden name and better examples of something-you-know identifiers come from "higher-order" transactions—that is, transactions with larger institutions in a sophisticated economy. This is not a coincidence. But something-you-know identifiers did not arise just for large institutions.

Let us return to the primordial family or clan of the last chapter. They needed to identify and distinguish family members from outsiders just for the sake of survival. Bodo and his kin used biometrics to do this, taking the measure of one another with their senses and using these measurements to make distinctions. Later, we imagined that Bodo's clan had progressed and grown in size and complexity, adopting a rudimentary language. It used this language to assign identifiers such as names, creating distinctions that could effectively be used more broadly.

Knowledge-based identifiers take identification a step further, going beyond the use of names. Though still in prehistoric terms, they rely on an increasingly sophisticated language system, and they are useful for relatively widespread interaction and commerce. Something-you-know identifiers are a social tool that probably roughly correlates with the transition of humans from fearful, antagonistic groups into early "societies" that engaged in rudimentary trade and commerce.

One can imagine, for example, our friend Bodo going on a trading mission, seeking to exchange rams' horns and shiny white stones for baskets, animal skins, and such. Potential customers along his route might have known something about his home area, one of his neighbors, or a relative. By chatting with him about common knowledge or a common acquaintance, the customers could gain assurance of Bodo's bona fides.

Specifically, the conversation might have been about Bodo's village (something you are assigned), and it might have gone into specifics about an annual feast, a village elder, or recent weather patterns in that area (all something you know). As the customer sensed that Bodo was conversant with information matching his claimed village, trust—and a relationship—would begin to form. This is a primitive use of multifactor identification, which we will return to in chapter 9.

Because of the expense and difficulty of travel in early human history, commerce was quite a bit more continuous and repetitive than it is today. That is, traders and merchants developed customers and contacts with whom they did business year after year after year. There were no "fly-by-night" operators, of course. Nobody flew and few ever traveled by night.

This type of trade pattern was extremely fertile for the development of trust because once a trader was identified, the powers to withdraw from future dealing and to damage reputation were strong incentives holding people to their promises.[4] As we will explore in chapter 11, identification promotes accountability, which is a building block of trust.

In any event, we see that "something you know" plays an important role in higher-order transactions, such as commerce among relative strangers.

41

Passwords

Like the mother's maiden name, passwords and pass codes are another something-you-know identifier useful in higher-order transactions, such as remote commerce. Everyone who accesses e-mail uses a username and pass code to do so. That is, a computer logs onto an e-mail account by sending a name or e-mail address (something you are assigned) and a pass code (something you know). The combination signals to the Internet service provider with a requisite degree of assurance that the request to access e-mail service is from a particular user.

Passwords improve on other knowledge-based identifiers in some respects and, at the same time, lack qualities of other such identifiers. The mother's maiden name, for example, has two weaknesses: it is unchanging—that is, there is one such identifier that applies for a person's entire life—and it is relatively easy to research. This combination makes it easy for fraudsters to learn.

A password, on the other hand, is just a string of letters and numbers. It need not be static. Indeed, it is generally a good security practice to rotate through passwords. And a "brute-force" attack—the attempt to guess a password by trying all possible combinations—can be made very difficult by making a pass code relatively long and by using both letters and numbers. This practice drives the possible number of combinations sky-high so that attempts to guess a password will reveal themselves to responsible network administrators.

This strength is a weakness, however. To avoid having to memorize too many passwords, people may use the same one for many different systems. And they may write their passwords down in a place where wrongdoers can find them. Users may weaken or break password systems for their own convenience. Striking the right balance is important: finding a password scheme that is difficult for outsiders to navigate, but not too difficult for insiders to navigate.

Cryptography

The science of cryptography has created cutting-edge uses for something-you-know identifiers. The keys used in modern cryptography are essentially passwords that can identify the author of messages and text if used properly.

Cryptography is the use of mathematical formulas to convert readable text into an unintelligible form and back again. In traditional cryptography, two people share a "key" that helps them encode and decode messages they send to each other. The best example is the "secret decoder ring" children have used for years. Two children use the same key to encode and decode messages. A third child without the key will have a hard time reading the messages and the first two can say mean things about him. If he gets that key or solves the code, he can easily decode and read the messages—and all three will probably end up crying to a parent.

Public key cryptography is a newer, more complex, interesting— and grown-up—form of cryptography. In public key cryptography, one person has both a private key and a public key. He or she keeps the private key secret and makes the public key widely available. A message scrambled using the private key can be descrambled only by the public key. Likewise, when a message is scrambled by the public key, it can be descrambled only by the private key.[5]

Provided a person keeps his or her private key private, anyone who receives a message that can be descrambled using the corresponding public key can be certain that the message is from that person. The private key is like a signature. It scrambles text in a way that indicates exactly whose key scrambled it.

Sets of keys like these are issued as digital certificates by certificate authorities. Public key infrastructure assures Internet users that they are dealing with people whose real-world identities have been validated (to the extent certificate authorities have done so). As long as the private key is kept private, messages decrypted using a person's public key are verifiably from that person and messages encrypted using that person's public key can be read only by that person.

Thus, private keys act as identifiers. They are used to confirm the authorship of text, as well as to confirm the integrity of messages that have been in transit across the Internet and other networks. Public key encryption ties remote transactions to real people and institutions.

Knowledge and Authorization

Although passwords often act as identifiers, they are just as useful as nonidentifying signals of status or access rights. As we discussed in chapter 2, the ATM card and PIN code are not an identification system, but rather an authorization system. A person who carries an ATM card and knows the associated PIN code is authorized to access the account regardless of who he or she is. This system is useful because it allows a person to share his or her bank account with someone else.

We also talked earlier in this chapter about how knowledge is used not just as identifying information, but information that confirms the role or authority people have. The police officer who knows the way is more credibly a police officer than the one who does not. The status of the violin teacher as such is more credible given her good ear. And the postal worker who knows the price of a stamp is one who we are going to accept walking up to our front doors. They each have characteristics that help qualify them on the merits for the roles they are playing. We use their knowledge as a characteristic that qualifies them directly for transactions and access, rather than identifying them as an intermediate step in doing the same thing.

This is an important attribute of the something-you-know category of identifiers—their parallel utility as nonidentifying signals. As will be discussed in chapter 24, knowing the identity of a person is often unimportant. Rather, what matters is his or her entitlement to access benefits, infrastructure, or goods.

When used for identification, "something you know" is an important and distinct characteristic. It is highly ingrained in human interaction, if not quite as much as biometric identification is. Certainly, Penelope appreciated using it to verify that her true Odysseus had returned home from his epic voyage. Most importantly, something-you-know identifiers are very useful in higher-order transactions. They facilitate transactions among relative strangers, dealings between individuals and institutions, and remote transactions such as online access to e-mail and Web services.

The qualities of something-you-know identifiers differ from other identifiers, such as something you are or something you are assigned. They are stronger in some senses because they can be very well obscured or randomized. On the other hand, they can be compromised by their own users, typically for the sake of convenience.

This is an important challenge for security experts. We students of identification must complete our study of identifiers, however, by examining the final category: something you have.

6. Something You Have

When a pope dies, the College of Cardinals ensures that the funeral rites and election of his successor are carried out in accordance with the *Ordo Exsequiarum Romani Pontificis* (the Order of Service for the Burial of the Roman Pontiff). When Pope John Paul II died in 2005, they also followed the *Universi Dominici Gregis* (apostolic constitution), written by him nine years earlier. These documents lay out elaborate instructions for the funeral of the deceased pope, selection of a new one, and passing of authority to the new pontiff.

For burial, a pope is traditionally dressed in formal papal robes, with two veils of white silk placed over his face and hands. The pope's body is placed inside a series of three nested coffins. The first is of cypress, signifying his humanity. It goes inside a second made of lead and adorned with the pope's name and dates of his pontificate, as well as a skull and crossbones. Those two are then placed inside a third, unadorned coffin made of elm, meant to symbolize dignity.

Funeral rites are to be celebrated for nine consecutive days. Burial should take place no sooner than four days and no later than six days after the pope's death. The coffins are placed at the entrance to the Basilica of St. Peter in Vatican City where the dean of the College of Cardinals presides over a funeral mass. Finally, the pope is interred within his tomb beneath the basilica.

These rites occur several days into the *sede vacante,* or vacant see, the period of time when there is no pope. The procedures to be followed during this period are carefully prescribed. The camerlengo is the official who informs the cardinal vicar for the Diocese of Rome about the death of the pope. The cardinal vicar, in turn, formally notifies the people. But before this happens, the camerlengo must verify the pope's death.

He does this at the pope's body by calling out his name three times and receiving no response. In the past, this was done by striking the pontiff's head with a silver hammer. The camerlengo then seals the pope's private apartments and residences.

Before formally announcing the death, the camerlengo destroys the pope's lead seal to prevent anyone else from using it and he breaks the Ring of the Fisherman. This is a gold signet ring engraved with the pope's name and an image of Saint Peter casting his net from a fishing boat. The ring is a singular symbol of papal authority. Its destruction in front of the other cardinals symbolizes the end of the deceased pope's authority. The search for a new pope officially begins.

Why should baubles like a seal and signet ring stand for so much that their destruction is a specific step in the transfer of power between popes? The answer has to do with the variety of roles played by something-you-have identifiers.

Tokens

"Something you have" is the fourth major category of identifier that people and institutions use to sort among one another. People are routinely distinguished by the things they possess.

At the simplest level, identifying people by their possessions is as simple as using any of the other identifiers we have discussed so far. It involves comparing the items possessed with the items that would be possessed by a known identity.

So a businessman meeting a colleague in person for the first time over lunch may use something-you-have identifiers. He may say, "I am in a gray suit, white shirt, and green tie today." This makes him easy to find at the appointed time even in the waiting area of a busy restaurant. People regularly take advantage of something they have (on) to distinguish themselves.

As with the other categories of identifiers, many somethings you have are used for authorization rather than identification. These identifiers are used when someone seeks particular attributes useful in a limited transaction rather than using identification to build a longer-lasting relationship.

The trademark brown uniform of UPS drivers is a good example of nonidentifying use of something you have. A brown-uniformed worker carrying a parcel up the walk signifies clearly to Americans that something is being delivered by this professional courier service. The characteristic that is communicated by the uniform is status as an employee of UPS. This is useful information that smoothes the exchange of the parcel. It does not mean that the recipient will recognize that particular deliveryperson later, out of uniform, at the grocery store—at least not without using other identifiers.

These comparative uses of something-you-have identifiers and nonidentifying authorization are extremely rudimentary, of course. The possessions we consciously use to identify ourselves rarely function this simply. Most something-you-have identifiers are objects that have been designed for a wide variety of uses and purposes related not only to identification and authorization but also to commerce and communication.

The word "token" is often used for identifiers from the something-you-have category because a wide variety of physical things can act as identifiers. The most common tokens used as identifiers today are cards such as driver's licenses or other government- or privately issued cards, but tokens on the near horizon include all kinds of gadgets and devices into which computer chips can be placed. Token-based identity systems use physical objects to help identify the bearer of the item.

Signet rings like the pope's Ring of the Fisherman illustrate some of the complexity and utility of manufactured identifier tokens. A signet is usually a ring with a flat surface on which a crest, shield of arms, or other signal is engraved in reverse. Pressed into sealing wax or clay, the signet ring produces an impression the right way around.

Signets probably emerged from cylinder seals, which date back to several thousand years BC and are found among the antiquities of ancient Egypt, Babylonia, and Assyria. These seals were images cut into a wide variety of hard stones. When rolled onto softer materials, they made an easily recognizable impression. Other seals revealed by archeology include images of the scarab beetle, popular in Egypt, and precious stones or pebbles with carvings in them. In ancient Greece, an image carved into a thin slice of stone was conveniently adapted to the bezel of a ring.

Before the wide availability of metallurgy, gemology, and quality stone carving, rings such as these were available only to the very wealthy. There were also strong social customs about who could own or wear rings and other jewelry. And because each seal was uniquely engraved, they were very hard to forge.

The rarity of signet rings (in early history), their individual uniqueness, and customs pertaining to their usage combined to create a

49

close correlation between a signet ring and an individual. Possession of a certain signet has historically served as a distinguishing characteristic. In other words, having a signet ring is a something-you-have identifier.

Identifiers with Ingenuity

But a signet ring is much more than an identifier. A product of human design, it serves a variety of different human needs and purposes. Signet rings demonstrate the high level of sophistication and complexity that go into manufactured identifiers.

One of the most obvious uses of the signet ring beyond identification is as decoration. Human vanity has a deep historical pedigree that is better exhibited nowhere than in signets, which have been designed for both their beauty and their power to say something about the bearer.

Signets are often made of precious metals and stones, both to lend to their rarity and because of their use as decoration. The design of the signet itself has often been quite decorative. Reportedly, in ancient Rome, Pompey's signet ring displayed a lion bearing a sword. Julius Caesar's was an armed Venus. Augustus had a sphinx at first, then the head of Alexander the Great, and finally his own image. Nero wore a signet ring representing the flaying of Marsyas by Apollo. Signets illustrated how closely great figures associated themselves with other great figures and the gods.

A signet ring might have been evidence of who a person was when other methods failed, but its more common use was probably to conduct remote commerce of various kinds. When a new signet was produced, the engraver or owner could make many impressions of it and distribute them among friends, family, traders, and officials to let them know the relationship between the impression of the signet and its owner—much like the public key in public key encryption is distributed today. Subsequently, the impression of the seal on a document would attest to the presence or authority of the person. A signet served the same purpose as a signature does on many documents today.

One example of this use of the signet comes from the biblical story of Daniel and the lions.[1] Because Daniel had violated an edict, King Darius reluctantly had to put Daniel in the lions' den. He shut the den with a stone and used his seal on the stone to show that the stone was placed there under his authority. Darius broke the seal in the morning to find that Daniel was still alive, protected from the lions by the will of God.

But use of seals continues today. In Japan, seals called *inkan* are a common business tool, used like a signature to indicate the presence or authority of executives and officials on documents. The seal is carved on the end of a stick of jade and used as a stamp with red ink. The owner of a new *inkan* will strike it violently so that small cracks develop, giving the *inkan* a unique "fingerprint" that is very hard to copy. When an *inkan* mark appears on a document, others know it has been reviewed or agreed to by the executive who possesses the *inkan*.

Signet rings and seals are security tools as well. They have been used historically to ensure the validity of communications and the integrity of goods.

Wax and clay are delicate materials that will crumble if people try to deform them after they have cooled or dried. This characteristic gives them use, in combination with a signet, for securing documents and goods.

A person who wants to communicate securely can use a signet to make an impression on the wax seal of a letter, folding the paper in such a way that it cannot be opened or read without breaking the seal. Seeing the undisturbed impression of the sender's signet on the wax seal, the recipient can be certain not only that the owner of the signet produced the document, but also that it has not been read or altered by outsiders. Similarly, for goods, a container can be sealed with cords or cloth that pass under a wax or clay seal. If anyone has opened the container, the seal and the impression left by the signet will be destroyed, revealing tampering to the recipient.

Considering all the uses of the signet—for decoration, for contract and agency, and for security—it is no wonder that the device has been regarded in many historical periods as highly powerful. And, indeed, symbolizing power has been another role of the signet ring. In countless historical examples, possession of a signet ring and other precious items has stood for the authority and power of the owner, including the power of an office or throne.

This is true with the Roman Catholic papacy today. Thus, when the camerlengo destroyed Pope John Paul II's seal and signet ring, the body that had worn the ring no longer held the papacy and the College of Cardinals was set the task of finding a new pope.

"Something You Have" in Historical Context

Recall how in previous chapters we postulated a primitive family, clan, or tribe headed by our faithful friend Bodo. The group did fairly well using the original something-you-are identifiers—biometrics— because biometrics allowed family members to recognize one another while distinguishing outsiders. But as their social group and the reach of their activities grew, they needed to extend their identification capabilities.

They did so with identifiers that we call "something you are assigned." Using names, for example, they distinguished among people who were not present for immediate observation. This adapted to the larger world in which more-advanced, but still primordial, humans lived. It required somewhat advanced language and communication skills.

Something-you-know identifiers represented another step forward. By comparing knowledge, people could judge the likelihood that another was the particular person he or she represented him- or herself to be. This required more advanced comparison among high-level concepts that might have included relationships, history, and other complex knowledge. "Something you know" probably coincided with the emergence of humans from clans into societies and the early stirrings of rudimentary trade and commerce.

Something-you-have identifiers, such as the seal and signet ring, took identification processes a step further, into the age of tools. Happily, this advance allows us to stop guessing about Bodo and the primordial groups that used such identifiers. These tangible items left tangible traces, and archeologists have studied signets and seals, revealing the use of these identifiers dating back several thousand years. At this time, commerce and communication had grown past what we might call primitive. The combination identifier/decoration/communications tool/security device/power symbol of the signet ring was an important tool for commerce and communication.

It was not the last identifier that humans invented, of course. The most common something-you-have identifier in use today is the identification card. Often, cards combine different categories of identifiers. Cards themselves are something you have. They are embedded or imprinted with information like account numbers or biometrics, such as a picture, from the something-you-are (or are-assigned) category. This is multifactor identification, a topic in a future chapter, as are identification cards themselves.

And the advance of human-created identifiers has not stopped. Mathematicians are working on new digital identifiers that may serve a variety of purposes and strike a balance between the interests that are served and threatened by identification in the digital age. The consequences of emerging digital identification systems and responses to them, including new digital identifiers, are discussed further along in this book.

We now have solidly in hand the concept of identifiers, the building blocks of identification. Every identification system uses facts about people that come from one or more of the four categories: something you are, something you are assigned, something you know, and something you have.

The divisions among these identifiers are not absolute. The private key in public key encryption is a password—something you know—but it is functionally similar to a signet ring. Perhaps this shows how, in the digital age, knowledge and facts are a form of property—something you have.

The identifiers available to us are not static. They are products of advancing technology. Newly created identifiers like encryption keys are slowly seeing adoption in ordinary life. And the way all identifiers are being used is changing with advancing technology. This raises important issues about the changed meaning and consequences of identification.

Before reaching those issues, though, we must study the quality of identifiers, how they are used in combination to identify reliably, and how they ride on one another to accommodate the complexities of our society. Today's pervasive and important identification system, the identity card, which we will return to later, sits at the pinnacle of all this complexity.

7. Identifiers in the Fourth Dimension

Inspector Clouseau spun the large globe at his office window and turned to look pensively out across Paris. Turning back toward the room and his assistant, Henri, he shook his finger in the air and commanded, "We must find that woman!"

Putting his hand down to lean on the nearest object, Clouseau was propelled to the floor by the spinning globe.

Righting himself quickly, he straightened his coat. "What's that? What did you say?"

"Uh, we don't have much of a description," replied Henri. "About five foot seven. Black hair. Wearing a light beige coat."

"We must find that woman! She is our first positive link with the Phantom!"

Just hours earlier, this mystery woman had approached a man reading a newspaper at a wall along the river Seine. The headline on the paper read " 'The Phantom' Strikes Again; Half Million in Gems Stolen." She handed him a small box wrapped in plain brown paper, saying, "They're worth half a million but we'll settle for three hundred thousand."

"I'll do what I can but the merchandise is extremely hot."

Just then, the Paris police and a carload of inspectors from the French Sûreté came upon them. The chase was on.

The woman—sporting shoulder-length black hair, a beige coat, black gloves, dark sunglasses, and a large black bag—ran into a nearby hotel. The police were in hot pursuit but she reached an elevator and its doors closed before they caught her.

As the elevator rose, the woman threw off her gloves, glasses, and wig. She snatched the false collar from her coat and bent down to take a blue turban and a pair of shoes from her bag, which she then turned inside out. While hurrying to change shoes, she put on the turban. Then she quickly reversed her coat so that the exterior was black.

As the elevator doors opened a few levels up, the mystery woman desperately collected her things from the floor and hopped off the elevator as the doors closed behind her. Barely composing herself, she turned around and pushed the call button just as the police, who had been running up the stairs, arrived at her floor.

She greeted her pursuers politely, as they did her. The elevator had gone back downstairs and the police turned to run after it, oblivious that the woman they sought was standing right there.

Inspector Clouseau's intercom buzzed. He pressed the button. "Yes?"

"Your wife to see you, Inspector."

"Send her in, please."

Inspector Clouseau dismissed his assistant Henri, who exited as Madame Clouseau came in.

"Hello, my darling," said his wife, the mystery woman.

"My angel," Clouseau cooed in his exaggerated French accent.

In this scene from Blake Edwards's classic movie *The Pink Panther*, Madame Clouseau successfully used low-quality identifiers to elude the police and continue her double life as the wife of a prominent French police inspector and an accomplice to the debonair international criminal, Sir Charles Litton. During the chase scene along the Seine, the French police had little identity information to go on, and she abandoned those identifiers in the time it took to ride an elevator up a few floors.

As we have discussed in earlier chapters, identifiers are any characteristic that can be used for sorting. A truly wide array of characteristics are used as identifiers. These identifiers can be gauged along a number of scales that tell us how well they work as identifiers and what they might be good for.

Some identifiers are permanent and fixed to the body, for example. In the absence of accident or disease, a person's brown eyes are permanent and fixed. Others can be permanent but unfixed. A person's birth date will never change but it is not connected to the person in an objectively measurable way. Rather, it is based on social concept of day and year represented in the calendar. Still other identifiers are fleeting, like Madame Clouseau's clothing, which she purposefully selected so that it could be changed in a brief instant or two.

Some identifiers are common among large groups of people, while others are not repeated twice among any two individuals on the planet. The given name "John" is very common in the United States.

A person's DNA or fingerprint is believed to be completely, or almost completely, distinct.

Some identifiers are hard to copy and others are relatively easy. A person's signature is a behavioral biometric identifier that is hard to imitate well. The state-issued driver's license in the United States has long been relatively easy to alter, forge, or falsely procure, as generations of college students can attest. This has become harder with advances in card technology, but there is a burgeoning international market for fake identification cards.

These variations all influence the *quality* of an identifier—that is, the assurance it brings to the connection between a person and an identity. From one interaction to the next, the likelihood that the same identifier will be found on the same person, and not found on another, goes to how strong an identifier it is.

A high-quality identifier is one that creates a high level of assurance about the identification that is made with it. A low-quality identifier is one that does not create such a high assurance. A higher-quality identifier is more useful for ensuring that the correct person is encountered on a second meeting, a third, a fourth, and a fifth. In short, quality is the measure of how useful an identifier is over the fourth dimension: time.

High-quality identifiers are not always the most convenient or the most appropriate identifiers to use. Identification has some adverse consequences to important human interests, so there is no natural superiority to using high-quality identifiers in every case. As we will discuss in the next chapter, low-consequence transactions generally require low-quality identifiers, if they require identification at all. Many transactions can be undertaken based on the substantive characteristics of the parties rather than their identities. In these cases, authorization rather than identification is more appropriate. In any event, understanding the elements of quality in identifiers helps reveal further how identification processes work.

Fixity

In the scene from *The Pink Panther*, Madame Clouseau had prepared herself well for the possibility that the police would chase her. She had purposefully selected clothing and accessories that were reversible and changeable. She used them to distance herself from the identifiers the police collected when she was spotted handing off the box of gems at the Seine. This allowed her to make her escape.

Madame Clouseau was able to do all that because clothing and accessories are unfixed to the person. Unfixed identifiers are low quality because they might only be associated with a person for a short period of time. Fixed identifiers are higher quality because they are attached to the person.

The most fixed of identifiers are, of course, biometrics. These something-you-are identifiers are defined by the fact that they are attached somehow to the body. As noted, fingerprints and DNA are high-quality identifiers because they are literally "of" the body. Signatures and voice prints are also fixed to the body because they are produced by particular movements of the body. This renders them fairly high on this measure of identifier quality. Skin color, height, weight, hair and eye color, likewise, are all fixed.

There are plenty of commonly used and useful identifiers that are not fixed, of course. Names, birth dates, Social Security numbers, ATM cards, and passwords are all unfixed identifiers that are in common usage. Their location on the scale of "fixity" is low but that does not render them useless by any means. In fact, they are very useful for many purposes, such as simple or remote interactions.

One of the important qualities of fixity is that fixed identifiers are relatively hard to remove. To avoid fingerprint identification, a person might have to burn or scar his or her fingertips. There is currently no known way to change the marker genes used in DNA analysis. Not all biometrics are inexorably fixed, however. Shaving off a mustache can change the appearance of the face when the authorities are circulating a mustachioed mug shot, for example.

Another of the important qualities of fixity is that fixed identifiers tend to be nontransferable. That is, one person cannot give a fixed identifier to another. It may be possible to forge a fixed identifier, such as a signature or a tattoo, but it is often difficult. Forgery of a signature is the attempt to overcome both the fixity and the "distinctiveness" aspect of identifier quality, discussed next.

Some fixed identifiers change over time. Height, weight, signature, gait, tattoos, piercings, hair color, and hair pattern are all examples of fixed identifiers that can change. That is why permanence is another important element of identifier quality, discussed further in the chapter.

Distinctiveness

Try looking for a brown-eyed person in Zambia, and you will not have much success. That is not because there are no brown-eyed people there, of course. It is because nearly everyone in Zambia has brown eyes. You will have *too much* success. This identifier does little to distinguish among people there. An identifier's being fixed does not mean it is inherently a high-quality identifier. How distinctive it is has an important role.

An identifier is higher quality if it is exclusive to one or a small number of people. An identifier is lower quality if many people may have it or because people may be able to acquire it.

Nondistinctive identifiers are useful for their purposes. How many times has "Check out that blond" served two American men pursuing a favorite male pastime? The same phrase spoken on their vacation in Sweden might not be as helpful because blondes are more common there. The distinctiveness of an identifier helps determine its quality and how valuable it will be for identifying someone.

Just as they are fixed, many biometrics are also very distinctive. DNA, fingerprints, and elements of the iris appear to be unique to each person. Thus, they are high quality along the distinctiveness scale, in addition to their fixity.

Some biometrics are quite distinctive, but not entirely so. The signature, for example, is a commonly used identifier, prized for its distinctiveness. Yet it is possible to forge signatures. Forgery is an attack on the distinctiveness of an identifier. It is an attempt by someone other than the person associated with an identity to proffer an identifier linked to that identity.

Many other biometrics are not at all distinctive. Nearly all hair colors, eye colors, skin colors, heights, and weights are repeated many times even in relatively small populations. That does not disqualify them from use as identifiers in particular circumstances. It just limits them to use in lower-consequence transactions.

The password is an identifier that can be highly distinctive and thus high in quality along that vector—at least if people and institutions are using good security practices. The Latin alphabet has 26 letters and the decimal numbering system 10 numerals. Including capitalized letters, 62 different characters are available for use in passwords. That means that someone trying to guess a one-character password has a 1 in 62 chance of getting it right. Most passwords are much longer, of course, and the difficulty of guessing them goes up exponentially. A two-character password has 3,844 possible combinations and a four-character password nearly 15 million. An eight-character password has over 218 trillion possible combinations.

This property makes random passwords potentially very distinctive. Many people use common names, words, and phrases to create their passwords, which drives the distinctiveness of their passwords down and makes the job of a password cracker much easier. Still, when used correctly, passwords can be as distinctive as DNA.

The highest-quality passwords are long and use random combinations of letters, capitalized and lowercase, and numbers. Many people devise mnemonics to help them remember their passwords.

Alas, people who do not understand the role of passwords write them down and leave them in inappropriate places, such as in their wallets or near their computers. This behavior risks breaking down the distinctiveness of the password. A roommate, spouse, maintenance person, or coworker who acquires a password may use it to access computer files, programs, or databases that he or she is not authorized to see, acting as an impostor of the authorized person. Writing down passwords and storing them insecurely threatens the distinctiveness that gives this identifier high quality.

The relative distinctiveness of an identifier lends to its quality. Identifiers that are highly distinctive are high quality, while identifiers that are common are relatively lower in quality.

As with fixity, it is unnecessary to gravitate toward total distinctiveness in the identifiers used for every transaction. The quality of identification needed varies from one circumstance to another, and overidentifying someone may be inconvenient or contrary to their interests in privacy and autonomy, for example.

Permanence

Permanence is the final scale along which the quality of identifiers can be measured. Many identifiers are permanent and lifelong. Many more last only briefly and plenty fall in between.

Many biometrics again lead the pack along this measure of quality: DNA remains largely the same through a person's lifetime, though in the future gene therapies may exist that change the molecules used as "markers" in DNA analysis.

The fingerprint, also nominally permanent, changes in some respects over long time periods. Older people's skin gets thinner and their fingerprints less pronounced. Over lifetimes, a small but relevant minority of people suffer injuries to their hands and fingers, burns or cuts that may obscure, change, or remove their finger-prints—and some may suffer these injuries on purpose.

Many other biometrics are challenged as identifiers by the passage of time. People's signatures, voiceprint, gait, height, and weight all change over time, as do hair color, hair pattern, and other features. Some of them are altered by surgery, dyes, prosthetics, and exercise.

Several assigned identifiers, on the other hand, are impervious to the passage of time. The Social Security number, mother's maiden name, and birth date all remain static throughout a person's life, with rare exceptions for the Social Security number. Given name and surname often remain unchanged for long periods, though they may change a few times because of marriage, divorce, and adoption or through court action.

Physical addresses, telephone numbers, e-mail addresses, and job titles are all identifiers that fall in between long- and short-term on the "permanence" vector. The same identifiers may be kept for anywhere from days to decades. The relative quality of each identi-fier depends on how often the identifier changes and how easy it is for someone to change it.

Each circumstance dictates the relative need for permanence in an identifier. Often, permanence does not matter but sometimes it does. Each transaction will dictate the level of quality that is called for in identifiers and which aspect of quality is most important.

By wearing a wig, Madame Clouseau confounded the Sûreté's attempt to collect an identifier that was useful when chasing her. They believed that they had the right kind of identifier: Hair and its color are fixed to the body and certainly permanent enough for a foot chase. Hair color is not very distinctive, but that is no matter in a hot pursuit.

But the fact that Madame Clouseau wore a wig meant that the identifier was not fixed at all. She removed that identifier and replaced it with another as she rode the elevator. The French police misjudged the quality of identifiers they had acquired in looking at her "hair" and clothes. These identifiers were much less useful, over even the short duration of a foot chase, than they thought. Thus

Madame Clouseau was able to elude them and carry on with her double life. The success of her and her compatriots in stealing the famous Pink Panther diamond and avoiding punishment would turn on many other, similar deceptions, as well as the famously bumbling ineptitude of her husband, Jacques Clouseau.

It is exceedingly rare that identifiers are falsified during in-person contacts because that is difficult and risky to do. Madame Clouseau was quite lucky to escape. It is somewhat easier when people interact with institutions and when they deal with each other remotely. These contexts raise the specter of fraud and similar wrongdoing because the quality of identifiers used in these environments can be low. Institutional and remote transactions require some very sophisticated approaches to identification, including accepting some risk of misidentification. We turn to these issues in the next chapter.

8. Identification, Risk, and Authorization

In ways we often take for granted, modern technology and business practices have opened up a wide new variety of options for work and lifestyle. The life of J. Trevor Hughes provides a good example.

Trevor is the executive director of the International Association of Privacy Professionals, a group whose membership includes many of the largest companies in the United States and the world. Each year, the association holds conferences in Washington, D.C. and elsewhere to address privacy, information security, and related topics. It offers a daily newsletter, conducts regular audio conferences and continuing education programs, and offers certification to those who wish to be recognized as highly trained privacy professionals.

Trevor is also the executive director of the Network Advertising Initiative, a consortium of online advertising companies. That group has negotiated important agreements with the U.S. Federal Trade Commission that shape the practices of online advertisers. On behalf of the Network Advertising Initiative, Trevor has testified before Congress a number of times.

As busy and active as he is in cutting-edge business and public policy issues, one would expect Trevor to live and work in Washington, D.C.; New York; San Francisco; or some other center of business and technology. But then one would be wrong.

Trevor, his wife, and their two children live in York, Maine, a small town in the southwest corner of the state, about an hour and a quarter outside Boston. Not far from Long Sands Beach, York's small business district has a few multistory buildings, a gas station, and a few shops. It is a quaint and neat, if sleepy, New England town.

Trevor knows a great place to get fresh Maine lobster, of course. Patrons bring their own beer, bread, salad—whatever suits their tastes—and select a few live crustaceans for cooking. The lobsters are served to diners at picnic tables on a deck overlooking Chauncey Creek near where it runs into the harbor. On occasion, Trevor has been known to play hooky from work and spend a morning kayaking there in York Harbor.

Just a few years ago, this New England idyll might have been too out-of-the-way for business activities of national scope, but with modern communications and technologies that is no longer true. E-mail, the Web, and mobile phone service, as well as regular air transportation out of Boston, mean that Trevor Hughes conducts business with the same connectedness as anyone anywhere else in the country. He just does it from a better-than-average place.

Trevor interacts with a lot of people remotely, over the phone and through e-mail. When he does, he may be using modern technologies, but his identification practices follow a framework that people have used for generations, even if almost no one ever articulates them.

Trevor is a soccer fan. He is one of those quirky few Americans who follow "real" football more than American football. So in mid-2004, as the Euro 2004 championship was about to begin, Trevor organized a small, informal betting pool among other American soccer watchers. The Euro tournament is played every four years among national teams in Europe to see which one is the best.

Trevor put an e-mail out to a group of people who had participated in an earlier pool and added a few names: people whom he thought might join in the fun. He invited everyone receiving the e-mail to send it on to others as well. Each participant would pick results throughout the tournament and the one with the most accurate picks would receive a soccer jersey from each of the other participants.

Sure enough, Trevor got an e-mail from someone he did not know but who had received a forwarded copy of his e-mail. When the invitee sent in his picks for the Euro 2004 pool, Trevor had a decision to make, a decision that centered on identification.

Trevor knew that the invitee was a friend of a friend, but he had never met him, never talked to him, and never corresponded with him online before. Should he trust this person? Would doing so present an unacceptable risk of fraud?

Trevor allowed this stranger into his football pool because of some commonsense judgments about identification and risk. Trevor felt he had enough identification of the participant to go forward.

As we discussed briefly in chapter 2, identification occurs when one person or entity compares the identifiers of another with a set of identifiers that he or she has previously recorded and finds a match between the two. To "identify" someone does not mean knowing everything about them, or the person's whole identity. Rather, "identification" is having enough assurances of who a person is to proceed with a transaction. What constitutes "enough" assurances is very contextual. It turns on the risk of misidentification.

Risk Management

"Risk" and "risk management" are difficult to define because they crop up in so many different fields and are used so many different ways. Roughly, though, risk management is the practice of studying and suppressing risks to the functioning and success of institutions, processes, technologies, and transactions. In essence, it is the study of bad happenings and how to deal with them.

Risk management starts with threat assessment. This is figuring out all the different bad things that could happen to the thing you are trying to protect. Threats are the vectors by which harm could come to something—in this case, a process like Trevor's football pool. The Euro 2004 competition could have been cancelled, for example. Trevor's computer might have crashed, erasing the records of who was participating and their picks. A participant might say he will participate but then refuse to fork over a jersey at the end.

The next step is risk analysis or risk characterization as to each significant threat. This explores and combines the likelihood that the bad thing will happen and the consequences of it happening.

Consider the following combination of general risk scenarios for a particular threat:

- The bad thing is *unlikely* to happen, and it would have a *small consequence*.
- The bad thing is *likely* to happen, and it would have a *small consequence*.
- The bad thing is *unlikely* to happen, but it would have a *large consequence*.
- The bad thing is *likely* to happen, and it will have a *large consequence*.

Of course, likelihoods and consequences do not fall into a four-step pattern. The likelihood of a bad thing happening falls along a continuum and the consequences of it happening fall along another continuum.

To illustrate how risk assessment factors into a simple transaction, assume that the seller of an exotic car stands to make a $5,000 pure profit from selling it for $100,000 to a wealthy-looking person who has offered to pay using a personal check. There is a threat that the check will bounce and the buyer will disappear, leaving the seller with no recourse. The seller has done a quite magnificent risk assessment revealing a 0.5 percent chance of that happening. That is, 1 out of every 200 transactions of this type will result in a total loss to the seller of $100,000.

This risk information reveals that the actual expected profit from each transaction is not $5,000. It is $4,475, because 199 times out of 200 the seller will gain $5,000 and, 1 time out of 200, will lose $100,000 [((199*5,000) + (1*–100,000))/200 = 4,475]. This is a worthwhile transaction to enter into because chances are that it will result in a profit. Yet there remains a chance that it will result in a substantial loss. The statistical expression of these chances is to place the expected profit at $4,475 rather than the $5,000 figure representing sale price minus cost. The risk assessment has revealed a lower statistical profit from the transaction than it would otherwise appear.

Risk assessment or risk analysis may reveal ways forward that reduce or prevent risk or that mitigate likely harms. That is, the seller of the exotic car may alter the transaction in some way to reduce the risk of being defrauded, or she may prepare for fraud in a way that prevents it having the anticipated consequence.

Using the risk information the seller has developed, she will spend anything less than $525 to totally eliminate the risk of being defrauded. She may spend $524 on an investigation into the buyer that fully proves his bona fides. She may charge the buyer $524 less for paying with a cashier's check or other guaranteed instrument. These steps go by various names: risk prevention, harm prevention, risk suppression, and so on. Whatever the name, they diminish the risk of fraud in the transaction.

Alternatively, she may spend $524 on insurance that will make her whole if the check bounces. For her, this is risk (or harm) "mitigation" because it reduces the consequences of the bad thing when it actually does happen. (For her insurance company, this is not mitigation; it is risk transfer because it will now have to pay.)

Of course, risk prevention and mitigation techniques do not fall into an all-or-nothing pattern. The seller may divide up the $524 with a little investigation that suppresses some of the risk, a little price break for surer payment that suppresses some more of the risk, and a little insurance that mitigates some more of the risk. She will likely spend less than $524 to partially reduce the risk. She will choose the quantity and types of risk suppression and mitigation that most efficiently address the risk of fraud.

Spending up to $524 to totally avoid the risk of fraud in the sale of the car will lower the seller's profit from an apparent $5,000 to $4,476, but that lower profit will be guaranteed. Without taking these risk-avoiding measures, the seller's guaranteed profit is just $4,475. Spending more than $525 would leave the seller worse off, of course. Spending $600 to avoid a statistical loss of $525 would be a waste of $75.

Returning to our general risk scenarios, consider how they might be addressed:

- The bad thing is *unlikely* to happen, and it would have a *small consequence*. Risk suppression and mitigation procedures are probably not necessary.
- The bad thing is *likely* to happen, and it would have a *small consequence*. Modest risk suppression and mitigation procedures might be appropriate.
- The bad thing is *unlikely* to happen, but it would have a *large consequence*. Modest risk suppression and mitigation procedures might be appropriate.
- The bad thing is *likely* to happen, and it will have a *large consequence*. Only a fool would not take steps to suppress or mitigate the risk, or consider avoiding the transaction entirely if possible.

The array of decisions among these risk scenarios—which risks to address, how to address them, and so on—is risk management. Risk management and decision analysis are complex and fascinating fields of study that have been badly oversimplified here. But in summary, a person considering a certain course of action will go forward if he or she believes that, in the end, the transaction will create a greater chance of gain than risk of harm or loss.

We are almost ready to understand Trevor's decision to allow a stranger into his football pool. First, let us apply some of these basic risk management ideas to identification.

Misidentification Risk

In the context of families, friends, and acquaintances, the risk of misidentification is almost always small: The person in the kitchen of your family home who looks and acts exactly like your mother is almost certainly your mother. The people at your favorite coffee shop who look like your friends and talk to you familiarly are almost certainly your friends. You use some of the highest-quality identifiers to interact in these ways with them and the likelihood of misidentification is very, very low. The consequences . . . well, they would just be weird.

But among strangers and in remote contexts—among humans who are not face-to-face, between individuals and institutions, or between institutions and institutions—there is a greater likelihood of misidentification because the processes used are not innate and have not been refined for millennia like in-person identification has. The consequences of misidentification can be small or they can be large.

Individuals selling their cars do not generally have good information about risk, such as the risk of being defrauded by a wealthy-looking purchaser offering a personal check. But institutions that engage in hundreds or thousands of transactions per week or day can develop fairly good statistical analyses of the risks to their systems from misidentification and fraud. They can determine what risk suppression and mitigation techniques are most appropriate for their processes.

The considerations they must take into account are much more complex than those in the car-selling example above. A bank whose risk suppression techniques look more deeply into a customers' identity or background, for example, may create more than just monetary costs: it may inconvenience customers or offend their privacy sensibilities, driving them to competitors.

Too much risk suppression is bad for everyone. Identification techniques aimed at reducing fraud may turn customers away and reduce their ability to enjoy goods and services disproportionately to the fraud that is suppressed. This is like spending $600 to eliminate a $525 statistical risk.

The identification that is appropriate for any given transaction comes from comparing identifiers with tolerable risk levels rather than with nearly perfect knowledge of a total identity. Spending insufficient time, effort, or money on identification will lead to mis-identification, error, and fraud. Spending too much time, money, or effort on identification will make transactions unnecessarily expensive, inconvenient, or intrusive.

Returning to the football pool conducted from York, Maine, Trevor was assessing fraud and misidentification risk. He knew that a friend of a friend might participate in his football pool. Most people are honest and, among the small number of dishonest people, only a very few would know about his football pool. Even fewer would open new e-mail accounts or forge e-mails to get the chance of winning some jerseys, while planning to vanish without paying in the event of losing. Fewer still would take over the e-mail accounts of other people to throw the results or steal winnings.

There are so many better opportunities for fraudulent behavior—and productive honest behavior—that defrauding Trevor and other members of his football pool would have been wildly inefficient thievery. Accordingly, there was an infinitesimal likelihood of someone falsifying an identity or fraudulently adopting another person's identifiers just to participate in Trevor's football pool. When he received the pool entry via e-mail, common sense (a colloquial name for risk analysis) told Trevor that there was an exceedingly tiny chance of hearing from an impostor or a scammer.

The consequences of a scammer participating in the football pool were also quite low: someone would come up short a jersey or, if the winner was the fraudster, he would get free jerseys without risking one himself.

Trevor balanced this small risk of fraud against risk-avoiding techniques, such as demanding more identification information, which would entail a good deal of inconvenience and make Trevor seem rude. Refusing this outsider participation would be a lost opportunity; the reward of having another participant in the football pool was relatively high. Trevor wisely accepted an e-mail address as sufficient identity information for this low-risk endeavor.

In day-to-day life, we are all good risk managers. We know without thinking too hard which risks are good to take and which risks are bad. When we choose to cross a city street, it is because we are better off on the other side even though we risk being hit by a car. When we consider crossing a freeway, the risk calculus is different, and most of us look for an overpass or tunnel rather than dodging among cars hurtling by at 70 miles an hour. We will take a longer route, using precious time, to avoid the relatively high risk of death from cars speeding along the freeway.

It is nearly a waste of precious time to parse the identification issues in Trevor's football pool so carefully. But it is a simple version of a typical modern transaction conducted remotely among strangers. Much of modern commerce, including remote transactions and interaction with institutions, requires some articulated thinking about the risks of misidentification.

Identification and Authorization

In the most consequential transactions, the need to identify a person accurately is very important. Criminal prosecution, for example, involves the rights and freedoms of individuals so accurate identification is essential. The criminal justice system has been an early adopter of high-quality identifiers like fingerprinting and DNA. Courts of law spend many hours ensuring that a person who may be incarcerated is accurately identified. When a person is inaccurately identified and wrongly held as a suspect, jailed, or put to death, we regard this as a grievous injustice. It is worth a very high investment of time and money by courts, law enforcement, lawyers, and jurors to ensure that identification is done well.

The issuance of a mortgage typically involves a very large amount of money and a personal obligation that may take decades to meet. Mortgage issuers require many identity checks, including information that allows them to pull a credit score (which, along with needed creditworthiness information, incorporates many different identifiers). They check identification cards, meet the prospective debtor in person, and so on. The costs in time and money of all these identification processes are worth it in light of the consequences of misidentification or fraud.

The type of identity information required for particular transactions can vary widely, however. Even relatively valuable transactions may not require bulletproof identity information. Consider, for example, that no actual identifying information is required to withdraw money from an ATM. Through experience and study, banks have made a judgment that the holder of an ATM card who knows the associated PIN is, within tolerable levels of risk, probably the account holder or someone authorized by the account holder to access it. Requiring more identifying information would inconvenience ATM users. It would also strengthen even further the ability of ATMs to track people's movements, raising well-placed privacy concerns. These costs are disproportionate to the amount of fraud that better identification would suppress.

The risk calculus is constantly shifting based on fraud techniques and the costs of suppression and mitigation, including nonmonetary costs like privacy. Personal preferences vary: Many people probably feel that requiring better identification at ATMs would make them worse off on the whole. Many may feel that the security benefits outweigh any privacy costs. Biometric ATMs may be on the near horizon because of the convenience and antifraud benefits they offer.

As we have discussed in earlier chapters, a card-and-PIN ATM transaction is not as much an identification process as it is an *authorization*. Authorization is the idea that a person with particular traits should be allowed certain privileges regardless of whether he or she is linked to a precise identity. When a woman gives her husband her ATM card and PIN so he can withdraw cash from her account, possession of the ATM card and knowledge of the PIN are sufficient indicators that he should be authorized to withdraw money, regardless of who he is. Authorization is an important alternative to identification.

The identifiers Trevor used in allowing a stranger to participate in his football pool were of such low quality that the transaction could be characterized as using authorization rather than identification. The characteristics that this person had were the ones Trevor was looking for: interest in participating, a sufficient knowledge of European soccer, and a modicum of reputation for honesty (suggested by the relationship between the invitee and the friend who had forwarded the e-mail).

In the end, the greatest threat to the integrity of the pool may have been Trevor himself. He did not publish his own picks in advance but won the pool by a narrow margin. A jealous participant who did not know Trevor as honest and fair might suspect that he had selected his picks as game results were announced, keeping his lead to a narrow margin just to stay credible. His closest rival in the pool was the author of this book who sent Trevor a lousy T-shirt in payment of his winnings as a mute protest of the potential impropriety.

There are thousands of contexts in which identification and authorization are used. In each of them, the likelihood of misidentification or fraud is different, as are the consequences should misidentification happen. The appropriate risk suppression and mitigation techniques are also highly specific to each circumstance.

Analyzing the appropriate methods used to identify people in various contexts is complex. Verifiers must choose identification methods that suitably avoid the risks involved in misidentification. Going too far, though, is inefficient. On the "cost" side of the ledger are things like the consequences of more precise identification to privacy, anonymity, convenience, and other consumer and individual interests, which we will discuss in chapters 19–22. As Trevor did, it is often best to use relatively weak identification in many transactions.

A number of advanced techniques and practices adjust the quality and efficiency of identification to suit different circumstances and risks. We turn to these in the next chapter.

9. Advanced Identification Techniques

FlexCar is one of several "shared-car" services that have cropped up in American cities over the past few years. Shared cars are vehicles that are available to rent for short durations—an hour or two for a trip to the store or the airport—rather than requiring customers to take, and pay for, a full day. Users pay hourly and mileage-based fees. The services take care of gas, tune-ups, insurance, and all other expenses. Most shared cars can be reserved using 24-hour phone and Internet reservation systems. Cars are conveniently placed throughout a metropolitan area for easy self-pickup and -return.

The idea of a shared-car service is a small but significant innovation in the car rental business model. It offers many attractions and benefits to consumers. Some are motivated by the environmental and aesthetic benefits, not having to own a car, removing cars from city streets. Many more find that they can save a tremendous amount on the cost of car ownership—including upkeep, gas, insurance, and parking—by using public transportation, bicycles, other transport, and a shared car for a few hours when the need arises.

One aspect that makes shared cars more convenient than traditional car rentals is that the cars are located throughout metropolitan neighborhoods rather than at airports and remote parking lots. This creates a problem, however, because placing an attendant with each car would be prohibitively expensive, undoing most of the benefits of the shared-car business model. The solution is preregistration—checking users' driving records and credit—and some technologies to make the cars easy to pick up and return without assistance.

Until it changed to a new system in mid-2006, FlexCar operated as follows: At the time reserved, the FlexCar driver went to the place where the car was parked and placed a special card next to a clearly marked reader in the corner of one of the car's windows. This prompted the car to unlock its doors. Once inside, the driver got the ignition key from the glove compartment and entered a code on a keypad located either in the glove compartment or on the dashboard.

Entering the code allowed the driver to start the car and drive it away. Do-it-yourself pickup and return is central to the success of the shared-car model.

Multifactor Authentication

Obviously, this sequence is an identification system. The card and code represent identifiers that help make sure shared car users, and nobody else, will gain control of the cars. Shared-car services would have a serious problem—indeed, there would be no possible way for the business to succeed—if they could not limit access to registered users.

FlexCar's identification system is a particularly clear and simple example of "multifactor authentication," the use of identifiers from different categories to lower the risk of misidentification or misauthorization.

In chapter 2, we briefly discussed the term "authentication," which is most commonly used in online commerce. In that usage, it can mean both "identification" and nonidentifying "authorization." Because there are important differences between identification and authorization, we have avoided using the term to avert ambiguity.

Correctly, though, the word "authentication" admits the possibility of error—that is, reasonably accepted risk of misidentification or misauthorization. "Authentication" is best thought of as the step in either identification or authorization where the verifier considers the provenance of offered characteristics or identifiers. We use it here because the multifactor technique works in both identification and nonidentifying authorization.

The FlexCar card is a something-you-have identifier. Each card is issued by FlexCar after it has qualified the customer to use its service through a review of his or her driving record, creditworthiness, and so on. The card contains a chip that carries a distinct serial number or string of characters correlating to that specific user. That serial number is transmitted to the car via radio frequency, telling the car (and, in turn, FlexCar) that the person opening the car is *likely* that particular user.

Cards can be lost or stolen, and the FlexCar card is a bright blue, with the company's trademark emblazoned on it. This distinguishing feature creates a risk that someone unapproved by FlexCar might use a lost or stolen card to enter a car and drive off with it. The

74

FlexCar code that must be entered onto the keypad before the car will start suppresses that risk.

The code is a something-you-know identifier. Like the card, it is issued to drivers after they have been qualified for the FlexCar service. When a driver enters a code, the system correlates the code to the card that was used to open the car. Only the code that matches the card will allow the vehicle to start. This combination of identifiers creates a very high probability that the person in the FlexCar is an authorized driver. An impostor would have to acquire both the card and the code from the authorized user.

FlexCar users are not identified to an absolute certainty. There is a risk that a burglar could steal a card and fish the code out of his victim's files, leading to theft of the cars. Another risk is that users will give their cards and codes to unapproved people, which can increase the liability associated with operating the service. But the risk of misidentification under this system appears low enough to make shared cars viable as a business and as a service that makes life a little easier, more convenient, and more aesthetic for urban dwellers.

FlexCar's access control mechanism illustrates how multifactor authentication helps lower the risks of error or fraud in identification and authorization. Using identifiers of different kinds lowers the likelihood of improper access to FlexCars.

Multifactor authentication can also be explained in numerical terms. Let us say a private club with 300 members requires members to give their names and a pass code to an attendant at the door. About 3 in 10,000 people in the United States have the name John Smith, one of the most common names in the country. There is a 1 in 10,000 chance of guessing a four-numeral pass code on the first try. The combination of this something-you-are identifier and something-you-know identifier makes it very likely that a person who arrives at the door, identifies himself as John Smith, and knows a certain pass code is the John Smith who is a member of the club. Someone who knows that John Smith is a club member has a 1 in 10,000 chance of impersonating him. An outsider who does not know the names of members may guess John Smith because that is such a common name, but he still has only a 9 in 1 million chance that there will be a John Smith and that he will guess John Smith's pass code correctly.

Pass codes are not so high quality as identifiers that they guarantee this level of protection, of course. As discussed in chapter 5, people often weaken or break password-based security systems for their own convenience by using default or easily guessable passwords, by sharing passwords, or by writing down passwords and leaving them accessible to others. Still, codes are often successfully used as part of multifactor authentication schemes.

Multi-Identifier and Uni-Identifier

Multifactor is an important model for suppressing the risk of misidentification and misauthorization, but the quality of identifiers is probably more important than their diversity or number.

Consider an identification system that uses two something-you-know identifiers: father's middle name and a pass code. The first identifier is unlikely to be known widely beyond a family group, and the second is hard to guess if it is properly created and secured. This pair of identifiers are from the same category but they probably provide better assurance of an identification than, for example, father's middle name and hair color. Hair color is from the something-you-are category, but it is relatively low quality because it is not distinctive. Even though it is from a different category than something you know, its use is not inherently better for identifying someone.

The important part of multifactor is really the "multi" piece of it. Multi-identifier identification can be just as good as, or better than, multifactor, depending on the quality of the identifiers used.

Earlier, we supposed that the use of a name and a short pass code could lower the chance of impersonation to 1 in 10,000 on the first try, or much lower depending on the circumstances. A lone high-quality identifier like DNA or a fingerprint can lower the risk of impersonation or error to one chance in several billion. Even a single identifier can be higher quality than multifactor.

As mentioned in chapter 7, the highest quality of identification is not always necessary and is often undesirable. Chapters 19 through 22 in this book will examine how identification may negatively affect important human interests like privacy, autonomy, and obscurity. The multifactor or multi-identifier technique can make good identifications without resorting to "overqualified" identifiers like biometrics. Multifactor authentication is an important tool for suppressing the risk of misidentification and misauthorization. Suppressing risk is important, in balance against the other qualities that are needed and desirable in transactions.

Piggybacked Identification Systems

Other qualities that are important for remote and institutional identification include speed, convenience, and low cost. Most of the benefits of transacting over distance would disappear if the parties had to meet in person, look each other over, and develop the kind of relationship that family members and friends have.

To accommodate these needs, nearly all human-designed (as opposed to spontaneously adopted) identification techniques and systems rely on other identifications or identification systems to do their work. One identification system will look to the fact that another has identified someone and will rely on the previous identification in making its own. Identification processes piggyback on one another constantly. This piggybacking reduces the cost and inconvenience of identifying people.

Many identifiers, such as titles, phone numbers, and e-mail addresses, exist because someone has been suitably identified by an entity such as a business or service provider. A phone number at an office, for example, tends to confirm that a person works in that office—that he or she has been suitably identified, vetted, and given access to the company's infrastructure.

FlexCar does not use in-person interviews to screen potential new members. That would be prohibitively expensive. Rather, it piggy-backs on several other systems. FlexCar may check prospective members' credit and employment histories, driving records, insurance claims reports, and insurance scores. And it requires a credit card for payment purposes. Those information and payment systems use identifiers like the Social Security number and the state-issued driver's license. They also produce identifiers of their own, like account numbers in the case of credit cards.

FlexCar uses these identifiers to suitably identify its users, then issues new identifiers of its own: the FlexCar card and pass code. Those identifiers piggyback on a host of other identification systems.

There are a variety of other examples. The domain name in an e-mail address signifies with a certain level of assurance that an identifiable person has been heard from and can be reached at that same address. People know how to "read" e-mail addresses and use them as identifiers for piggybacked identification. Several large Internet service providers offer free e-mail service. A username and pass code identify users to the ISP. With less assurance than the corporate environment, but still enough for low-consequence purposes, recipients of e-mail from such a domain can be reasonably confident that an identified person has been heard from and can be reached at that e-mail account. Free e-mail services are not careful about confirming identity information, so it is riskier to rely on e-mails from such accounts, otherwise unidentified, than on e-mails from corporate accounts. They may be inappropriate for higher-consequence transactions.

In turn, many websites use an e-mail address and pass code to identify or authorize users. This process piggybacks on identification or authorizations made by other entities' e-mail systems. And the piggybacking goes on and on.

Thoughtful readers have been noting the weaknesses in these identification systems, and there are plenty. Piggybacking on an identification system incorporates the weaknesses of that system into the new identification system. If a previous identification has been fraudulent, the current one may be too.

In favor of substantial cost savings, convenience, and speed, piggybacking injects misidentification risk into identification systems. It is by no means wrong to piggyback identification systems, though. Many modern conveniences would disappear, and the prices consumers pay would rocket skyward, if identification systems did not rely on one another. But it is important to understand the practice and its results for both good and bad.

Ride Refusal

As with so many other examples of identification systems so far in this book, the FlexCar system could be used equally well as a nonidentifying authorization system. A couple, family, church, or neighborhood association may wish to use one FlexCar card and pass code for all their drivers. Assuming all qualified for the service, FlexCar gave them permission, and they controlled the card or took liability for its misuse, different individuals could use the service and FlexCar would not know which had used it. This system would help obscure from corporate surveillance which particular person had used the FlexCar service on any given day.

Likewise, the FlexCar system could be used for nonidentifying authorization with other institutions. A FlexCar card could be used as a substitute library card for example. Tapping the card on a reader and entering the code could authorize a person to borrow a book without informing the library of the person's identity. FlexCar would be liable to the library for overdue books and fines and could charge the customer accordingly. It might guarantee, in the meantime, that once a book has been returned, the record of who borrowed it would be destroyed.

Between FlexCar and the driver/patron, the system is used for identification. As to the library, however, the system would be used solely for authorization. The design of such systems would allow people to share information and identification with the organizations they trust and avoid sharing with those they do not, an idea we will return to in chapters 25 and 26. Piggybacking identification systems is important and useful, but often people may not want their identification card to give other systems a ride. Preserving thousands of small facts as secrets will be increasingly important in the advancing digital world, as we will also discuss in later chapters of this book.

Piggybacking and multifactor authentication are advanced, but common, techniques in identification and authorization. Piggybacking is a way of reducing the cost, difficulty, and time consumption of identification or authorization. It tends to increase the risk of misidentification and misauthorization.

Multifactor authentication uses identifiers from different categories to drive down the risk of misidentification. Multiple identifiers from the same category can achieve the same result if they are substantially different. Even single identifiers can be quite useful. The important thing is to be aware of the resulting quality of the identification and the consequences of overidentification.

Piggybacking tends to lower the quality of identification because it can create a long, potentially flawed "chain" from an original identification to the immediate one. Without piggybacking, however, many of the benefits of remote commerce would be lost. The risks to identification systems from piggybacking are significant but assuming those risks in many cases will be the best way to proceed.

Perhaps the most important and most piggybacked-upon identification systems are government-issued drivers' licenses and identification cards, which are also multifactor and multi-identifier. For this reason, licenses and ID cards merit special attention. They get that attention in chapters 14–18.

First, though, let us turn to the purposes and roles of identification. We now know much about how identification works: we have a theoretical framework that helps us understand the different techniques used in identification, factors that make identification reliable or unreliable, and techniques that help set the balance between efficiency and authenticity in identification processes.

Next we must ask why we use identification and why sometimes we do not. The following chapters look at the roles identification plays in our personal, social, commercial, and political lives. As we will explore, identification fosters social and economic interaction. It is essential for accountability. But preserving anonymity is equally important because it protects individual autonomy and personal power. Anonymity promotes full participation in society. Our challenge is to strike the balance between identification and anonymity that best promotes individuals' interests in things like tangible wealth, personal security, individual autonomy, and liberty.

PART II

THE ROLES OF IDENTIFICATION AND ANONYMITY

10. Identification and Relationships

"Thea, it's me. I've been shot. And the only reason I'm still alive is because of you."

It's a bad line from a bad film with an improbable plot.

Minotaur is a 1995 movie starring Mili Avital and Joshua Lucas about an affair of sorts between an Israeli secret agent named Alex and the woman he becomes obsessed with after spotting her on the subway. Apparently because he is in a dangerous line of work, Alex cannot just introduce himself and talk to Thea. Instead, he writes her letters.

And she writes letters back. They conduct a supposedly intense liaison over a period of years through these letters. There is one phone call after Alex is shot in a parking garage. For some reason, the phone call is okay.

When he was a child, Alex's mother had told him the story of how the Minotaur, a creature from Greek mythology that is half man and half bull, was saved from death by a woman's touch. Among the things Alex sends Thea is a line drawing of a Minotaur with a woman reaching toward it.

While Alex is conducting this odd pseudostalking of Thea, she has a couple of normal relationships as well: with G. R., a fellow student, and Nicos, a professor of Spanish literature. G. R. is killed by bad men who probably had it in for Alex. There is little character development where Nicos is concerned, but there is no need: he has a Spanish accent and a thick mane of shoulder-length black hair.

Alex finally decides to reveal himself to Thea. She pretends to care about leaving Nicos behind—or perhaps bad acting makes it seem a pretense. On the street in front of her house, she gets her first look at Alex, but before they can speak he is felled by a hail of bullets. Though Thea is in the line of fire, none of the machine-gun spray strikes her. She reaches out to touch him, drawing a too obvious analogy between Alex and the Minotaur.

Minotaur is an improbable movie on several levels. Much richer storytelling is needed to explain what Alex is actually doing when he assassinates people and why he cannot approach Thea. Odd flashbacks to Alex's childhood make clear that the moviemakers saw something intense in what they were doing. They just didn't get it across in the film.

Most of all, the movie does not explain why Thea would enter into this odd correspondence with a man who would not identify himself to her. Thea is by no means starved for companionship, and most people would reject a one-sided arrangement like this out of hand. In real life, Thea would probably have gotten a restraining order against Alex instead of accepting his creepy notes and gifts, which show up at her family home and in her locker at school.

The relationship between Thea and Alex is so improbable because nearly every relationship begins with identification. Shared identifiers are the building blocks of connection. Think of anyone you know—any member of your family, any friend from work or school, your spouse, or a loved one. Down to the very last one, you have collected in your mind the group of identifiers that distinguish that person or entity from all others. You have his or her identity suitably captured for the relationship you have. Indeed, saying that you "know" someone almost always means you can identify them. Thea and Alex did not have this, and their relationship made no sense.

Personal relationships start with the collecting of identifiers that allow memories and knowledge to be cataloged. In *Minotaur*, for example, Thea's normal relationship with G. R. began when he said to her, "Hi. I'm G. R." Sharing that common, something-you-are-assigned identifier got their relationship off on its first baby steps. As they talked to each other, of course, they shared and collected many more identifiers. All the flashed smiles, winks, and other displays involved in flirtation are just the exchange of dozens of biometric identifiers to passionless students of identification theory. As the relationship progressed, they shared and collected more and better identifiers, along with all the substantive information—the facts, stories, opinions, aspirations, and shared experiences—that accompany a deep personal relationship.

A good illustration of something-you-know identifiers appears at one point in the developing relationship between Thea and G. R.: At first, Thea mistakenly believes that G. R. is the writer of Alex's letters. She tries to establish his identity as such by quoting from one of them. When she says, "I hope it is not 'far, far too late,'" and sees that G. R. does not recognize the phrase, she is quite shocked. This attempt was to use knowledge as an identifier—their common knowledge of the text of a letter.

Studying the unusual case portrayed in *Minotaur* illustrates how identification is a crucial dividing line between having and not having a relationship or connection with another person. Identifying someone commences a relationship, and failing to be identified prevents a full relationship from forming. In the movie, Alex and Thea had a relationship premised on little or no identification, and it was not believable. In all but the most exceptional circumstances, identification plays an early and ongoing role in binding people to one another. Identification is a sort of social glue.

Identification is an invaluable tool. In its lowest form—things like the nametag—the use of identification greases happy hour conversation. The use of names and visual identifiers allows people to talk to and about one another in ways so obvious that their absence would be absurd. Imagine a cocktail party where guests could not tell whom they had spoken to just the moment before. Imagine the difficulty university students would have comparing professors if there were no standard ways of distinguishing one from another. Identification dispenses with these absurdities.

Relationships with Institutions

Identification plays a similar role in forming relationships between people and institutions, as well as forming relationships among institutions. Just as people use identification to catalog memories and knowledge of one another, institutions use it to catalog and remember people. People likewise use identification to catalog institutions.

Employers, for example, check the references and educational backgrounds of people they might hire for positions of trust. To do that they must accurately assess the background of the person they are considering rather than someone else. They use identification to ensure that the reference they call or the transcript they inspect is about the person they are considering. That is important to get right. Identification allows them to do that.

Even more is at stake in lending, so identification is even more important. Misidentification can mean the entrustment of money to someone unlikely to repay it or the denial of a loan to a deserving person. There are serious negative consequences when identification is not correctly made and the characteristics of one person are applied to a decision about another.

Think of any business that might characterize itself as having a "customer relationship" with you. When that business identifies you, it starts treating you in a particular way. Your Internet service provider delivers your e-mail when your computer presents your e-mail address and pass code. Perhaps your grocer, barber, manicurist, or host greets you with friendly and familiar chitchat when he or she sees you. Or it could be the credit card issuer whose representative calls your phone number asking whether you want insurance protection for your account. Their identification of you is the first essential step in tailoring your experience of them in some way—and building on your relationship, they hope.

Different institutions use other identifiers, of course. The U.S. federal government and many state government programs use the Social Security number as a primary identifier, with other identifiers sprinkled in for good measure. When these institutions use these identifiers to distinguish a particular person from all others, it can be said that it has a relationship with that person. Interacting a second, third, fourth, and any subsequent time, the government agency can refer to records of past interactions and other information to decide whether the person qualifies for benefits, should be incarcerated, and so on.

This is a different kind of relationship, of course: the relationship between sovereign and citizen. If, during any particular contact, a government agency has not identified a person, the agency is not in the same role as it is when it has identified the person. Generally speaking, it has less power to control the person and dispose of his or her freedom and assets.

Individuals use identifiers to distinguish among institutions, too. Trademarks are the words, phrases, slogans, designs, or symbols used to identify the source of goods and distinguish them from other sources. These are identifiers that corporations create and use to help ensure that consumers will recognize them as distinct from one another. Companies hope that consumers will associate good memories and feelings with them so that they will do more business.

One of the most memorable trademark cases dealt with whether the Owens-Corning Fiberglas Corporation could get a trademark on the use of the color pink in its insulation products. This was certainly a distinctive color for home insulation. The company's advertising had featured the Pink Panther cartoon character and encouraged homeowners to "add another layer of pink." A federal court of appeals found that a color could be the subject of a trademark.[1] This advance in trademark law also helped solidify the remarkable relevance of the 1964 movie *The Pink Panther* to identification theory.

Trademark law prohibits the use of confusingly similar marks because they make it difficult for consumers to identify the sources of goods and services. In other words, trademark law protects the identifiers that consumers use to identify corporations and to maintain relationships—of a commercial sort—with them.

The role of identification in relationships of all kinds can be shown through counterfactual examples. This chapter opened with the story of a "relationship" in which identification played a minimal or negligible role. It was not believable. This example helps show how comprehensively people use identification in interpersonal relationships.

Businesses can certainly pursue customers without developing relationships. There are roadside fruit stands, for example, that neither identify particular customers nor make available identifiers such as brand names, websites, or phone numbers. But most businesses do push identifiers out to consumers and seek to identify their customers to build relationships.

And, of course, it would be impossible for a government or government agency to collect taxes, distribute entitlements, or collect fines and jail criminals without properly identifying the subjects of those actions. The point is simple but essential: identification is at the core of all relationships, be they among people or between people and institutions.

Identification and Boundaries

Identifying someone commences a relationship and refusing to be identified prevents a full relationship from forming. But it is more complicated than that. The kind and quality of identification control the scope of relationships. Identification varies with context and thus helps to support or delimit relationships, allowing them to reach the levels that the parties think appropriate.

A couple in an intimate personal relationship uses plentiful identifiers in wide varieties for all the contexts in which they encounter each other. They use multiple biometrics, specially assigned identifiers, shared knowledge, and much more. This contrasts with the relationship between, say, an Internet service provider and an Internet user. The provider uses a simple e-mail address and passcode for nearly all interactions with customers. Once in a while, it may use a physical address or a payment card account number. This is a shallower, less intimate relationship, to be sure. The different identification practices among different parties in different contexts illustrate how identification puts boundaries on relationships.

The connection between Thea and Alex in *Minotaur* was odd because the sharply limited identification between them was inconsistent with the deep love relationship they supposedly had. More often, when people withhold identification information, it is to delimit the extent of a relationship. Think of a woman in a bar who declines to give a drunken suitor her last name or tell where she works—or who gives a fake phone number. These are all customary and appropriate ways of preventing a relationship from continuing beyond that one awkward conversation.

It is increasingly common—if still too rare—to see corporations ask consumers how they might wish to be contacted on the webpages where they sign up for subscriptions or buy goods. This is a welcome adoption of tact by consumer-oriented businesses, many of which have long failed to recognize the boundaries that many consumers would like to see on the "customer relationship."

A company that agrees not to contact a person by telephone is showing the courtesy of not pushing the relationship beyond the customer's tolerances. It is not exactly the withholding of identity information because the business probably still has that contact information, but the gist of the agreement is, "Don't think of me as a person you can reach by telephone. Contact me only by mail."

Technology and Identification

Changing technology has the potential to change the relationships between businesses and individuals in fundamental ways. Radio frequency identification (RFID), for example, is a technology that uses tiny computer chips and radio transmitters to individually identify the objects to which they are attached. The use of RFID is likely to see substantial growth in coming years because of the great efficiencies it will bring to logistics, retail inventory control, and many other economic segments and functions.

It will be possible to tie goods to individuals through RFID: If a person buys a chipped item and uses a store loyalty card in the purchase, for example, the RFID chip could be associated with that person in the store's records. RFID infrastructure might be used to track people and goods quite comprehensively. That could dramatically change the relationship between shoppers and stores. Stores might be able to identify returning customers and treat them differently based on past transactions or other information.

A person walking into a store and being recognized is in a different relationship with the store and its salespeople than an unidentified person. This relationship is illustrated by a scene in the 2002 science-fiction thriller *Minority Report,* in which John Anderton (Tom Cruise), on the run from authorities, enters a store where eye scans (called "eye-dents") allow the store to display ads personalized for the identity they have assigned to his retinas.

Some consumers may prefer browsing a familiar store in relative anonymity. They may want to reveal themselves only when they have selected an item for purchase, or not at all. Other consumers may enjoy the special treatment and customer service available to them if they are in a close relationship with a store.

Consumers may ultimately reject RFID tracking, acquiesce to it, or demand it. No one knows what the consuming public will prefer or how those preferences may evolve,[2] although plenty of people are willing to project their own preferences—both out across the population and forward into the future. The nub of the question is whether commercial entities and governments should have greater ability to identify people. The use or limits on RFID for identifying people will help define the relationships of people to institutions in the future. RFID is controversial because of its power to change relationships.

The distinction that we have mulled in this chapter—between being connected to, or separate from, others—is crucial in a number of ways. We will explore more of its meaning and consequences in later chapters. Suffice it to observe here that identification is the key social practice that connects people to one another, allowing them to form relationships. It also connects people to institutions and institutions to people. The methods used for identification in a given relationship help define the nature of the relationship, and many connections are bounded by limiting or withholding the identifiers or identification processes that the parties use.

The movie *Minotaur* provides an interesting case study because it attempts to portray a strong personal relationship in which one of the lovers cannot identify the other. Without better storytelling, this plot does not work. (Incidentally, the film has also bad sound design: characters' footsteps can be heard when they should not be and glasses clinking together don't sound right. All in all, it gets a thumbs-down.)

Identification is an essential part of personal and economic relationships, but that is not its only role. As we will see in the next chapter, it also allows governments to visit accountability on wrongdoers, and it allows people to hold one another accountable in commercial and social contexts.

Then we will explore some reasons not to prefer identification. Anonymity, or the absence of identification, has many benefits. Succeeding chapters discuss how anonymity permits people the fullest range of choice in personal and social development. It also has functional benefits: anonymity protects people who engage in dissent, whistle-blowing, and other controversial activities that challenge, and ultimately strengthen, our institutions.

11. Identification and Accountability

In a little over two months, Thomas Jennings would be dead. So ordered the Illinois Supreme Court in December 1911, affirming his conviction and death sentence for the killing of Clarence Hiller 15 months before.

Clarence Hiller was not perfect, but he was a good family man. He lived with his wife and four children in a two-story frame house on the south side of West 104th Street just east of Waldon Parkway in Chicago.

Clarence and his wife shared their bedroom with their two youngest children. Their modest home was well within earshot of the Chicago Rock Island and Pacific Railway line just on the other side of the parkway. On summer nights like that one in September 1910, when the family slept with their windows open, they were sure to wake to the sound of the trains. Their life was not opulent.

But Thomas Jennings was not after money when he climbed through the Hillers' kitchen window that night. Earlier, he had snuck into the McNabb place, just two lots to the south. Mrs. McNabb would later testify that Jennings had placed his hand on her shoulder twice then under her clothes against her bare body.

Jennings was doing more than this to one of the Hiller daughters, a terrified Florence, when Mrs. Hiller awoke and noticed that the gaslight at the top of the stairs was out. She woke Clarence, who went to investigate. Hearing him, Jennings retreated from Florence's room. The two met at the top of the stairs.

In the struggle that followed, Hiller and Jennings fell to the bottom of the stairway. There, Jennings managed to turn his gun on Clarence Hiller. Jennings shot Clarence twice, grazing himself in the process.

The neighbors awoke to the screams of Mrs. Hiller and her family. John Pickens dressed hurriedly and ran to the Hillers'. Pickens's son Oliver was returning from the train station and heard the commotion, as did a police officer on patrol nearby. They all arrived at about the same time, but Thomas Jennings had already fled the scene. Mrs. Pickens fetched a blanket from upstairs to cover Clarence's body.

Three-quarters of a mile east, 15 minutes later, four police officers just off their shift were waiting for a streetcar on Vincennes Road. Slightly concealed as they sat on a bench, they watched Jennings walk up with his right hand fixed in his pants pocket, holding something. He was perspiring and fresh blood was on his clothing. The officers did not know about the murder of Clarence Hiller, but they searched Jennings, found a gun, and arrested him.

A doctor who examined Jennings later found a fresh injury to his left arm that looked more like a bullet wound then something that would happen falling off a streetcar, as Jennings had claimed. He strongly denied being involved in Clarence Hiller's murder.

The Hiller house had recently been painted, with the back porch done last. It had been finished on the Saturday just before the shooting. One of the porch railings was near enough to the kitchen window that a person climbing through it might use the railing to support himself. There was an impression in the fresh paint on that railing from the four fingers of somebody's left hand.

Officers from the Chicago Police Department's identification bureau took the railing and made enlarged photographs. They also enlarged photos of Thomas Jennings's fingerprints, taken after he was arrested and also several months earlier when he had been returned to prison on a parole violation.

Four expert witnesses testified at Jennings's trial that the fingerprint images from the Hillers' railing and the images from prints taken while Jennings was in custody were the same. On this and other evidence, Thomas Jennings was convicted. The Illinois Supreme Court affirmed the use of fingerprint evidence and ordered his execution to occur on February 16, 1912.

People v. Jennings[1] was one of the earliest and most influential court cases dealing with the use of fingerprint evidence in American criminal law. It illustrates well one of the most important purposes of identification: making people accountable.

Most Americans understand the basic principle of justice that punishment for wrongdoing can only be fairly meted out to the actual wrongdoer. Group punishment is anathema to our system, as is punishment of anyone who has not been proved beyond a reasonable doubt to have committed a crime. To uphold this principle of justice, our criminal law system devotes substantial resources to careful, high-quality identification.

Yet there remain strong arguments that the legal system does not do enough to ensure correct identification. Recent revelations of wrongful convictions, turned up by DNA evidence, show that justice can be better administered with better-quality identification, in terms of both convicting the guilty and exonerating the innocent.

In the case of Thomas Jennings, the Illinois Supreme Court sanctioned the use of an identifier that was controversial at the time but is now widely accepted. It is probably accepted for good reason: the fingerprint, a something-you-are identifier, meets high-quality standards because it is fixed to the body, it is permanent, and it is highly distinctive.

Accountability in Daily Life

People have a general duty not to do violence to others or to perpetrate theft or fraud. The criminal law appropriately punishes people, holding them accountable, when they violate this duty. Identification of wrongdoers is an essential step in this process.

But accountability, and the identification necessary for it, is certainly not confined to criminal matters. In nearly every commercial contract, every purchase and sale of goods, and every promise to perform services, accountability is also needed. Nearly all commercial transactions involve some kind of promise or guarantee that might be broken. Nearly all commercial transactions require at least a modicum of identification so that the parties can hold each other accountable.

For example, the seller of a lamp may guarantee explicitly or implicitly that its wiring is safe. A chimney sweep may require half of the money for his work before he begins, the other half to be paid when he finishes. The mortgagor of a house may promise to make regular payments for 30 years.

Each of these transactions may require the parties to hold each other accountable if something goes wrong. Thus, each of these transactions requires a requisite level of identification between the parties. Only the rarest commercial transaction is structured so that neither party can have recourse against the other.

A problem that has become acute with the growth of remote commerce is the need to ensure that the people who enter into contracts and transactions are who they say they are. Imagine arranging to sell your car online, for example, with the buyer agreeing to come to your house and pay for the car the next weekend. If the buyer does not show up and you sue for breach of contract, he might repudiate the contract by arguing that it was not him who had agreed to buy it. You would need to prove that it was really him with whom you had been dealing.

For generations, contracts and transactions of all kinds have been formed by parties interacting in person. They may have signed a document or shaken hands, looking each other in the eye. In these cases, identification has not been difficult. But the ways people conduct business are changing so proving that a person is who he or she claims to be is more important than before.

It is difficult to ascertain identity in remote transactions. Nonrepudiation is a highly sought after quality in such interactions. That is, it is essential to have proof that people are who they say they are and have agreed to be bound by a contract. Identification is an essential part of this process, explicitly required by new forms of conducting business.

In June 2000, the U.S. Congress passed the Electronic Signatures in Global and National Commerce Act,[2] also known as "ESIGN." This law was designed to give explicit recognition to contracts entered into and agreed to online. This was an important step forward for remote commerce, and at the time there was much talk of multimillion-dollar mergers, car sales, and mortgage closings rapidly moving to the online environment.

That has not happened all that quickly. Consumers and businesses have been reluctant to trust the online medium for large transactions. The reason is, in part, because of the potential for imposter fraud and the difficult problem of ensuring nonrepudiation in large contracts. It is also because the online medium can be used for comprehensive tracking, which goes too far for many people's comfort.

Better online identification systems may yet allow the vision of large-scale remote commerce by creating nonrepudiation of online contracts while protecting people's interest in privacy and anonymity. Perhaps coming technologies will make it so that real people are accountable to each other in some of their dealings online, but they are not even recognized by each other in others. We will look at some of these systems in the final chapters of this book.

Reputation

Identification also allows for the creation and use of reputation. Think, for example, of the common practice whereby companies check the references of potential new employees. Accurate identification means that a worker who has been fired for stealing or consistently shirking his or her duties will receive unfavorable recommendations, thus being held accountable for his or her malfeasance. Identification is an integral part of the trust building that is necessary for commerce among relative strangers. Identification allows people's reputations to be used in their favor, or against them, as the case may warrant.

Reputation is important in commerce, of course, but it is just as important in social environments. Think of a party, for example, where someone has said something rude. The victim may tell others about it, tying the perpetrator to his act through identification. People may treat the ignoramus differently, knowing what poor manners he has. They may shun him, scold him, or conveniently forget to invite him to future parties. All these reactions hinge on proper identification and show its integral role in enforcing and strengthening social mores. Identification allows people to be accountable in social systems, just as in legal and commercial ones.

In short, just as identification brings people together for their productive purposes, it holds them together when things go badly. We talked in chapter 10 about the role identification has in facilitating interaction and relationships, both social and commercial. It has an equal role in promoting accountability.

Again, identification is a sort of social, economic, and legal glue. It holds people to their words and actions so that there can be reputations and consequences. It holds people to their promises so that there can be commerce. And it holds people to their law breaking so that society can punish them. Accountability is an obvious, but important, function of identification.

This does not mean that identification is always a good thing. In the next two chapters, we will explore how remaining unidentified fosters full personal development and autonomy, as well as the full exercise of legal rights and public participation. It is often just as important to remain anonymous as to be identified.

The family of Clarence Hiller would certainly have preferred having its patriarch alive to the small glory of having his name associated with a landmark case about the use of fingerprints in American criminal law. But perhaps it is a small tribute to Clarence Hiller's modest and honorable life that the story of his killer's capture and conviction makes an essential point about the relationship between identification and accountability.

12. Anonymity and Personality

In 1961, Jane Jacobs turned the world of city planning on its head with her book *The Death and Life of Great American Cities*.[1] This one-time writer for architectural magazines in New York City debunked conventional wisdom about how cities should be organized—indeed, whether they should be organized at all. City planning had been developed up to that time by a series of "utopian" visionaries, each of whom believed he had come up with a master plan for designing urban environments. Those master plans did not work.

Through example after example, Jacobs showed fatal errors in how planners build cities. She found parks placed in the shadows of skyscrapers or on dead-end streets, narrow sidewalks that could not carry heavy foot traffic, and city blocks so long that people avoided walking down them. These and other elements led city spaces to fall into disuse, abandonment, and disrepair, which cultivated crime and blight. Then, when planning failed, the planners came back to do it some more.

The key to a successful city, Jacobs showed, was diversity: different buildings, residences, businesses, and uses in any given area, dictated by no one master plan. That is the opposite of what we still see today in many downtowns, where office buildings are packed together, apartments are packed together, and stores are packed together—each in its own sort of ghetto.

The International Network for Traditional Building, Architecture & Urbanism is a UK charity dedicated to the support of customary architecture around the world, the preservation of local character, and the creation of better places to live. The organization's patron is His Royal Highness, the Prince of Wales, better known as Prince Charles. Prince Charles has had a long interest in preserving the unique character of towns and cities. He has made himself a bit controversial in architectural circles by anointing the buildings he thinks too modern with florid descriptions like "monstrous carbuncle" and "giant glass stump."

Among many other things, the charity publishes essays about traditional design and planning. One such essay, written in 2003 by Israeli architect Hillel Schocken, is called *Intimate Anonymity: Breaking the Code of the Urban Genome*.[2] In this essay, Schocken builds on Jane Jacobs' criticism and explains cities in terms of human needs. His theory: "the city is a place that allows human beings to form relations with others at various levels of intimacy while remaining entirely anonymous."

This theory bridges the two extremes between relations in village life and those in city life. Although village life offers many comforts and benefits, it can be limiting and claustrophobic because neighbors there know so much about one another's business. Gossip and social pressure make it very hard to deviate from social norms.

In cities, on the other hand, life can be alienating and lonely, with people losing themselves in the massive urban environment. The implication behind this theory is that urban spaces should bring people together into a welcome mix while preserving maximal anonymity.

The Jerusalem Municipality Piazza is beautifully detailed and proportioned, according to Schocken, but it fails as a space because it serves only a single use. Everyone there has some municipal purpose, such as paying taxes. Indeed, just by being there, individuals reveal their Jerusalem citizenship. Similarly, a person in a business district reveals something of his or her occupation or social standing. A person on a university campus is probably a student or academic. A person in a neighborhood zoned for housing probably lives there. Because it stratifies people and separates them by class, status, ownership, and interest, rigid zoning is an anti-urban practice.

Cities and Freedom

People go to cities in search of freedom. This is counterintuitive, of course, because cities teem with people. One might think that the presence of other people—who vie for limited space, overhear conversations, and constantly observe one another—would suppress freedom. But they do not. Cities support people's ability to live as they wish, choose among different modes of living, and express themselves more fully. Cities offer room for anonymity.

City residents can access the necessities of life while identifying themselves to only a tiny cadre of people, each of whom needs to know very little about their lives and few of whom will compare notes with one another. A city dweller may talk to a landlord once every few months, rotate among grocers and restaurateurs regularly, switch jobs often, and never acknowledge a neighbor, if he or she chooses.

This flexibility leaves city folk free to live as they choose, select companions that are best suited to them—or avoid companionship altogether. They can adopt the social norms that they prefer, with a minimum of societal pressure. City dwellers avoid the constraints that come from being readily identified as people are in small communities. In cities, people can resist being drawn into the relationships and encumbrances that are practically required in other settings. Thus, the relationships they have are largely voluntary.

Anonymity is not an unalloyed good for people who cannot make mature and healthful decisions on their own. Social pressure guides many people in ways that benefit them. But for the rest, the anonymity allowed by cities is fresh and invigorating. The ability to choose with whom and with what institutions one has relationships is an important protection for individuality and social freedom.

This exploration of cities and urban *non*planning helps illustrate the value people place on having the freedom to select their social and commercial relationships. People desire and deserve substantial control over their society. All people do not naturally conform to the customs and lifestyles of their families, peers, and communities. The choice to do so is what makes the conformist an actor with free will rather than a cowed follower of fashion.

Each of us consistently uses our power over relationships to shape our lives. More often than we realize, because we are not conscious of the process, we decline to be identified. For example, we abandon websites that require personal information in exchange for content that is not important enough to us. We take natural offense when a phone caller says, "Hi, who is this?" without first identifying himself or herself. As we discussed in chapter 10, we decline identification or limit the release of identifiers to control and delimit relationships.

Just as often, people decline relationships entirely through the absence of action. They constantly shun proffered attachments. They do not join social or business groups, do not shop, and do not interact when they do not want to. They do not respond to the catalogs and flyers sent daily to their homes, each an invitation to engage in new relationships with clothing retailers, nonprofit organizations, real estate agents, publishers, and political groups.

When people pick up and move from one town to another—to a place with better schools, for example—they are breaking a relationship with one local government in favor of another. They may also be choosing a lower tax rate, a better business and employment climate, better police and fire protection, and so on.

Each of these choices—whether they are actions or inactions—structures our material lives and our personalities. When we do not have these choices, our power to make ourselves who we are is reduced. Although the power to refrain from relationships is not well articulated and understood, it is very important to protect and to foster.

Lessons for Identification

The lesson for identification is this: Identifying people contrary to their needs and wishes erodes their ability to craft their lives as they wish. To maintain the greatest freedom for personal development, relationships should be, as much as possible, a product of choice.

So should be identification. Identification should occur when it offers those being identified a benefit that they either choose or acquiesce to and benefit from.

Identification should be avoided if it does not offer something in return. It should not be used if it commences a relationship that a person does not prefer. Identification should not be required or coerced as a condition of enjoying access to the wealth of goods, services, interactions, and experiences that societies have to offer. Identifying people when it does not benefit them would apply this "social glue" to people too often and make society far too "sticky" for many people.

"City air makes one free after the lapse of a year and a day." This principle, recognized in 12th-century Bremen, Lübeck, and other cities around Europe, claimed that a person residing in a city for more than a year was entitled to stay and enjoy the benefits of city life.[3]

Those benefits were substantial because city dwellers at the time had a special kind of life. The legal relations among them were governed by contract rather than status. While their peers in the countryside were subjects of kings and feudal lords that may have been only slightly less rapacious than Viking raiders and pirates, people inside city walls had lives and property that were much more secure, legal equality was the norm, and relations among people were voluntary.

During that period, the church was asserting its independence from the secular power of kings, and the burghers in the cities were asserting their independence from both. The voluntary relationships found in early cities were the stirrings of what we know of today as civil society.

The liberal social order that we take as a given in the West today, and that is on the rise elsewhere in the world, started in early cities. One of its hallmarks is voluntary choice in the relations among people and institutions.

A deep strain in modern Western culture holds that people should be able to identify themselves—and refuse to be identified—to shape their lives as they see fit. That is a power worth preserving. Forcing identification on people would undo that power and would return people, in a small but important degree, to the subjection that Westerners have been climbing out from for centuries.

13. Anonymity and Immunity

The initials AG conventionally stand for "attorney general" but they often seem to stand for "aspiring governor." State attorneys general have a natural proclivity to run for higher office: for Congress, for the U.S. Senate, but especially for governor. The experience AGs gain as a state's top lawyer suggests their executive ability. AGs can project a tough-on-crime populism that often works for getting votes.

John Malcolm Patterson was that kind of attorney general. In fact, he was the first AG in Alabama to move directly from that office into the governorship. He served as Alabama's governor from 1959 to 1963.

As attorney general, Patterson built a name for himself a couple of different ways. For one, he developed a reputation for being tough on organized crime. He also stridently opposed the civil rights movement, with its insistent demands for racial equality in the South. The images of police siccing dogs and spraying fire hoses on protesters are matched behind the scenes by the political and legal maneuvering of people like John Patterson, who lined up to staunchly defend the status quo. Obviously, he was on the wrong side of history.

Like most professional politicians, Patterson was quite crafty and aggressive. He used his role as attorney general to battle institutions such as the National Association for the Advancement of Colored People, demanding in a 1956 lawsuit that the NAACP qualify in Alabama as a foreign corporation.

The NAACP had been founded in 1918, was headquartered in New York, and had opened a regional office in Alabama in 1951, five years earlier. Attorney General Patterson began looking after the legal niceties when the NAACP supported black students seeking admission to the state university and promoted a boycott of the bus lines in Montgomery.

The NAACP denied that it was required to comply with Alabama's foreign corporation law. To adjudicate the dispute, the attorney general's office demanded a wide variety of the association's records and papers, including bank statements, leases, deeds, and lists of the names and addresses of all its members and agents in Alabama. This way, Patterson would kill two birds with one stone: he could burden the NAACP with litigation costs while turning up a trove of information about its membership. He and his allies could exploit this information to undermine the group's resolve and strength.

The NAACP decided to comply with the Alabama foreign corporation law and offered to settle the dispute by filling out the required forms. The judge in the case, however, fined the NAACP $100,000 for not producing its membership lists. The NAACP appealed this ruling all the way to the Supreme Court. It had an idea of what the attorney general and his allies might do if the identities of its members were revealed.

The Supreme Court did too. The NAACP won.[1]

The Court's opinion summarized the NAACP's argument as follows: "[T]he effect of compelled disclosure of the membership lists [would] abridge the rights of its rank-and-file members to engage in lawful association in support of their common beliefs."[2] Expanding on this, the Court wrote the following:

> Effective advocacy of both public and private points of view, particularly controversial ones, is undeniably enhanced by group association. . . . It is beyond debate that freedom to engage in association for the advancement of beliefs and ideas is an inseparable aspect of the "liberty" assured by the Due Process Clause of the Fourteenth Amendment, which embraces freedom of speech. . . . Of course, it is immaterial whether the beliefs sought to be advanced by association pertain to political, economic, religious or cultural matters, and state action which may have the effect of curtailing the freedom to associate is subject to the closest scrutiny. . . .
>
> Petitioner has made an uncontroverted showing that on past occasions revelation of the identity of its rank-and-file members has exposed these members to economic reprisal, loss of employment, threat of physical coercion, and other manifestations of public hostility. Under the circumstances, we think it apparent that compelled disclosure of petitioner's Alabama membership is likely to affect adversely the ability of petitioner and its members to pursue their collective effort to foster beliefs which they admittedly have the right to advocate, in that it may induce members to withdraw from

the Association and dissuade others from joining it because
of fear of exposure of their beliefs shown through their associations and of the consequences of this exposure.[3]

This boils down to a simple, but essential, notion: People are freer
to speak and act if they can do so anonymously.

For this reason, U.S. law has recognized the importance of anonymity in speech, in association, and in other constitutionally protected behaviors. There are many negative consequences of being
identified when engaging in controversial or unpopular, but legal,
behavior. In *NAACP v. Alabama ex rel. Patterson,* the Supreme Court
appreciated this, which is why it granted constitutional protection
to the anonymity of NAACP members.

In chapter 11, we talked about how identification promotes
accountability. It does, and accountability is essential in many cases.
But there is equal merit to not being accountable in other cases.
Resisting identification is often just as important as being identified.
U.S. constitutional law protects the anonymity of people engaged
in protected behavior to keep them from being penalized for it.
Anonymity creates a special zone of protection for legal but unpopu-
lar speech and action.

Anonymity and Free Speech

The practice of anonymity has a long and highly valued pedigree,
particularly in the area of anonymous speech. *Cato's Letters,* for
example, were an influential series of essays about freedom of speech
and political liberty that first appeared in 1720. They were written
by two British men, John Trenchard and Thomas Gordon, who called
themselves "Cato" rather than identifying themselves.[4] If they had
been identified, the authorities might have been quite harsh in rebuk-
ing them for their opinions.

These works had a wide following in America. John Adams and
Thomas Jefferson both quoted them, and they were among the most
influential 18th-century works on political liberty, freedom of
speech, and freedom of the press. The practice of anonymity is
woven into the framing of the U.S. Constitution.

This is just one example of many instances where unidentified
speakers laid the groundwork for freedom in the United States.
The Federalist Papers were published anonymously under the
pseudonym Publius.[5] Many other publishers, both favoring and

opposing the new American government, wrote anonymously or pseudonymously.

Legal defenses of anonymity have a deep history too. In 1735, John Peter Zenger was arrested for seditious libel for publishing pseudonymous essays attacking New York governor William Cosby. Zenger was a German immigrant printer who also republished several of *Cato's Letters*. His lawyer, Andrew Hamilton of Philadelphia, defended Zenger by asking the jury to lay "a foundation for securing to ourselves, our posterity, and our neighbors" the right of "exposing and opposing arbitrary power . . . by speaking and writing truth." The jury acquitted.[6]

Modern American constitutional law still rests on this foundation. In a landmark 1995 First Amendment decision, *McIntyre v. Ohio Elections Commission*, the U.S. Supreme Court held that pamphleteers did not have to register or sign their documents, saying, "Under our Constitution, anonymous pamphleteering is not a pernicious, fraudulent practice, but an honorable tradition of advocacy and of dissent. Anonymity is a shield from the tyranny of the majority."[7]

Anonymous speech had a significant role in the founding of the United States and maintains that role in public advocacy today. Anonymity underlies the freedom and prosperity that all Americans enjoy.

As typified by the *NAACP* case discussed above, the constitutional right to free speech enshrined in the First Amendment clearly encompasses anonymous speech and anonymous association related to speech. Requiring identification risks the possibility of censorship, self-censorship, or husbanding of speech-related associations and activities. Accountability tools like mandated identification are described as having "chilling effects" on speech because they would induce this self-censorship and excessive caution. In cases where governments have sought to require identification and registration of speakers, the Supreme Court has held this to offend free-speech rights.[8]

Stated in the terms laid out in this book, there can be no requirement that people must have some special relationship with, or accountability to, government or broader society in order to speak. Because of the benefits of robust speech and criticism, our law deems that there can be such a thing as too much accountability for speech.

Especially, but not exclusively, to get the benefits of a full airing of people's views about important topics, political issues, and public figures, our nation has made a judgment that it is important to have people free of encumbrances on their willingness to speak. The connections or relationships that are created by identification can hinder the exercise of civil rights like free-speech. Anonymity is a core tool of free peoples.

A Right to Anonymity?

So, is there a right to anonymity? Many advocates claim there is, or should be. Before we address that, let us briefly discuss the concept itself. Anonymity is probably best described as a condition a person enjoys when he or she is unidentified to a relevant person, group, or institution. Anonymity arises from withholding identifiers to prevent a usable identification from occurring. A person who has withheld identifiers from others is anonymous to them.

In the scheme of negative rights that makes our Constitution what it is—rights that protect us against government interference in the way we live our lives—a "right to anonymity" would probably be better described as a right to be free from mandatory identification. If there is such a right, it seems almost exclusively to be honored in the breach.

Aside from the small swath of cases like *NAACP ex rel. Patterson,* where anonymity provides practical protection for recognized constitutional rights, little legal or constitutional protection for anonymity exists on its own. With the personal income tax, the growth of the welfare state, and the vast expansion of both state and federal police power in modern times, there is little chance that claims of a general right to withhold identification information from the government could possibly pass muster.

Even in the criminal law area, rights that we have long believed sacrosanct—like the "right to remain silent" repeated millions of times a year in *Miranda* warnings—are in retreat. In the 2004 case *Hiibel v. Sixth District Court of Nevada,*[9] the U.S. Supreme Court found that a person can be required to identify him- or herself to police under a state "stop and identify" statute if an officer has just a small amount of suspicion that the person may be involved in a crime.[10]

In a telling passage, the Court said,

> Knowledge of identity may inform an officer that a suspect is wanted for another offense, or has a record of violence or mental disorder. On the other hand, knowing identity may

help clear a suspect and allow the police to concentrate their efforts elsewhere. Identity may prove particularly important in cases such as this, where the police are investigating what appears to be a domestic assault. Officers called to investigate domestic disputes need to know whom they are dealing with in order to assess the situation, the threat to their own safety, and possible danger to the potential victim.[11]

The Court begins with the critical error of assuming that getting identity information itself reveals substantive additional information—whether a person is wanted for other offenses, the level of danger a person presents, or the person's role in a crime. Identity information alone is not those other facts. It is just glue.

To learn those facts, officers must divert themselves from investigating the particular crime and particular scene to investigating the person that they happen to have stopped. Rather than gathering evidence of the instant crime, officers will use identity information to research warrants, mental history, or other information on innocent people like Dudley Hiibel. As a policy, the *Hiibel* case invites law enforcement to develop passing suspicions of anyone and everyone because that opens the door to general investigation. It rewards trumped-up suspicions.

When police officers are actually investigating a discrete crime, as they were supposed to be doing when they investigated Dudley Hiibel, identity information is relevant only when one of the clues that officers have is the name (or other identifiers) of a suspect. This was not the case in *Hiibel*. Poor understanding of concepts in identification degraded the Supreme Court's analysis.

Anonymity has not been recognized by the Court as a freestanding right, though it is important for many, many reasons. Except when a narrow band of particular constitutional rights is involved, anonymity is routinely trampled by law enforcement, taxation, and the many government programs that thrive on citizens' personal information.

Sweet Freedom

Being protected against sanctions is not just important in legal environments, but in economic and social ones too. Think of all the different times in your life when you have done something that might have been unpopular or uncomfortable for you to reveal to your employer, your parents, a teacher, or your friends. Anonymity gives people greater freedom of action by releasing them from the influence of others.

If a corporate whistleblower cannot afford to go without his or her job, for example, anonymity protects freedom from accountability to the employer (who would probably exercise it wrongfully). This promotes exposure of wrongdoing or illegality. Internet discussion boards that host anonymous discussions of disease or sexuality allow people to discuss sensitive topics free of the chance that they will have to explain their thoughts or questions to people in their social circles.

Civil and criminal law enforcement often justifies stripping away anonymity. But it is important to recognize the general protection that should be accorded to anonymity because it provides people with shelter for the freedom to act without unwanted outside pressure.

Of course, people choose social and commercial relationships, or acquiesce to them, all the time. When they do, identification serves extremely valuable purposes. The point of protecting anonymity is to preserve people's fullest range of choices as to when they are identified and when they are not. Identity information given or released voluntarily is usually used for purposes that serve the individual and the rest of society very well. Neighbors who greet each other in the street can do so because they acquiesce to the release of their "neighborly" identity—biometric measurements of their faces, bodies, and movements, plus a well-manicured lawn. This benefits everyone because it knits neighborhoods with bonds of sociability.

But anonymity is a practice that empowers individuals against encroaching social pressures and unjust use of state power alike. Our policies and practices should favor voluntary relationships and voluntary identification, while disfavoring mandatory or unwanted relationships and identification. The former maximize people's freedom of action, personal power, and political participation.

As we saw in chapters 10 and 11, the case for using identification is strong. It is the starting point for relationships of all kinds: social, commercial, and institutional. Identification is also essential for accountability—not only accountability to the state for criminal law enforcement and administration, but accountability in commercial and personal relationships. We now have a better understanding of why identification is important.

But we have also explored why avoiding identification is important. Anonymity is a normal and beneficial social practice that people use to retain power over their lives and to shape their society. Our law recognizes the importance of anonymity for more explicit functional purposes, as well. Anonymous people are freer to speak their minds, to criticize public officials and corporate wrongdoers. This tests our institutions, exposes their flaws, and forces them to adhere more closely to our laws and values. The testing we give our institutions—governments and corporations alike—make them better. We live in a stronger, more healthy, and more wealthy society because we shelter critics behind veils of anonymity.

The difficult problem that remains is to find the right balance between identification and anonymity. Before we turn to that problem and consider the system we might use to solve it, it is important to go further into modern identification processes and their meanings. The chapters that follow explore identification cards and tokens, the advanced technologies going into modern identification processes, and how these advances are changing and heightening the consequences of identification.

PART III

IDENTIFICATION CARDS

14. Identification Cards

John Gilmore does not carry a driver's license. He suffers from epilepsy and it was suspended. It is doubtful that Gilmore would show a driver's license if he had one, though. He is a little bit disobedient about things like that.

Gilmore is a high-tech multimillionaire turned civil liberties activist and philanthropist who has challenged the rules requiring people boarding airplanes to show identification. What he characterizes as his "regional arrest" began on July 4, 2002, when he attempted to board a Southwest Airlines flight in Oakland, California, bound for Washington, D.C. There, he planned to visit his member of Congress.

When asked by airline personnel for identification, he politely refused and was denied boarding. Later that day, at the United Airlines counter in the San Francisco airport, he was told he could fly without showing identification, but only if he agreed to an unusually close search. He declined and was not allowed to fly.

So began Gilmore's long legal exploration of whether identification is required, and can be required, by the federal government when Americans travel domestically. He is battling in court for the right to travel without showing identification.

There is much more to Gilmore's case. What it illustrates, though, is the pervasiveness of identification cards like the state-issued driver's license that today control access to many different goods, services, and locations.

People are regularly required to show identification. Public and private entities require identification to get into office buildings, to open bank accounts, to enter courthouses, to participate in elections, to access college buildings, to join in ski trips, to get into bars, to check into hotels, to carry weapons, to attend music festivals, and so on, and so on, and so on. Identification by card is a pervasive demand in society today.

But government-issued identification cards are not required by nature or ordained by God. Indeed, prescriptive regulation of mobility and regulation of travel through licensure are nothing more than a pair of historical accidents. These combined to create the document that nearly every adult American carries today.

The Driver's License

No horse-and-buggy driver ever needed a license. But when the automobile began sharing roadways with horse-drawn conveyances around the turn of the 20th-century, something had to give.

Noisy, fast-moving cars were the newcomer to the scene, of course. Belching smoke and steam, they could easily spook horses. Courts came close to classifying autos as inherently dangerous instrumentalities. That would have made their operators strictly liable for any harm resulting from using these contraptions. Horsemen also argued that the automobile was a nuisance, but this ran up against the common law rule that any mode of locomotion is proper, provided it does not interfere with the equal rights of others.[1]

In a series of cases, though, courts cited the dangerousness of automobiles as the basis for regulating the operation, speed, and location of their use. The logic necessary to support this prescriptive regulation was that driving was a privilege granted by the state and not a right. Because the state could theoretically ban the use of cars entirely, it could condition their use in any way it deemed appropriate.

When cars were a novelty, that might have made sense. The result of such logic, applied today, though, is that Americans' chief source of mobility could be banned, which would effectively ban mobility itself. Courts have elided past this problem by finding that regulation of driving and licensing is subject to due process limits.[2]

However, the early precedent for licensure was set. On the theory that driving was a privilege, first localities and then states began requiring drivers to be licensed. Government certification of automobile operators was well established in Europe by the turn of the century. The first examination and licensing ordinance in the United States was instituted in Chicago around 1899, modeled on the law in France.[3] In other words, the practice was a European import. Beginning in 1903 with Massachusetts and Missouri, U.S. states began requiring drivers to be licensed. Wyoming did not require drivers' licenses until 1947.[4]

It is easy to assume that the driver's license was a safety measure, but the evidence is mixed. Early operators of automobiles were either rich, using their vehicles in business, or both, and licensing brought in revenue. In New York and Chicago, the license fee was three dollars, not an insubstantial amount in 1900, and Chicago's annual renewal fee was one dollar.[5]

Casting further doubt on the safety motivation, driver competence examinations did not adjoin licensing requirements, but followed them, in some cases by many years. Missouri waited 49 years after it began licensing drivers to examine their competence. The average state waited more than eight years. South Dakota did not have a driver's license exam until 1959.[6]

Some insight into the delay—or perhaps into the basis of the testing requirement itself—is revealed in a 1939 document lamenting the relatively sparse and inconsistent examination standards in many states:

> Lack of appropriations to pay for a sufficient number of examiners is the most common reason. A number of states have started so recently and have been so handicapped by limited funds that they have not had an opportunity to bring their examination systems up to a point of reasonable efficiency.[7]

The author of this document was no road safety group. It was the American Association of Motor Vehicle Administrators, representing the most direct beneficiaries of government spending on licensure: department of motor vehicles bureaucrats.

AAMVA has been nothing if not consistent in its effort to expand regulatory control of drivers and driving. In a 1956 document, it defended the theory that driving is a privilege, saying "if driving were not merely a privilege but a legal right, licensing would be unnecessary. . . . The public must constantly be reminded that a license to drive is only a privilege—not a right."[8] This rather transparent argument for department of motor vehicles job protection admits Americans' doubts that their ability to move about the country is a gift from the government.

The highways should not be a free-for-all, of course. Licensing and prescriptive regulation is just the most intrusive option among several that driving policy could have taken. It is easy to conceive of alternate historical routes that driving policy might have traveled.

Tort liability rather than regulation might have predominated. Networks of private road systems might have produced customary and contractual driving practices.

On our government-owned and -operated roadways, though, AAMVA's promotion of regulation has been successful. As far back as 1968, a report issued by the Department of Health, Education, and Welfare noted that, thanks to driving regulations, "the incidence of arrest by armed police in the United States has undoubtedly reached the highest point for any civilization, democratic or totalitarian, in recorded history. . . . One may well question whether the instincts of a free people will not one day be impaired by the habit of being arrested without protest. . . ."[9]

Along with driving controls, AAMVA is a consistent promoter of national identification cards and, indeed, international identification card systems.[10] Although it claims motor vehicle administration, police traffic services, and highway safety as its aims, its activities are much broader. Before September 11, 2001, AAMVA promoted a national identification card as a solution to illegal immigration. After September 11, 2001, it promoted a national identification card as a solution to terrorism. If national identification cards are a hammer, AAMVA sees every public policy problem as a nail.

Identification Cards

Thanks to AAMVA's years of diligent work, every adult is familiar with identification cards like the driver's license. But few understand them in depth. Little analysis has gone into how they work, the quality of identification they provide, and for what they are appropriately used. Nor have government-issued identification cards been compared with the other cards and tokens that people commonly carry. Nor has there been much exploration of using authorization instead of identification—that is, providing access based on characteristics rather than identity. Let us start by analyzing what an identification card is and how it works.

We will call the person showing a card the "ID subject." This is the person who uses a card to assert his or her identity (that is, enough identity information to substantiate a transaction). The person or institution who uses the card to identify the ID subject (sufficiently) is a "verifier." The producer of the card is the "ID issuer" or "card issuer." We will speak about identification cards and drivers' licenses here because they are so common, but the same thinking applies to other tokens that achieve one-stop identification.

In the absence of identification cards or similar tokens, people and institutions collect identifiers during a first contact for use in the second and all subsequent contacts. Identification cards are unique because they are used to establish all the identity information needed for a particular transaction all at once. In essence, the card allows a verifier in a first transaction to treat the ID subject as if he or she is already known. This represents a huge convenience because it allows strangers to transact with relative confidence in each other's identities. Identification cards are like the signet ring we discussed in chapter 6: an identifier with ingenuity.

Identification cards may be used by issuers themselves, such as a company that issues its employees identification cards. A human resources department might give employees a card so that the security guard at the front desk on Saturday, working for the same corporation, can verify that the ID subject is authorized to enter the building.

Many government-issued cards are issued by departments of motor vehicles, both for their own use and for the use of the police and highway patrol in administering driving control laws. These cards have come to be used as an identification document by many institutions for purposes well beyond the scope of motor vehicle administration, of course. For the convenience of those who do not or cannot drive, the department of motor vehicles also issues identification cards that do not indicate authorization to drive.

Identification cards incorporate most of the characteristics and advanced techniques of identification that have been discussed in earlier chapters. They piggyback on other identification systems, for example. This is a source of significant misidentification risk. An identification card is also a multifactor identification tool: The card itself is a something-you-have identifier and it has printed on or embedded in it a variety of other identifiers, usually from the something-you-are category—such as name, address, identifying numbers, and a variety of biometrics. In the coming chapters, we will discuss much more carefully how these characteristics and techniques affect identification cards.

A Communications Device

When you write a check on your bank account, it communicates your promise to pay money to someone else through your bank.

Figure 1.
IDENTIFICATION BY STATE-ISSUED CARD

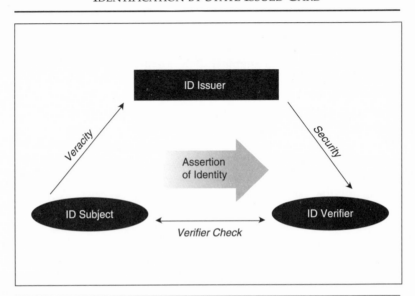

When the recipient deposits the check, his or her bank calls on your bank to collect the money.

An identification card is a similar sort of communications device. It conveys identifying information from the ID subject to the verifier through the card issuer. By proffering an identification card, the ID subject is seeking to communicate who he or she is with the level of assurance sufficient to go forward with a transaction.

Figure 1 illustrates this communication process in the example of the state-issued card. There are three important steps. First, the ID subject asserts identity information to the card issuer. Second, the card issuer communicates this identity information to the verifier by printing it on, or embedding it in, the card. Third, the verifier compares identifiers on the card with the ID subject. If all goes well, the verifier knows and has confidence in everything on the identification card about the ID subject, and that is enough to go forward with a transaction.

Each of these steps is a potential point of weakness, however. In the first step, false information may be submitted to the issuer by the ID subject or the ID subject may seek to corrupt the issuer. The primary question is the veracity of information submitted to the card issuer—whether the information the issuer ultimately puts on the card is true.

In the second step, there is the risk that the card has been forged or altered. There is an arms race of sorts under way, with card issuers and forgers constantly working to stay ahead of the other. The question here is the security of the card.

The primary question in the third step is whether the verifier properly compares identifiers on the card with identifiers proffered by the bearer. A smart verifier carefully ensures that the bearer of the card is really the ID subject.

Identification cards are subject to significant weaknesses, and there is a substantial risk of misidentification from using them. Each of the steps in the identification-by-card process has been the subject of recent attempts at "strengthening." Most notably, strengthening has been done by the REAL ID Act, which created federal standards for U.S. state-issued identification cards. We will discuss the REAL ID Act in chapter 18.

But these types of reforms do not address the root of the problem. The problem is that unified identification systems can be very profitable to break. The more roles a given card or identification system plays, the more value there is to breaking it, and the more investment people will make in fraudulently accessing the system. A better identification system would be heterogeneous, with separate systems controlling access to different goods, services, infrastructures, and opportunities. Current reforms to strengthen identification systems use brawn where they should use agility.

But before we get to those conclusions, let us examine each of these steps more carefully to see how identification cards work when they work and why they fail when they fail.

15. Data Veracity

Connecticut's governor was in a classic fix. An agency of her government was failing utterly in a basic mission and the news would break soon. She had a decision to make: Should she apologize for failing to oversee the agency? Call for downsizing, admitting her incompetence to manage Connecticut's sprawling government? Or should she seize credit by cobbling together a promise of reform?

In May 2005, Connecticut Governor Jodi Rell announced a series of changes designed to improve the process used by the Connecticut Department of Motor Vehicles to issue drivers' licenses and identity cards. The previous November, she had ordered a performance audit to look into allegations of fraud and abuse at the DMV. Conventional wisdom held that false identification cards issued in other states had aided the September 11, 2001, terrorists in their attack on neighboring New York, so the political stakes were high even though the conventional wisdom was mistaken.

In a news release, Governor Rell said, "Frankly, the findings in this audit are disturbing. They point to a system that is broken and reveal a licensing process badly in need of reform. The audit makes it very clear that we must keep working to build an up-to-date and secure licensing system—an issue I have been focused on since taking office."[1]

The state's Auditors of Public Accounts had found numerous flaws in the state's system for issuing drivers' licenses. Their report concluded that the DMV did not detect fraudulent documents submitted by applicants for new credentials. The DMV did not know whether fraudulent credentials were being issued to imposters. And it did not know when it was renewing or replacing lost or stolen licenses.[2] While other investigations were ongoing, at least one employee of the Connecticut DMV's Bridgeport office had been arrested on allegations that she had been selling drivers' licenses for up to $3,000 apiece.[3]

Connecticut was far from the only state with this problem. The going price for a DMV-issued false driver's license in Virginia was reported at about $2,500. That state's officials asked 250 licensees in December 2004 to return their documents and get new ones because a corrupt employee in Henrico County had issued them. A news report said that 13 drivers complied. The rest did not respond or the letters asking them to get relicensed were returned as undeliverable.[4]

This DMV corruption spree was not an aberration striking the Mid-Atlantic and Northeast in the middle of the decade. In October 2000, an *Orange County Register* investigation found that clerks in the California Department of Motor Vehicles were selling fraudulent drivers' licenses to undocumented immigrants, convicts, and identity fraudsters just two years after the end of an effort to stamp out corruption called Operation Clean Sweep.[5] There, licenses were reportedly selling for as much as $4,000. A December 2004 study by the Center for Democracy and Technology found bribery and physical security lapses "rampant" in DMVs.[6]

These anecdotes and the Center for Democracy and Technology study illustrate one way that the veracity of identification cards is compromised: corruption inside the card issuer. Obviously, if the issuer of an identification card can be convinced not to use true identifiers, the identification card it issues will be inaccurate and it will be an unreliable identifier itself. The "veracity" link of the identification card communication chain will be broken.

Corruption in card issuers is one way that the veracity link in an identification card can be broken. The other major way is fraud on the issuer.

Fraud on ID Issuers

Thanks to a high legal drinking age, generations of American college students have gone to great lengths to get fake identification cards for years. They have found that states' identification-issuing processes are notoriously susceptible to adulteration. As noted above, DMV employees are susceptible to corruption. But, just as much, these state workers regularly fail to catch fraudulent documents. In addition, authentic documentary identifiers can be fraudulently procured and used to acquire state-issued identification documents.

Before a move to federalize U.S. state identification card standards began with the REAL ID Act in early 2005, the requirements for issuing a state driver's license or identification card ranged widely from state to state. A typical pattern, though, was to require two pieces of identification (in more precise terminology, two identifiers). Often, one was from a "high-quality" category and one from a "lower-quality" category. Certain facts might have to be shown by the documents, such as name, date of birth, lawful presence in the United States, or residency in the jurisdiction issuing the card. These identifiers are often called "breeder" documents, a pejorative-sounding name that seems to admit their ability to infect state identification systems with fraud.

Take the identifiers required by the state of Colorado as a typical example. As of December 2004, Colorado required two documents that proved age, name, and lawful presence in the country. One document had to be from among the following list (summarized by the National Immigration Law Center):[7]

> An out-of-state–issued photo driver's license or photo ID card expired one year or less (out-of-state ID cards and licenses required additional documentation for proof of lawful presence); any Colorado driver's license, Colorado 7-day Affidavit and Notice of Revocation or Affidavit and Notice of Suspension, or Colorado ID card that matched the photograph on file with the Motor Vehicle Division (Colorado ID cards issued between June 1, 1997, and July 1, 1998, required additional documentation for proof of lawful presence); a certified birth certificate (federal-, state-, county-, Dept. of Justice–, Dept. of State–, or Bureau of Indian Affairs–issued; a birth certificate issued by a hospital was not acceptable); a U.S. passport expired less than 10 years; valid foreign passport with I-94 or valid "processed for I-551" stamp (no B-1, B-2, WT, WB, CP, or NC status; and H-1, H-2, J-1, J-2, F-1, F-2, etc., statuses required verification of Colorado employment or education); a Form I-94 (Arrival/Departure Record, refugee/asylee status version) (Refugees/asylees presenting such an I-94 were also to present either an employment authorization card or an original letter, on agency letterhead, from the legal agency providing assistance, which letter was to be surrendered to the Motor Vehicle Division); a valid I-551 (resident alien/permanent resident card) (no border-crosser or U.S.A B-1/B-2 Visa/BCC cards accepted); a valid I-688 (photo temporary resident card), I-688B and I-766 (photo employment authorization card); a valid U.S. military ID (active duty, dependent, retired, reserve, and National Guard); a tribal ID card; a U.S. or U.S. territory certified

court order of adoption (including DOB); or a Certificate of Naturalization with intact photo.

If the applicant was applying for a license under a name that was different from the name on the document presented as proof of age/ lawful presence, or if the applicant was changing the name on an established record, any of the following documents were acceptable in addition to the document presented for proof of age/lawful presence (no photocopies allowed):

A U.S. city-, county-, or state-issued, or foreign-issued, certified marriage certificate (foreign language documents might have required translation; no church-issued documents were accepted); a certified divorce decree, U.S. or foreign, with a case number and official signature; a certified court order of name change, U.S. or foreign, with case number and official signature (foreign language documents required translation); a valid U.S. military ID (active duty, dependent, retired, reserve, and National Guard); a tribal ID card; or an out-of-state–issued photo driver's license or photo ID card expired one year or less.

Wading through the intricate regulations regarding which documents are acceptable as proof of identity, legal presence, residency, and so on must certainly be mind numbing for Colorado DMV employees. Determining whether a rarely seen but acceptable document is authentic is not an impossible task, but surely it is not one that a DMV bureaucrat would take to with enthusiasm. The process used for state-issued identification cards is naturally prone to fraud.

In the next chapter, we will talk about card security, the second link in the identification card communication chain. This is the question whether an identification card is actually the card that the issuer produced, or whether it is forged or altered. When a forged or altered card is accepted at a DMV to establish identity, this fraud breaks the first link, the "veracity" link, in the new card.

Most DMV employees are nice, honest people, but their institutions do not have a reputation for crisp attention to detail or speedy customer service. And the evidence shows that their work is highly error prone. They have been easily victimized by fraudulent identifiers.

From July 2002 through May 2003, the General Accounting Office's Office of Special Investigations visited a number of states' departments of motor vehicles and applied for drivers' licenses using counterfeit documents, including counterfeit out-of-state drivers' licenses. The GAO found that DMV employees generally did not recognize counterfeit documents.[8] Whether due to negligence or lack of training, DMV employees are a weak link in the ID card issuance process, unable or unwilling to ferret out forgeries.

Verification processes are intended to shore up some of the weaknesses in document verification at DMVs but they have proved unreliable so far. The Social Security Administration provides an online Social Security number verification service designed to prevent the use of false Social Security numbers, but in September 2003, the GAO found weaknesses in its design and management that caused outages and cutbacks in states' usage of the system.[9]

The GAO also applied for and got drivers' licenses using the names, Social Security numbers, and dates of birth of deceased individuals. This, despite an online service the Social Security Administration offers to match applications against the SSA's Master Death file, which tracks by Social Security number who has died.[10]

These problems may be ameliorated over time with consistent oversight and pressure. Doing so would shade back on fraud on state-issued identification processes. But verifying Social Security numbers cannot control identifier fraud if authentic Social Security numbers and other identifiers can be obtained fraudulently.

Authentic Identifiers Fraudulently Procured

Identifiers that are authentic but issued based on fraud or mistake cannot be caught by DMVs or their employees. In a May 2003 report, the GAO described how it used counterfeit identification documents to obtain valid Social Security numbers for two fictitious infants. One Social Security number was acquired by investigators posing as parents and supplying a counterfeit birth certificate and baptismal certificate. GAO acquired a second Social Security number by submitting counterfeit documents through the mail.[11]

Authentic Social Security numbers and other genuine documents obtained fraudulently can be used as identifiers in applying for identification cards. The fraudster can then use the authentic but fraudulent identification card to get additional identification cards

125

and other identifiers. These can be used to open bank accounts and access other financial services. These are the mechanics of general financial and identity frauds.

The "veracity" step is a major weakness in state-issued identification cards. Authentic but inaccurate identifiers may be used to defraud DMVs in ways they cannot be expected to catch. These bureaucracies are also quite susceptible to being defrauded directly by forged documentary identifiers because they necessarily must accept relatively low-quality breeder documents. And, of course, if DMV employees are corrupted, false identification documents will issue.

Drivers' licenses and state-issued identification cards are classic examples of piggybacked identifiers. They are issued based on identifiers issued by other institutions and entities. The range and variety of identifiers acceptable for state-issued identification cards open the process to exploitation. Many of the documents accepted as proof of identity can be forged well enough to fool bored and indifferent DMV workers. The documents they then issue incorporate the weaknesses of the identifiers used to substantiate them.

For years, the common practice of using fake ID has acted as a release valve on arbitrary drinking-age laws in the United States. Or, perhaps, the practice has empowered the more careless, willing law violator to drink while infantilizing mature, law-abiding young adults. Either way, the identifiers that serve as the basis for issuing driver's licenses and identification cards are probably suitable for administering driving laws, but they probably lack the needed fixity, distinctiveness, or permanence for administering alcohol control, transportation security, financial services, immigration control, and the many other responsibilities that have been placed on, or proposed for, state-issued identification cards. By continually adding new roles and responsibilities onto this single identifier, the driver's license, policymakers have created an attractive target for corruption and fraud.

Private Card Issuers

We have focused on state-issued identification and driver's licenses because they are the most widely recognized identification documents and they are at the center of debates about identification policies. But when most people open their wallets, they find far more privately issued identification and authorization cards than government-issued ones. Interesting differences between privately and government-issued cards affect their strength in terms of veracity.

One of the most important differences is what is at stake when public and private entities issue credentials. When a government agency issues an identification or authorization card, it does not take on any risk. Though other government agencies and card users may, the agency itself and the people who work there risk neither direct loss if their procedures fail nor liability if someone relying on their system is harmed.

Indeed, government agencies tend to "fail upward," getting more funding when they malfunction than when they do not. Connecticut provides a good example. Governor Rell had indeed been as pro-active as she claimed in her press release: In her budget for 2005–06, she proposed creating 11 new positions in the Connecticut Department of Motor Vehicles to aid in the verification of background and identity documents of applicants. That would add more than $650,000 a year to the $50 million plus annual budget. She also initiated a $10 million capital upgrade for DMV computer systems.[12] Certainly, almost no one at the Connecticut DMV intended for the agency to fail, but the incentives to succeed were weak: the budget of the agency, and job security for its employees, *rose* when it failed.

Private entities enjoy no such windfall when their systems fail. A failed system threatens the income of the organization and the job security of its employees.

Take a system that is constantly besieged by attacks and fraud: the credit card system. In recent years, credit card fraud has caused around a billion dollars in losses annually. Credit card associations have spent hundreds of millions to identify illegal card use precisely because those losses accrue to their members and the merchants who use their systems—and can refuse them. Failing to continually address fraud and update its fraud-prevention systems would bring down the credit card associations and destroy the livelihoods of their workers.

The credit card industry's anti-fraud expenditures have worked. In 1992, fraudulent credit card transactions represented 15.7 cents of each $100 in sales. In 2004, fraudulent transactions had fallen to 4.7 cents per $100. The absolute value of credit card transactions

Figure 2.
IDENTIFICATION BY PRIVATELY ISSUED CARD

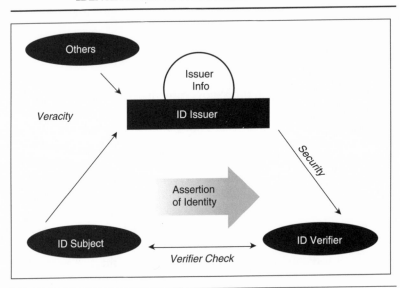

rose nearly 50 percent from 1999 to 2004, but fraud fell from $1.13 billion to $1.05 billion.[13]

In the last chapter, Figure 1 illustrated the process by which a state-issued identification card communicates identity information to a third-party, the verifier. It formed a neat triangle because the ID subject gives information to the issuer that in turn creates the card, passing information to the verifier. Upon comparing identifiers to the ID subject, the verifier has nominally identified the ID subject—barring all the fraud and forgery discussed above and in the next chapter.

The picture looks slightly different for most private issuers of identification and authorization cards, such as employers, banks, insurers, and credit card issuers. Whereas states rely mostly on information supplied by the ID subject, private issuers rely on information from ID subjects, information they develop themselves, and information they buy from third parties. This process has a major influence on suppressing fraud in the issuance of private identification and authorization cards. Figure 2 illustrates the process with privately issued cards.

Consider any company that is considering hiring a new employee. The human resources department or hiring manager will look at a resumé, which includes contact information, such as a physical address, phone number, and e-mail address. Each is a (piggybacked) identifier that can be verified—and they are often verified in the natural course of the hiring process, through phone calls, letters, or e-mails.

Companies will typically bring in the individual for an interview. This practice, as a matter of course, adds a collection of high-quality biometric identifiers to the identifiers collected in the preinterview process. The company may check references that the prospective employee submits, further confirming both identifiers and the substantive qualities of the candidate. Once the employee is hired, he or she will be seen at work regularly and interact constantly with naturally observant colleagues. Opportunities to commit identity fraud on the company, limited in the first place, shrink even further. An identification card issued by an employer has a much stronger "veracity" link than a government-issued card.

The credit card functions at different times as an identification card and an authorization card. It is issued after a card issuer has received an application and completed a credit check. To learn credit-worthiness information, the credit card issuer contacts one or more credit bureaus and uses a variety of identifiers to request the subject's records, including such items as Social Security number and physical address. Along with revealing substantive information, this process acts as independent verification of identifiers the subject has put forward.

When a credit card is issued, it is typically mailed to the card holder's address. For fraud-prevention purposes, the card will not work until the card holder has called from his or her home or business phone number to activate it. (Calling from a specific phone number shows that the recipient of the card has access to the facilities of the person to whom the card was sent.) These steps serve naturally to confirm identifiers that the card holder has asserted. They suppress the kind of fraud to which state-issued cards are so subject.

There are problems with accuracy in the credit-reporting industry, and identity fraud is a fascinating and difficult problem. The dollar amounts involved make it easy to assume that credit cards are issued to fraudsters more often than driver's licenses and that credit card issuers are more susceptible to fraud and corruption than DMVs. But it would be an error to assume that. Many variables must be corrected for to make an apples-to-apples comparison.

First, ordinary credit card fraud is not identity fraud (as we will discuss in chapter 22). Credit card fraud exploits weaknesses in the security link and, most often, the "verifier check" link in the card communication chain. The credit card fraudster typically uses a stolen card or a stolen card number in a remote transaction. The verifier's failure to check the signature or willingness to accept the card number without checking identifiers breaks the verifier check. In identity fraud, on the other hand, a person acquires a card fraudulently. That is an attack on the veracity link, which is all that is relevant here.

Next, it is important to account for the incentives that fraudsters face in the two contexts. Identity fraud can pay tens of thousands of dollars, perhaps even a hundred thousand dollars or more. Thus, criminals will invest a great deal of time and effort in defeating credit card systems. Defrauding a DMV is sometimes a constituent of identity fraud, but more often teenagers and 20-year-olds do it just so they can drink with their older friends. The average payoff is lower so the incentive to crack the system is not as great. If defrauding DMVs could net fraudsters hundreds of thousands dollars, these agencies would have been swarmed over with crooks. The state-issued identification card system would have collapsed long ago.

Because they are designed and operated in light of the specific, often high, threats that face them, credit cards are far less susceptible than government-issued cards to fraud and corruption that breaks the "veracity" link in the card communication chain. Other privately issued cards are each designed for a separate, lower-value purpose and so avoid the battle over veracity and security entirely.

In chapter 18, we will examine whether the processes used in the issuance of private cards can be incorporated into state-issued cards. There may be some lessons that state officials like Governor Rell could have learned, and that the U.S. Congress could learn. But first, we will examine the other steps in the identification card communication chain.

16. Card Security

U.S. Interstate 15 runs from the Mexican border up to Canada, making its way through San Diego, Las Vegas, Salt Lake City, Idaho Falls, and Butte as it heads to Sweetgrass, Montana.

Passing through Las Vegas, motorists may be tempted to stop off and enjoy the all-night hustle of the Strip. Exit 36 to Russell Road is the best route to Mandalay Bay, the Four Seasons, and the Luxor. Tropicana Avenue/Frank Sinatra Drive will get you to New York–New York, Excalibur, and the classic Tropicana. The Bellagio has a pair of huge, bright signs enticing you off the interstate at Flamingo Road. That exit will also get you to Caesar's Palace, Treasure Island, or the Venetian.

The gambling, dining, and shows on the strip and down in old Las Vegas offer something for everyone—everyone of legal age, anyway. And if the legitimate diversions in this adult playground aren't strong enough for you, hawkers line the streets with cards and flyers advertising stronger entertainment—entertainment that isn't even legal in Sin City. Rightly or wrongly, Las Vegas is known for some exotic crimes.

But Las Vegas is a big town getting bigger. Much of its large and growing suburban population doesn't have much to do with the lights and glitter of the Strip. The size of the metropolitan area becomes clear as you continue on Interstate 15 over the next 10 miles. After crossing Route 95, the freeway falls alongside the Union Pacific Railroad tracks. The construction along the highway starts to thin out and becomes a little more industrial. You get the sense that you'll soon be back out in the high desert.

Out here toward the edge of town, some exotic crimes have taken place as well. But these crimes are very different from what goes on downtown.

Just before the Craig Road exit, the freeway and railroad track peel apart. If you exit at Craig and take a left over the freeway, then another left, you're on Donovan Way, a dead-end road that fills the spit of land between the railroad and the interstate.

Sometime late on Saturday, March 6, or early Sunday, March 7, 2005, someone drove down dark, empty Donovan Way with a curious plan. The Peterbilt dealership was closed and no one was around the department of motor vehicles office. They rammed their truck into the DMV, gaining access to the darkened bureau.[1]

It was a blunt and low-tech way to embark on a quite high-tech crime. The criminals stole a computer, a camera, 1,700 license blanks, and laminated plastic covers bearing the embossed seal of the state of Nevada.

When the theft was discovered, the press immediately fixed on the possibility that data on the computers might be used in identity fraud. Many recent data breaches in private companies, public universities, and other institutions had highlighted the risks of having sensitive personal information fall into the hands of crooks.

But, just as likely, these thieves were after the blank cards and laminated covers used by the Nevada DMV to make licenses and identification cards. Producing false identification is an increasingly lucrative crime, with the price of good quality cards reaching into the thousands of dollars. At those prices, the loot stolen from the Donovan Way DMV could have helped the thieves gross millions of dollars.

Forged and altered identification cards represent a break in the "security" link of the identification card communications chain. That means that the integrity of the communication between the card issuer and the verifier has been broken. The verifier has been fooled into believing that the card it sees was issued by the third party—in this example, the state of Nevada. The security link is also broken if a legitimate card can be altered well enough to fool the verifier.

Advanced Identification Card Security

Card issuers use a wide array of techniques to ensure the security of cards, but an arms race is under way between the card issuers and the forgers. The break-in at the Donovan Way DMV was just a small skirmish in a very large war.

Drivers' licenses used to be printed on paper. Sometimes they were laminated between plastic sheets. Today, the typical construction of a card will be a center layer of durable, printable material like Teslin, with a polycarbonate layer on the front and back, and possibly an additional layer of laminate.

Especially when used on the inner layers of the card, a wide array of printing techniques and practices make forgery and alteration harder. Redundant and overlapping data are one such technique. On many drivers' licenses, a second, smaller image of the ID subject may appear behind some of the printed material. That practice makes it very difficult to cut out and replace the picture of the person to whom the card was issued. Some information may be printed twice in different places on the card. Some printing on a card may be in a slightly different font than the rest of the card, revealing forgeries and alterations to the trained eye. Controlled misspellings or other "defects" can turn up the heat just a little more on attempts at forgery.

Card issuers have a stunning array of inks at their disposal. They may produce cards with colors that cannot be replicated by the mixture of cyan, magenta, and yellow used by most color printers. Some inks will color-shift, varying in shade with the angle of viewing. Ultraviolet or infrared inks are available, meaning that they can be read under black light or by a laser scanner. Even full-color ultraviolet printing is now possible. Some of these inks are tuned to particular wavelengths, making them even harder to forge accurately. These latter inks obviously require special equipment to read.

Card issuers can use a wide variety of high-quality printing techniques to inhibit forgery as well. Gradient printing is the process of changing the color of ink as it is laid down (rather than printing different colors at different times). This produces a unique appearance that is difficult to copy. Guilloche printing involves extremely fine concentric circles that are very hard to copy or replicate. Microprinting makes very small images, visible only under magnification, which cannot be replicated by commonly available printers or copiers. What appears to be an ordinary line on an identification card may be the name of the card issuer printed over and over again.

A number of other techniques go into card security. Many cards today have holograms or kinegrams in the card or laminate. These are images that reflect light in distinct ways or that shift appearance at different angles. The exterior of cards may be laser engraved or etched so that they feel differently in certain places or so that images or letters have a different feel than the rest of the card. The adhesive between layers of the card may even contain tiny, barely visible microtaggants.

Another advanced technique for ensuring card security is the placement of pixels on the card in an arrangement that is invisible to the naked eye but readable by a scanner or computer. The arrangement of pixels represents a code. This digital watermarking can carry an encrypted message that guarantees that the issuer produced the card—provided the issuer maintains the security of its encryption keys, at least.

To limit the risks to card security exemplified by the break-in at the Donovan Way DMV, in recent years card issuers have more closely controlled their card stocks and laminate inventories with serial numbers and better physical security at places where identification cards are made. A general shift to centralized card issuance may supersede the immediate over-the-counter issuance people are increasingly used to. That will enable the use of the most advanced security techniques, at a cost in convenience to recipients of identification cards and drivers' licenses.

Each of these security techniques—overlapping data, specialized inks, high-quality printing techniques, and so on—makes it more difficult to forge or alter identification cards and drivers' licenses. On a technical level, they largely work. That is, they make forgery harder.

But they don't make forgery impossible. Nearly all of the techniques available to card issuers are also available to card forgers, at some price. Low-quality off-the-shelf printers may no longer allow college kids to print their own identification cards but criminal groups have the resources to acquire most of the hardware needed for forgery. If specialized inks cannot be acquired lawfully, criminals will seek to corrupt employees of card issuers and ink producers just like some DMV employees have been corrupted.

Each step that is taken to secure identification cards will be met with a countermeasure aimed at breaking that security step. It is possible to make cards quite secure, but there will always be a technical arms race on card security.

The Weakest Link

Probably, the physical security features of identification cards and licenses are not their weakest link. Rather, it is the ability of verifiers to determine whether a card is forged.

Recall the discussion in the previous chapter about the classic American college ritual: acquiring a fake ID. The most brazen college kids may go to the DMV with false documents to procure a genuine card but, more often probably, minors alter their genuine identification cards or get cheaply forged IDs. All they need is a card good enough to fool bouncers. That is not hard to do given the quality of the personnel, the often difficult lighting conditions, and the fact that violating anti-drinking laws carries little or no moral opprobrium.

In more serious circumstances, people may be trained to recognize security features in identification cards. With education, the average person can get good at recognizing common forgeries, but it is unlikely over time that the millions of people who check identification cards can be kept on the cutting edge of card security.

In more and more cases, the card security arms race will be fought on the terrain of computing and encryption. More and more cards are likely to contain computer chips. Devices like mobile phones may adopt an expanded role as identifiers. These identifiers will use algorithms, networks, and mathematics, rather than human eyeballs and brains, to keep forgery in check.

Chapters 19 through 22 examine the consequences of this trend. Better security is not an unalloyed good, though it will be an inevitable demand if the policy of driving multiple uses onto a single, ultra-high-value card or token persists.

Inhibiting Forgery by Design

Many of the anti-forgery techniques described earlier are used in the printing of paper currency, which is evidently a hot and innovative area. Obviously, designing a card the way you would design currency can make it hard to forge. But identification cards are not money. Other, more subtle design steps can inhibit forgery and related threats to the security of identification cards and tokens.

Two things dictate how well anti-forgery technologies and practices inhibit forgery: the cost of the countermeasure and the motivation of the forger. How hard does the technique make forgery? And what does a forger get if he or she succeeds?

Consider currency. To thwart forgery, the Treasury Department's Bureau of Engraving and Printing began updating the design of U.S. currency in 1996. Among other things, it started embedding polyester thread in notes, with the denomination of the bill printed on the thread. You can see them by holding a modern $20 bill up to bright light.

Seven years after that program began, the Series 2003 $1 bill still did not contain that security thread. But this is not an example of government bureaucracy, sloth, or incompetence. The $1 bill does not need security features like this because it isn't very profitable to forge. Twenties and hundreds are profitable to forge so better security features are needed on those bills.

The same dynamic applies to identification cards. A card or token that controls a lot of value—access to work, travel, public areas, and so on—is going to see forgery attempts; a low-consequence card will not.

Governments will always need to issue high-denomination currency. It would be a practical nightmare if everyone had to carry all their cash in singles. But is having high-"denomination" identification documents necessary?

Consider how the overall design of identification or authorization systems affects the risk of forgery: If a single card could give unfettered access to Fort Knox, a lot of criminal investment would go into forging that card. If a single card could give access to one person's financial assets, or several people's, that would be a good investment of criminal time. This is very nearly the state of affairs today with the driver's license and Social Security number controlling nearly all Americans' financial and economic affairs. But if no single card, token, or system provided access to more than one or two corners of an individual's personal or financial life, the value of forging any card or access control would be quite low. Criminals' efforts would go elsewhere—perhaps even to lawful, productive enterprise.

The card security war is an attractive but unnecessary fight. It can be avoided by intelligent design choices, such as maintaining and increasing diversity in identification systems. This is an idea to which we will return in chapters 23 through 26.

In the end, the theft at the DMV on Donovan Way in Las Vegas did not result in a thousand fake identification cards. After North Las Vegas police and the Secret Service began conducting interviews and issuing search warrants, the stolen items showed up on the roof of an office building under construction. The authorities reported that the stolen goods were intact, and that the personal information on the stolen computers had not been accessed. Although this theft did not lead to widespread forgery of Nevada cards and licenses, it illustrated the challenges present in trying to ensure that identification cards are a secure way to transmit identity information.

17. Verifier Check

If you didn't know the whole story, you might think Jerry Iannacci was just a wise guy or a prankster. But his prank had a purpose. It illustrates the third challenge to card-based identification: the "verifier check."

Jerry Iannacci is a regular guy. He was born and raised in Brooklyn, New York. With his accent and easygoing demeanor, it is easy to picture him being a cop on Long Island—and he was for a while, before he came upon a better-paying and more engaging career. He's an Italian-American Catholic who, given the choice, will pick an unpretentious Irish-themed restaurant for lunch. Jerry is white, which matters for reasons that will be clear in a moment.

Around 1990, Jerry got a letter from his credit card company inviting him to apply for a new card with a special feature: a photograph, right there on the card. Photo credit cards have been around for several decades and they have a number of advantages. They help credit card companies build customer loyalty. People feel better about the issuer and more attached to their cards. Photo credit cards can serve as an additional form of identification. And people with photo credit cards are more confident that their transactions are safe, so they will use their cards more. Obviously, a merchant could compare the picture on the card with the person presenting it to prevent a stolen card from being used fraudulently.

Jerry jumped at the chance to have a photo credit card, but not for the usual reasons. He is a corporate security expert, focusing on financial crime, access device fraud, and forensics. At the time, he was working for one of the nation's largest credit card issuers in a financial investigative unit assigned to work with the U.S. Secret Service's Task Force on Financial Fraud and he was president of the International Association of Financial Crimes Investigators (Mid-Atlantic States). Jerry wanted to prove a point about photo credit cards.

The picture that Jerry sent to his credit card company was of a Nigerian man named Charles Molen. Molen was a member of a fraud ring who had been arrested, charged, and convicted of various offenses. As you might guess, Charles Molen was black.

Jerry soon received a new credit card, issued in his name, with the picture of Charles Molen on the back. He used it for a variety of things, including his hotel on a trip to New York. At a Crate and Barrel store in New York City, he bought a hammock with his Nigerian-face credit card. When he returned home, he found that the hammock was damaged, so he returned it to the Crate and Barrel in Tysons Corner, Virginia. He received a credit on his Nigerian-face credit card.

In all those transactions, nobody ever asked Jerry Iannacci why the picture on his card was so different from his own face. Nobody questioned his authority to use the card. And nobody asked for proof that the card was his. Although he put a lot of charges on that credit card, the fact that someone else's face was on it never came up.

Weak Links in the Authorization Chain

To flesh out this story, let us step back and note how credit cards work: Credit cards authorize payments in much the same way that identification cards prove identity. In the first step, the credit card issuer collects information about the customer and issues credit to that person on appropriate terms. To do this well, they must know who the person is. In the second step, the card issued to the person communicates to a merchant that money for payment can be transferred. The third step requires the merchant to check the card against the bearer to ensure that he or she is authorized to use it. The traditional way this has been done is by comparing the signature on the back of the card with the signature on the receipt.[1]

The point Jerry was trying to make goes to the first step. If the credit card issuer does not control the picture that it puts on the card, it doesn't know who the person is and the picture will do little to control fraud. In fact, it might make it worse.

When First Hawaiian Bank started offering photo credit cards in March 1971—one of the first issuers to do so—that undoubtedly limited fraud because customers came to the bank's branch offices to get their pictures taken. Only the most audacious or reckless criminal would appear in person to perpetuate an identity fraud.

140

The number of fraudulently acquired photo credit cards was almost certainly quite low.

Because photo credit cards can now be obtained by mailing in a picture, the pictures on them are barely more fraud-proof than any other unverified datum a credit card holder might submit. If a fraudster has acquired a credit card under a false identity, he can send the issuer a picture with his or her face. The whole process does nothing to prevent use of the fraudulently acquired card. Indeed, it probably helps convince merchants that the card was correctly issued and is properly being used.

Photos have one slight advantage over no photo at all. They give the credit card issuer an idea of what the criminal may look like. But, overall: Score one for Jerry. The credit card issuer that allows the customer to submit a photo puts itself at risk of incorporating a fraudulent photo into its card.

Comparing Cards with Bearers, or Not

Jerry inadvertently proved another point in his experiment with the Nigerian-guy credit card. His trip to New York, purchases, and returns revealed that even obvious differences between card information and bearers often go unchallenged. This illustrates the final point of weakness in the identification card communication chain: When a verifier is presented with a card, it must do the verifier check. It must confirm that the identifiers on the card are the same as the identifiers of the ID subject. It must reconsider a transaction with this unknown person if they are not.

Again, step back to look at credit cards: The signature on the back of a card is a biometric authenticator.[2] It is there so that the merchant can compare it with the signature of the person bearing the card. The comparison of signatures is the final step in authorizing a payment. If the signature on the card and the receipt match, the bearer is authenticated as the rightful user of the card and the transaction can be safely authorized.

The process is the same with identification cards. The final step in identifying someone through a card is to compare the identifiers on the card with the bearer of the card, the ID subject.

In chapter 3, we talked about the natural skill people have for using biometric identifiers. We can recognize close friends and loved ones instantaneously thanks to our senses of sight and hearing, and the skill our brains have developed for collecting and organizing identifiers like facial appearance, gait, voiceprint, and so on. It would seem like a card with a photo on it would be just as easily compared with characteristics of the bearer. It turns out that is not entirely true.

Our skills with facial recognition are not unlimited. The quality of execution will vary, particularly due to social circumstances and economic pressures. For a variety of reasons, a verifier may fail to second-guess or interdict an ID subject who presents a document, even if, as in the example of Jerry Iannacci, the card does not seem to match up with the appearance of the person's face.

The primary reason why the verifier check fails is probably boredom or lack of care. In bars and airports, bouncers and security people spend hour after mind-numbing hour checking identification cards in variable light conditions. They are prone to error. Many of the eager-to-socialize college students we love so well rely on such mistakes to get into bars. They use older siblings' identification cards to prove a false age, or they use the card of anyone who looks roughly similar. Our natural biometric training does not translate terribly well to the artificial practice of comparing a single, small photograph with the face of someone standing there in person, under different light, wearing different clothes, and adorned by different tresses.

Courtesy and embarrassment probably play strong roles in reducing challenges to proffered identification documents. Consider the fact that people are better at recognizing faces of their own race than faces of other races.[3] (This effect is stronger for European Americans who may have limited experiences with African-American faces, for example, than for African Americans who generally have greater experience with European-American faces.) In cases where the verifier and ID subject are of different races, the verifier may lack confidence in his or her ability to compare identifiers. He or she may be concerned that questioning or challenging the proffered documents of an ID subject may be viewed through the lens of race and create the appearance of discrimination or animus.

Here is another possibility: If the verifier perceives himself or herself to be of a lower social standing than the ID subject, he or she may be under strong pressure not to interfere with the ID subject's desires. It may seem risky for a person at the low end of the socioeconomic ladder to challenge the identification documents of someone who is well dressed and well connected or powerful. Although some probably love the idea, the average low-dollar-per-hour security guard probably feels some compunction about holding up a corporate CEO for a third look and some hard questioning about his identification card.

Add to these concerns the social and institutional pressures on the people who check identification cards. If the verifier is under time pressure—at the head of an airport security line, for example—challenging identification documents may slow the line and inconvenience everyone waiting in it. Because of the demand for quick comparison of many people, the verifier who questions identification documents every few hours will probably come under strong peer pressure to be less cautious about comparing identifiers—that is, pressure to be faster or just let questionable cases go.

At the same time, verifiers are under little pressure to actually interdict people using false documents. In most cases, there are no repercussions to the person doing the verifier check if he or she gets it wrong. Airport security may be technically breached, or an office building may have impostors in it, but the harm coming from these occurrences is exceedingly rare, in some cases speculative or nonexistent, or not terribly proximate to the identification. Little or no direct recourse will reach those verifying identification documents even if they do a poor job.

The same things are true of the store clerks and hotel receptionists that Jerry Iannacci encountered with his Nigerian-guy credit card. They were not keen to turn up fraud. If they even noticed the picture, they risked being rude in questioning an amiable guy like Jerry. He looked honest. In fact, if they had had the gumption to do something, they would have learned that Jerry was really just doing his job. He was not a fraud threat to their companies.

The verifier-check leg of the card-based identification chain is a significant source of weakness. As Jerry Iannacci's story helps illustrate, people presented with cards may not examine them carefully and may hesitate to ask difficult questions about them. Even if an identification card is based on sound information, and secure, the fact remains that someone can use someone else's card to gain access and benefits wrongfully.

Like the security link in the card communication chain, computers are beginning to do more of the verifier check step, using machine-readable biometrics, such as fingerprints and iris scans to tie tokens to their bearers. Machines can do repetitive, rote tasks like comparing identifiers better than humans.

They lack judgment, however, which would be a mistake to overlook. The clerks who allowed Jerry Iannacci to use his Nigerian-guy credit card probably thought he "looked honest," a judgment that was correct, and that usually is, though it can also import unfair prejudices.

The machine-identification route subjects all people, honest or not, to the same scrutiny. Eliminating the role of judgment in these systems disserves the honest people who will be treated as slightly more suspect than they are in today's systems.

To get at the small number of dishonest people, honest people like Jerry Iannacci may find themselves paying the price of being biometrically tracked. Greater surveillance of all, and treatment of all with greater suspicion, are themes of the improvements and fixes being proposed for identification systems, as we will see in the next chapter.

18. Can Identification Cards Be Fixed?

In early 2005, American troops were deployed in Iraq and Afghanistan, coming under routine fire from Iraqi insurgents and occasional remnants of the Afghan Taliban government. The American presence in those places followed the September 11, 2001, attacks on the World Trade Center and Pentagon, which had awakened a stunned United States to the specter of international terrorism.

It was about the midpoint of the 2005 fiscal year and the military had been spending heavily on its part in the "War on Terror." The funds that had been designated for this purpose in the regular appropriations process were giving out. Legislation was pending in Congress to provide more money—and to fund aid efforts after a devastating tsunami hit the Indian Ocean at the end of 2004. It was clear that this $82 billion spending bill would pass. Opposition to it, even principled responses to important details, could easily be spun as "not supporting the troops."

Consistent with usual practice, the Iraq spending bill came before the Rules Committee on its way to the floor of the House of Representatives. But the committee added a curious note to the rule governing debate on the bill. The committee instructed the Clerk of the House to append the text of a different bill at the end once the bill had passed the House.[1] This new bill was called the REAL ID Act.[2] It would not be open to amendment or separate consideration on the floor of the House of Representatives.

The REAL ID Act was nominally aimed at preventing terrorists from entering the country. But this was a rather small fig leaf covering a broader attempt to curtail illegal immigration. To do so, the REAL ID Act sought in various ways to shore up the weaknesses in state-issued identification documents.

Since 1986, one of the ways Congress has attempted to prevent illegal immigration is through surveillance of workers. In the Immigration Reform and Control Act, Congress required employers to collect proof of citizenship or legal residence from new employees on pain of fines and even prison sentences. That requirement is a subtle, if not too successful, conscription of the business sector into federal surveillance for the purpose of immigration law enforcement.[3]

One of many reasons that federal surveillance of workers has had so little success at stemming immigration is the wide availability of false identification papers. People who enter the United States illegally are unlikely to feel much compunction about procuring false documents while families wait in their home countries for badly needed remittances.

Certainly, employers have little incentive, absent the penalties, to be zealous guardians of the law either. Reporting on workers is at best a distraction from running their businesses. It is not in their interest to turn away people eager to work hard at competitive wages producing the goods and services that American consumers want. But with the REAL ID Act, Congress pressed forward with the policy of identification-based surveillance for immigration law enforcement. The military spending bill with REAL ID's new identification provisions passed by overwhelming margins in both the House and Senate.

As a practical matter, the REAL ID Act federalized the rules for state-issued identification cards. Under REAL ID, any state-issued identification card that does not comply with the act cannot be used to access federal facilities, board commercial aircraft, and enter nuclear power plants or for any other purposes that the secretary of homeland security determines.[4] The REAL ID Act formalizes and symbolizes how state-issued identification cards have come to control access to a large and growing quantity of goods, services, and infrastructure.

Identification Card Reform

In the last three chapters, we looked at the three different steps in the process by which a typical government-issued identification card communicates information from an ID subject to a verifier: First, the ID subject communicates information to the card issuer. Next, the issuer produces the identification card, which communicates information to the verifier. Finally, the verifier compares the identifiers on the card with the ID subject. If the identifiers and the

ID subject match up, the information on the card is accepted as true and the ID subject is identified.

As we have seen, each of these steps is a point of weakness. And each seems to be under growing attack as government-issued identification cards take on greater roles in regulating life and trade. There are ways to steel identification cards against the fraud, forgery, and carelessness that weaken each step in the identification-by-card process, though. The REAL ID Act sought to address each of them. Nothing will ever perfect identification cards, but these reforms sought to make them stronger. Unfortunately, doing so will magnify the negative consequences of our nation's identification system.

ID Card Veracity Reinforcement

The obvious weakness in the ID-subject–to–card-issuer step is that ID subjects are allowed to submit the information that goes into the card. As we saw in chapter 15, this opens the window to corruption and fraud. The information on the card can be falsified.

The REAL ID Act addressed this several different ways. First, it mandated collection of four different items of information:

- A photo identity document, except that a nonphoto identity document is acceptable if it includes both the person's full legal name and date of birth;
- Documentation of the person's date of birth;
- Proof of the person's Social Security account number or verification that the person is ineligible for a Social Security account number; and
- Documentation showing the person's name and address of principal residence.[5]

Along with increasing the number of identifiers, REAL ID also required evidence of lawful status[6]—that is, the legal right to be in the country. It required states to issue temporary cards, conspicuously marked as such, to anyone in the country temporarily.[7] Regulations pending when this book was published would determine the specifics more precisely.

Further, the REAL ID Act required departments of motor vehicles to capture digital copies of source documents (identifiers) and retain paper copies for 7 years, images for 10 years.[8] DMVs can no longer accept foreign documents other than passports. Each person applying for a driver's license or identification is also subject to "mandatory facial image capture."[9]

The REAL ID Act also required DMVs to verify "with the issuing agency, the issuance, validity, and completeness of each document" presented.[10] At a potentially huge expense—few institutions have the resources or infrastructure to confirm their authorship of documents—this could suppress the easiest attack on data veracity: presenting DMV workers with fraudulent identifiers.

The REAL ID Act also sought to suppress fraud on DMVs by improving their employees' ability to detect false identifiers. Among other things, it required states to "establish fraudulent document recognition training programs for appropriate employees engaged in the issuance of drivers' licenses and identification cards."[11]

If carried out properly, each of these steps would make it harder for ID subjects to inject false information into new identification cards and drivers' licenses. With constant oversight, they would make it harder to defraud DMVs.

In chapter 15, we noted how private issuers tend naturally to use a variety of data sources for the cards they issue. They gain information from data subjects at the start, of course, but then confirm it in many ways, adding additional information that they develop themselves and that they get from third parties. This practice reduces the opportunity for fraud by ID subjects.

The REAL ID Act mimics that process in small ways. It requires states to routinely use the Systematic Alien Verification for Entitlements system, which confirms the legal presence of foreigners in the country.[12] It also requires them to confirm Social Security numbers with the Social Security Administration. In the event a Social Security number is already associated with another license or identification card, the state must "resolve the discrepancy."[13]

These processes attempt to use information held by governments to check the identifiers proffered by an ID subject. They help reduce one or two avenues for fraud.

The REAL ID Act does not take the additional step of requiring crosschecking of data held outside of government by private data aggregation firms. That step is regularly taken by the private sector for employment and tenant screening, for issuance of credit, and for other reasons, but it is a controversial process when done by governments.

The CAPPS II (Computer Assisted Passenger Prescreening) program, also named Secure Flight, was a program put forward by the Department of Homeland Security's Transportation Security Administration in the early to mid-2000s. Although its policies were constantly in flux, at times it would have checked data in airlines' passenger name records with data held by private aggregators to figure out how "real" the identifiers and passenger were and to reduce errors when the government matched travelers against various "watch" and "no-fly" lists.[14]

Government background checks on people who are under no suspicion raise significant concerns. And there is a difference in kind, not degree, when governments use data aggregated for marketing or financial purposes to control people's access to goods, services, and benefits. People in the United States are entitled to due process when governments make these types of decisions about them.

An alternative is for governments themselves to collect more information and develop the records needed to prevent fraud in card issuance. As noted, the REAL ID Act requires DMVs to verify the issuance, validity, and completeness of breeder documents with the issuing agency and to keep copies of these documents. The REAL ID Act also requires states to contribute information to a nationwide database of driver information.[15]

These data collection and retention requirements show the unwelcome trajectory of our national identification policy. The logic of a strengthened national identification system goes this direction: If a high-quality biometric like DNA were included in the reporting requirement, a national register of all births in the United States could be developed. Deaths, likewise, could be reported so that a master list of living Americans, and appropriate records about them, would be available whenever an identification document were needed. A system like this, carefully designed and operated, could thwart fraud on issuers of identification documents by removing ID subjects from their current role in providing the information that goes into cards.

It would also be the Big Brother database that Americans so rightly resist—but it is inevitable if the policy of a single, government-issued card used for identification and access to society continues to advance.

The REAL ID Act does many things to strengthen the "data veracity" portion of the identification card communications chain, at least as far as fraud on DMVs is concerned. It does little about corruption, however, except requiring "appropriate security clearance require-ments"[16]—whatever those may be—for the people who produce drivers' licenses and identification cards. As discussed below, if opportunities for fraud drop, corruption will likely rise. These reforms may make the identification card system "stronger," but at the same time make it brittle.

Card Security

The REAL ID Act did a few things to address the security of identification cards. It required state-issued drivers' licenses and identification cards to use physical security features designed to prevent tampering, counterfeiting, or duplication of documents for fraudulent purposes.[17] It required physical security features at the locations where drivers' licenses are produced. And it required secu-rity to protect the materials and papers from which the documents are produced.[18] As mentioned above, the REAL ID Act also required "appropriate security clearance requirements" for people who man-ufacture or produce drivers' licenses.

In chapter 16, on card security, we discussed all the countermea-sures against forgery that are being taken. The identification card security arms race will undoubtedly continue. One of the directions in which this arms race is heading is to use encryption. For example, a card could have a computer chip embedded in it containing all the information printed on the card, including the ID subject's pic-ture. These data could be encrypted using public key encryption. Thus, using the issuer's public key, the verifier could decrypt the data on the chip making certain that the data on the card and chip were published by the issuer in the form they appear.

Other data structures could do the same things as quickly or more quickly and conveniently. The chip could contain a serial number, or standard identifier like the Social Security number, also encrypted. A reader operated by the verifier could query a central database using secure communication over the Internet and retrieve the identi-fication information and verifying identifiers. Assuming well-con-structed and secure databases and communications, this procedure would virtually ensure the security of identification cards against forgery.

150

Going beyond the REAL ID Act, these are just two of a number of ways that the security problems with identification cards and tokens could essentially be solved. They would, however, tend to lock in the government's control of the identifiers and identification documents that Americans use. The use of chips, encryption, and other such technologies would also make the identification process opaque to average Americans. Far from an identification system that works for them, the national identification system would work *on* them.

Verifier Check

The weaknesses in the "verifier check" step can also be solved by using newer technology. Relying on humans to look at pictures of one another is outdated, slow, and incautious compared with using today's high-quality, machine-readable biometrics. The REAL ID Act called for "a common machine-readable technology"[19] that may or may not be used at some point to improve verifier checks.

Fingerprint scanning, iris scanning, hand geometry, and a number of other machine-readable biometrics are already in use or coming into broader use shortly. Although they do not have the mathematical certainty of encryption because they interact with the human form, these processes are likely to provide very highly ensured comparisons between the biometric information stored in identity records and the information found on people when they present themselves for identification.

In other words, a card could be issued with an embedded chip that contains biometric information about the bearer, such as a fingerprint, encrypted for security. (The card would not actually contain an image of the fingerprint, but a mathematical description of the fingerprint—distances and angles between and among key features.) When someone presents himself or herself for identification, he or she could place the card in a reader and his or her finger in a separate reader. The machine would compare the information on the card with the person's finger and confirm a match. This procedure would prove that the card is about the person presenting it.

Machines don't get tired, and they don't get bored. Nor are they subject to peer pressure, embarrassment, or other similar human defect. Using machines to do the verification step can vastly improve the quality of verification and probably accelerate it compared with current human verification processes.

As with card security, there are many different ways to structure the data in these transactions. A chip could contain a serial number, encrypted, and call on a database for the confirming biometric information along with the identification information. Indeed, a system could be designed requiring no card at all, just a chip. The chip could be embedded in a key fob, a watch, a mobile phone, or an arm.

The natural trajectory is obviously to dispense with the identification card, a familiar but unnecessary item. People's wallets might be getting thinner soon, as smaller, handier physical tokens take care of identification and authorization.

Why Bother with a Card?

Another variation on the data structures discussed above could do away with cards and tokens entirely. Already, people can identify themselves completely using a single biometric alone. Placing a finger on a scanner allows a machine to write a mathematical description of fingerprint features. That description can be compared with fingerprint descriptions on file in a database. When a match is found, the person whose finger is on the scanner has been identified with a very high probability of accuracy due to the quality of the identifier.

Already, high-quality, machine-based identification requires no physical items at all and only a small amount of human involvement. Indeed, all the identifiers needed for near perfect identification of all the humans on Earth could be stored in a single database.

The versatility of such a system would be incredible. Access to goods, services, and infrastructure could all be carefully controlled and monitored. So could the ability to enter into contracts and make payments. Identification and interaction data could all be housed in the same place, with notations made in associated records that reflect key life events, the legal status of the subject, and so on—all of this keyed to highly accurate biometric identifiers.

The national security potential is incredible, as well. Such a database would reveal the tracks of terrorists and other wrongdoers (once they were known), expose their whereabouts when they try to access the benefits of society, prove links between terrorists and their accomplices, and so on. A database like this could be applied equally well to general law enforcement—the tracking and exposure of child molesters, drug dealers, deadbeat dads, and people with outstanding parking tickets.

A perfect identification and surveillance system is a real possibility. But perfection is in the eye of the beholder.

Reforms That Do Not Fix

By now, careful readers have noticed the simple, straightforward progression from reforming identification systems to a worldwide database of identification and interaction information. Wherever it is used, identification is essentially the interface between people and the surveillance systems that watch them, whether benign or malign. Many people feel in their guts that the "reforms" described here would be too reminiscent of George Orwell's cautionary novel *1984*—and they undoubtedly are. We will return to concerns about uniform identification systems in later chapters. But this is the direction in which many identification policies and practices are headed.

Before getting to these concerns, a practical concern about a "reformed" national identification system stands out: As we alluded to at the end of chapter 16, a strong, unitary identification system is much more valuable to break. The more access it controls to goods, services, infrastructure, and employment, the more rewarding it is for people on the wrong side of the law to compromise it.

Consider surveillance of workers to control immigration, a technique used by U.S. law and a major impetus behind the REAL ID Act. If you assume that having an identification card makes the difference between black-market work that pays $15,000 per year and legitimate employment paying $35,000, the value today of working 20 years at that higher wage is more than a quarter of a *million* dollars. News stories reporting corruption at DMVs that reaches into thousands of dollars per identification card show that false identification today is probably selling at far below its actual value.

"Strengthening" identification systems by unifying and hardening them will drive more pressure onto their "soft" portions, such as the entry points (DMV offices) and back-end systems (databases and networks). They are, and always will be, controlled by fallible humans. They will always be corruptible and breakable at some price. And the price some people might pay could be very high.

The reforms embodied in the REAL ID Act do not address the root problem, which is the policy of using a single, state-issued identification card for more and more important purposes. The more valuable a driver's license is for access to work, mobility, goods, and services, the more likely people will seek to acquire this document illegally. Reforms of this type may "stiffen" state-issued identification card processes, but they leave it brittle.

Meanwhile, the expense and inconvenience of restricted access to identification cards will fall on all Americans—including the ones who need drivers' licenses for the simple purpose of driving. Honest, law-abiding Americans will suffer impingement on their freedom of action, their individual power, and their security from identity-based frauds. The REAL ID Act is full of reforms that do not fix.

Instead of "strengthening" our national identification system, policies that reduce the value of breaking identification systems will improve identification. Jujitsu is needed much more than brawn. The linear reforms of REAL ID are an error when more subtle and intelligent shifts in policy would truly improve identification.

Before we reach the policies that will actually improve our identification systems, we must complete our understanding of identification itself by exploring the costs of uniform identification systems. The following chapters examine the consequences of identification and the often high price people pay when identification systems are designed to serve something other than their interests.

With rapidly advancing digital technology, the consequences of identification are changing. People's lives are becoming more and more exposed to institutions, both public and private. Historically, uniform identification systems have been a handy tool for abusive governments. And modern criminals ply their trade more easily thanks to the poor security that uniform identification systems provide to individuals. We explore these problems in the following chapters.

PART IV

THE DANGERS OF DIGITAL AGE IDENTIFICATION

19. The Decline of Practical Obscurity

"Space. The final frontier."

As these words opened each episode of the *Star Trek* television series, viewers knew that Captain James T. Kirk would soon boldly go where no man had gone before. In part, that meant that he would be romancing some humanoid female on a new planet or a nubile member of his crew—outfitted like a go-go dancer on *Rowan and Martin's Laugh-In*. This groundbreaking science-fiction television series had some very down-to-earth plot lines.

Episode 11 of the original *Star Trek* series, broadcast from 1966 to 1969, was titled "Dagger of the Mind." In this episode, Kirk's accomplice in trysting was the dimpled and miniskirted Dr. Helen Noel. Kirk and Noel were about to beam down to conduct an investigation on the Tantalus Penal Colony. They had met before . . . at the science lab Christmas party.

"Problem, Captain?" Mr. Spock asked, pretending not to notice the sexual tension between the two as they met again on the deck of the transporter.

Later, as Noel and Kirk tested the neural neutralizer that Dr. Tristan Adams was using to rewrite inmates' memories on Tantalus, Dr. Noel would place the suggestion in Kirk's mind that their meeting at the Christmas party had ended in her cabin. But Dr. Adams would discover them at the neutralizer and take it a step further, diabolically forcing Kirk to believe that he has loved Dr. Noel for years and that he would sacrifice anything for her.

At the climax of the action, Dr. Adams himself is being neutralized. Spock bursts in, phaser drawn, on Kirk and Noel as they kiss in a sleeping chamber. The hint of embarrassed exasperation on Spock's face is classic Vulcan deadpan.

Earlier, back on the *Enterprise*, Spock and Dr. McCoy had been investigating the mental delirium exhibited by an escapee from Tantalus, Dr. Simon Van Gelder. Dr. Van Gelder had been a colleague of Dr. Adams but Adams had turned the neural neutralizer on Van

Gelder, making him a prisoner. Because of the extreme pain caused by recovering neutralized memories, Van Gelder could not describe what had happened.

The solution was Spock's first ever use of the Vulcan mind meld. He had never practiced this ancient secret Vulcan technique on a human but, placing his hands carefully on Van Gelder's neck and pate, Spock changed the pressure in Van Gelder's nerves and blood vessels, allowing the joining of their minds.

Using the mind-meld technique, Spock learned that the universally respected penologist Dr. Adams had become a megalomaniac, turning his planet into a tyranny. Captain Kirk and Dr. Noel were in grave danger on Tantalus. They had to be rescued . . . from that . . . awful . . . make-out session.

Understanding Practical Obscurity

Captain Kirk's conquests aside, the mind-meld technique exposes through contrast a central feature of the human condition that people rarely consider: nearly all of our thoughts, memories, feelings, and observations are known only to ourselves. The vast bulk of the things we experience and think are never communicated to another soul. We can talk for hours to friends and loved ones but share only thin slices of our most important and relevant ideas, experiences, and feelings. The rest remains on tap inside our heads, or it fades from memory forever.

What we do share is limited by our ability to communicate and by our intimates' abilities to perceive and understand. Even if it gets through, information about us might reside only briefly in others' thoughts and memories. Almost certainly, the people we share with cannot further communicate our experiences with any accuracy. Nearly all of our lives and experience are separated by a thick fog from ever reaching the minds of others. Probably out of psychological necessity and instinct, we ignore this and focus on our connectedness.

The same dynamic is at play in the relationships between institutions and people, without the emotional or psychological meaning, of course. The governments and businesses with which we interact capture only tiny slivers of information about us (again, measured against our total experience). What they do collect is important though—pieces of data that define our legal, social, and economic lives, such as income, health status, purchases, ownership, appearance, identities, and so on.

As they developed over the past few hundred years, institutions used paper and similar low-tech methods to record that information. The filing cabinets in government warehouses, courthouses, law firms, doctors' offices, banks, and department stores represent the "memories" of these institutions. Searching them has long meant sending clerks to dig through dusty piles of paper looking for notations in alphabetized files.

That method has not been easy or efficient. Even collected and recorded by large enterprises with smart organizational systems, information about us has been fairly obscure, as a practical matter. Although sensitive information may have come to reside with many institutions that could conceivably use it and share it with others, the substantial expense and difficulty of doing so has sharply limited the practice. As with individuals, our lives have been shrouded from institutions by a thick fog. Information about people has been practically obscure.

Practical obscurity has long provided a degree of protection to information about us, even information we have not guarded as private. Just as our thoughts are obscure to one another, our economic and social lives have been obscure to the government agencies and business enterprises that play such significant roles in our lives. This is changing, and the change affects every facet of information policy, especially identification.

Identification in the Digital Age: Biometrics

In earlier chapters, we roughed out the path of identification processes through human evolution and history. It started with "something you are"—those highly accurate human-read biometrics we talked about in chapter 3. Then, with the emergence of human society, we advanced to other things like names, statuses, and relationships. These identifiers we called "something you are *assigned*."

With increased mobility, "something you know" became another identifier, socially constructed, that helped people engage one another in more complex transactions over greater distances. Finally, "something you have" emerged: the trinkets, devices, and eventually cards and tokens designed specifically to identify people. The identification card is a complicated and highly sophisticated identification tool that incorporates multifactor authentication, that piggybacks on other systems, and that itself is heavily piggybacked upon.

The identification card is far from perfect, of course. It is susceptible to fraud, forgery, and carelessness. It can be misplaced. Importantly, it serves poorly in modern remote commerce, conducted online or over the telephone. The reason is that the identification card still relies on biometrics, which are typically still human-read. It does not cure the problem of distance and is subject to all the weaknesses that human participation imports into identification processes.

Those flaws have led to a resurgence in knowledge-based identification: not knowledge to validate kin relations and family history, of course, but things such as passwords. Key fobs that display a randomized number every few seconds—the number serving as a password during that few seconds—are fascinating devices that combine something you have with something you know. Financial services providers are using them not only for security but to build brand loyalty. These identifiers, too, are subject to weaknesses, however, such as insecure networks and loss or theft.

To overcome those weaknesses, identification is returning to its roots. The ultimate identifiers—just as they were at the beginning of history—appear to be biometrics. Biometrics appear to be returning as the preeminent way of positively identifying people. That is because many biometrics are immutable, they cannot be misplaced, and they are conveniently on hand—in some cases, literally—all the time. The difference today is that biometrics will increasingly be measured by machines. The index card variables on and about us will be used to plug us humans into our appropriate place in the datascape.

We have not reached the end of the story for identification. There is a future where biometrics may be forged, through manufactured DNA and fingerprints, for example. Individuals may use gene therapies one day to splice alternative genes into the portion of the genome used in DNA identification. But modern biometrics are the most significant current development in identification and the most important for the next few decades.

Two related elements make modern biometric techniques unique. First, modern biometrics use fully articulated and standardized measurements. The most advanced techniques, such as DNA analysis, are widely regarded as proving identity with near-absolute certainty. They use scientific processes that can be repeated by anyone with proper training. Biometric measurements can be implemented to minimize human error.

DNA identification enjoys substantial confidence among the public for accuracy. Because of long experience, the public has substantial confidence in fingerprinting also, though perhaps less than DNA. The standards used in other biometric techniques may not yet have gained the confidence of the public, but one can assume that they will.

Second, and more important, modern biometrics are machine readable and recordable. Biometric information recorded by machine, and the data linked to biometric observations, can be copied easily, shared quickly and widely, combined, and stored for long periods of time without degrading. That is how modern identification systems most threaten practical obscurity and the privacy it has afforded people for all of history.

Biometrically authenticating identification by machine is highly *accurate* and, more important, it is highly *usable* personal information. It allows institutions to collect data and index it to precise and highly accurate human identifiers, making it useful in countless ways.

We all know about the massive advances in computing power and data storage under way. Moore's law, so vaunted for so long (and expressed various ways), describes the advances in semiconductors as roughly doubling their power, or halving their cost per computation, every two years.[1] The same has been roughly true of data storage.[2]

Whether these technological advances continue at the same pace, computing and data storage are motifs of modern life that will only grow more prominent. They will have significant influence over our future lives by changing our relationships to information-collecting institutions. The linchpin of this process, which causes data to have this influence on all of us, is identification.

Machine-readable biometric identification represents a dramatic change from previous forms. As we have said before in this book, identification is a sort of social, economic, and legal glue. Modern biometrics are a particularly strong form of this glue. Modern computing means that a particularly large amount of information may be stuck to us for a very long time.

This idea—that massive amounts of data about people are becoming more and more readily available to more and more people and institutions—is one of the most important social changes under way as we enter the Information Age. This is the decline of practical obscurity.

The Decline of Practical Obscurity

Imagine a world where everyone did the Vulcan mind meld each time they touched. With all the handshaking and hugging going on, in a few days everyone would know everything about everyone else. Instead of the current version, people might play a sort of converse "six degrees of separation" in which they would struggle to determine who on earth they do *not* know.

When you went to the park, a stranger might walk up to you and say, "I hope you brought your bee-sting medicine. That was scary when you didn't have it and got stung out at the lake." She would know this and everything else about you.

That is a vast exaggeration of what is occurring with the decline of practical obscurity, of course. Many commentators paint a picture of an all-seeing corporate surveillance state. Most famously, George Orwell warned in his book *1984* against the growth of government power, implemented through comprehensive surveillance. That fictional account is nowhere near any likely future, though the concerns are legitimate and it provides useful rhetoric for debates about modern technologies.

Practical obscurity is a massive force. It is changing only slightly and rather slowly but, like the course of an iceberg or a planet, a minor tick in one direction or another can make the difference between smooth sailing and worlds colliding.

Practical obscurity has long ensured that even nonprivate information is not widely shared. An endless array of social, legal, and economic practices has developed around the assumption that the information collected about people will remain practically obscure. The things we wear, the places we go, the people we see, the things we say, and the things we buy have all been chosen in the past under the umbrella of practical obscurity.

Machine identification systems and better data collection generally are changing that. The websites we surf and the words we commit to e-mail are part of a world in which information is less obscure.

This information travels, persists, and sees reuse in ways few people yet fully understand, much less have adjusted to.

As practical obscurity declines, it becomes more likely that large quantities of data centered on identified individuals will be collected and more likely that it will be shared and used. With larger collections of data highly correlated to precise identities, the consequences of being identified are changing.

... Which Might Not Be All Bad

It would be easy to dismiss the decline of practical obscurity as inherently bad. It is not. It is just different. In a world of mind melds, everyone would know about your allergy to bee stings. You would be well assured of receiving appropriate medical treatment even if you were incapacitated. Everyone would know how to protect you and to serve your needs.

Arguably, the waning of practical obscurity returns people to a parallel of the social circumstances that probably dominated human existence for most of our past. When families lived in extremely close quarters, sharing one or two rooms, a cave, or the hollow of a tree for all activities, nearly all personal information was subject to scrutiny by their relations. Villagers who spent their entire lives in one small town were subject to constant observation by their neighbors, who would certainly share the best information in the form of gossip.

In other words, practical obscurity is a relatively new social circumstance enjoyed by the relatively small number of people with enough wealth to secrete their lives from family members, neighbors, and others. Obscurity and privacy are luxuries enjoyed only very recently, in historical terms, by a small part of the world's population.

Advanced technology and its use for identification do not mean that practical obscurity should be dispensed with, however. We should seek to preserve and extend obscurity as an option for all people to enjoy.

Preservation of Choice

Many people enjoy obscurity and the privacy that comes from acting anonymously. But just as many, if not more, prioritize other goods. As often as not, collections of data about people serve them. Consumers benefit from being identified when that improves their experience of customer service, their convenience, and allows them to receive specially tailored offers, products, and lower prices. Many people choose to be identified and enjoy the benefits from it. That is a rational choice.

Many, however, at least claim to prefer greater privacy, including the option of transacting anonymously and choosing whether to share certain information. Few markets recognize that preference, and there are few natural experiments that reveal consumers' true desires. Getting privacy protective options in homogeneous markets can be very difficult.

A rare exception (going to substantive information, not identity) is forming in the market for auto insurance. Some auto insurance companies are beginning to allow drivers the option of submitting digitally recorded information about their driving habits in order to get discounts. The car owner can install a device that collects and reports information about his or her auto usage to earn discounts of between 5 and 25 percent.[3] If they do not install the device, or if they remove it, they will receive no discount.

In this case, withholding information—that is, maintaining privacy—is the default option. Consumers must affirmatively choose the benefits of information sharing. Over time, consumer demand may converge on sharing information to get discounts; insuring a car without sharing driving information may become nearly impossible. Or consumers may resist this because of the Big Brother possibilities. Or the option to share driving information may remain an option, with different prices offered based on different information-sharing practices.

In many cases, consumers who seek greater privacy or anonymity do not constitute a significant market segment, or at least they have not been recognized as such. It would be gratifying to see more companies offering goods and services with tiered pricing based on varied information sharing (both identifying and substantive). If there is money to be made from serving people with high privacy demands, they should be served. The choices they make in the market will reward companies that offer services and goods without requiring identification and extra information.

If privacy demanders do not constitute a significant market, though, and are not willing to put their money where their privacy desires are, they will remain "outliers" whose preferences go unserved.[4] Their demands to be served without paying the full cost should not be heeded by imposing costs on the majority.

If enough consumers want them to, businesses will find that there are myriad transactions and interactions that require no identification. Instead of identification, authorization should be the key. Authorization occurs when an individual has the characteristics needed for a transaction to go forward. Most simple commercial transactions require only that a person pay money or guarantee payment. But billions of such transactions per year also incorporate identification. Whether that brings added security, enhances customer service, or lowers costs is debatable, if not actually ever debated. Alternatives to identification and other information sharing are rarely part of the mix of offerings that companies put forward.

The important thing is to preserve choice. The design of information systems and policies is very important to the type of world we will live in. If the default is for every encounter with business or government to commence with identification, people won't be able to choose anonymity. Advocates may have to fight for practices that the majority of people would enjoy. If the default is anonymity, people can choose to be identified and enjoy the benefits that provides. In other words, to preserve choice, anonymity should be the default. Identification should be used by default only when it is essential, not out of assumption or habit.

Monolithic Identification Systems

The consequences for practical obscurity are greatest in the case of monolithic identification systems. These are systems that use one identifier or the same set of identifiers, such as the Social Security number or name and mother's maiden name. Monolithic identification systems are the most promiscuous because their standardized identifiers facilitate record sharing and linkage among disparate databases and institutions. Identification by machine will hasten the decline of practical obscurity most if the methods used are uniform. Uniform identification systems unnecessarily drive a wedge between technological advances and the interests of people.

The alternative is to use diverse identifiers that make it difficult to identify an individual from one system to another. Using diverse identifiers is an essential protection, if not a complete one. A heterogeneous group of identification systems is a structural bulwark that—to an important degree—would protect the obscurity that people enjoy. A purchase at a store may be recorded by the store, correlated to an identified individual, and used to serve his or her interests. If the record is not shared—if it cannot be shared because data sets don't match—knowledge of a person's commercial behavior will be restricted to the appropriate realm. There are many costs to this approach, of course.

Identification systems and practices must be reconsidered in light of the increasing threat they pose to obscurity and privacy in the digital age. Although the structure and theory of identification has not changed rapidly over time, new identification processes are changing, in important ways, what it means to be identified. Foremost, identification processes are now being conducted by machines—machines that record, preserve, and copy information extraordinarily well. These processes are easily convertible to broad tracking schemes.

The increased availability of information about people is reducing practical obscurity. The chapters that follow explore the consequences of identification with new intensity in this light.

20. Dossiers and Surveillance

"How do you know all this stuff?"

"We just got wired into the system, sir."

"Oh. Well, I'd like to order a couple of your Double Meat Special pizzas."

"Sure thing. There'll be a new twenty-dollar charge for this, sir."

"What do you mean?"

"Sir, the system shows me that your medical records indicate that you have high blood pressure and extremely high cholesterol. Luckily, we have a new agreement with your national health care provider that allows us to sell you double-meat pies as long as you agree to waive all future claims of liability."

"What?"

"Do you agree, sir? You can sign the form when we deliver but there is a charge for processing. The total is sixty-seven dollars even."

"Sixty-seven dollars!"

"That includes the delivery surcharge of fifteen dollars to cover the added risk to our driver of traveling through an orange zone."

"I live in an orange zone?"

"Now you do. It looks like there was another robbery on Montrose yesterday. Hmmm. You could save forty-eight dollars if you ordered our special Sprout Submarine Combo and picked it up yourself."

This excerpt from a video distributed by the American Civil Liberties Union in mid-2004[1] illustrates and plays on the concerns people have with an economy and society that increasingly makes use of databases. Organized by personal identifiers, these databases operate as dossiers on each person.

If widely disparate databases were combined, as they are in the ACLU video, pizza parlors like this one would come to know far too much for our comfort—including customers' home and mobile phone numbers, home and work addresses, health status, travel plans, library reading, spouse's names, magazine subscriptions, credit card balances, and sundry other details. In the video, the tactless customer service representative notes her customer's waist size and says that tofu and sprouts are "like, *required.*"

This is the specific version of the general threat that uniform digital identification holds for practical obscurity, which we discussed in the last chapter. In the pizza video, the system recognizes the customer's mobile phone number, correlates it to his national identification number, and pulls up all the other information keyed to that identifier. The uniform national identifier is the structure on which the dossier is built.

The thrust of the video is that this kind of thing is bad, of course, and, in the extreme case, it certainly is. But databases and dossiers can be quite good too. Nobody knows how much our society and economy should rely on databases and dossiers. Finding the most desirable level of database use is beyond the capability of any analyst or advocate, especially while technology, information practices, and people's expectations are all changing.

The Good That Comes from Databases

Though it may be counterintuitive, think of all the good things that are done with databases. In the ACLU video itself, the pizza company knows the address of its customer so that it can provide faster, more convenient service. It recognizes its customer by name, which is often a welcome customer-service gesture.

In terms of customer well-being, it is appealing to have the pizza place recommend a more healthful alternative to its double-meat pie, though it is obviously troubling that a pizza company should have an information-sharing relationship with health providers and insurers. Local crime information is more available, which is a good thing for promoting responsive government. If this were routine, citizens might demand more effective crime control in their local neighborhoods because they would recognize even more of its costs. When local politicians heard from enraged pizza buyers, the politicians would pay the price for failing to provide adequate police protection.

At the end of the video, the customer service representative points out that a coupon is available in a magazine the customer's wife subscribes to. The fact that his credit cards are maxed out means that payment will have to be in cash. Again, it is disconcerting to have a pizza place know so much, but these two data points help the transaction go forward quickly, and at a discount to the customer.

While tweaking our information sensibilities, the ACLU pizza video illustrates how data aggregation adds brains to the economy and society and how it promotes seamless transactions. If each of the millions of transactions and interactions that occurred every day in the U.S. economy were "improved" this way—if consumers were offered better health and lifestyle choices, if services and risk were more accurately priced, if savings options were promoted, and if payment was smoothed and ensured—consumers would see enormous benefits. In the ACLU pizza example, they would be healthier, wealthier, safer, better informed—and less private.

"Unfairness" and Distrust of Data Aggregation

There is much distrust of data aggregation and the decisionmaking that comes from it—probably for a number of reasons. One is that it is a relatively new and unknown economic practice. Although credit bureaus have been around for generations, their role and the role of other data aggregators in marketing and decisionmaking have blossomed only recently thanks to advances in data collection, transfer, storage, and use.

Is data-based decisionmaking unfair? The ACLU pizza video plays on the fact that most people believe they would be worse off if insurance companies had more information available to them for assessing risk. Insurers could price their products more accurately if that were so, meaning that many people could pay less for their insurance. A significant minority would lose out, though, because they could no longer hide their drinking, smoking, and skydiving to impose the costs of their lifestyle on the broader insurance pool.

This minority would object vocally to the "unfairness" of the increased prices they would pay and the "privacy invasion" of having more accurate information in the hands of insurers. The majority of consumers, however, would enjoy reductions in premiums. Unfortunately, because those reductions would be relatively small compared with the minority's increases, even consumer interest groups might object to insurance pricing that is lower and, actually, fairer.

Likewise, crime surcharges of the kind illustrated in the ACLU pizza video would be regarded as unfair. There is greater risk to

169

the pizza company of losing a driver, a car, or its cash when it delivers to a high-crime "orange" zone. It asks the customer to share some of that risk by paying a higher cost. (The video sets the price wildly too high, of course, for dramatic effect.) This practice would disproportionately affect poorer communities that suffer more crime.

Protesters against this kind of "redlining" (by that name or some other epithet) would seek to prevent economic signals that bring the cost of crime home to the most interested citizens. Preventing this use of data in the name of "fairness" would, in turn, insulate people from information about the relatively poor service they receive from police departments, alleviating pressure on them to improve.

With good data, it is possible today to price products and risks much more accurately. However, more accurate pricing might offend people who have benefited from inaccurate pricing in the past. They would perceive unfairness as they lost implicit wealth transfers and began paying the full price for the goods and services they receive.

Add to this the real unfairness that exists in the data aggregation industry. Since 1970, the Fair Credit Reporting Act[2] has regulated the operations of credit bureaus. They are the organizations that collect information about people's payment behavior so that their credit risk can be gauged. An intricate set of regulatory procedures dictates how consumers can dispute items in their credit reports and what responsibilities credit bureaus have to respond or to change consumers' files. The FCRA sets low hurdles for the credit bureaus and, most importantly, insulates them from tort liability for defamation, invasion of privacy, or negligence.

Accordingly, ever since the FCRA was passed, the credit reporting industry has oriented itself to serve two masters: the financial institutions that furnish information and buy information products and the government regulators that enforce the FCRA. Consumers—who could be partners in maintaining the data that typically serve them so well—are an afterthought. They enter a confusing maze when they receive adverse credit scores based on bad data, when their files are mixed with other consumers' information, and when their corrected files are repolluted by data furnishers supplying incorrect information again.

When the arcane procedures in the FCRA work, that is well and good. They help consumers. But very often they do not. Stories of consumers wronged by indifferent credit bureaus are legion—more than 30 years after federal regulations nominally aimed at fairness went into effect. Widespread distrust of this industry, and data aggregation generally, is the result.

Making matters worse, amendments to the Fair Credit Reporting Act in the USA PATRIOT Act[3] made consumer information more readily available to government agencies for investigation and counterterrorism purposes. Several data aggregators make a substantial part of their income from selling data to law enforcement. It is no wonder that data aggregators are perceived as part of a growing corporate surveillance state rather than as a valuable service provided to consumers.[4]

In addition, recent times have seen a welter of security breaches from data-collecting institutions that built insecure data systems or failed to practice sufficient security procedures. Most consumers have learned about data stores containing information about them when the data has been lost or breached. That is no way to introduce an industry or a business practice to the consuming public.

Most people would regard it as intrusive and bizarre to have a pizza parlor know the magazines they read—even though they would also blithely tick off the same information in a telephone survey just for the asking or in exchange for a coupon. Likewise, it seems offensive for a seller to know in advance that a person cannot pay by credit card, even though the seller would surely find out if the buyer tried to use credit in the transaction. Society's expectations about who should know what information, and when it should be used, would be the subject of a fascinating sociological study.

Suffice it to say that our society is not ready to accept the changes that would make all the efficiencies made available by data aggregation a reality. Although many people accept and tacitly appreciate the convenience benefits from data aggregation, many also chafe at it—some do both. Many people are uncomfortable with the simple fact that calling from a certain phone number reveals to a business their names, addresses, past transactions, and other relationship information. Data-based business is of recent vintage and the consuming public is slowly but surely deciding what it thinks of it.

Data aggregators provide an essential service to a fully modern, remote-commerce economy: providing reputation and background information, marketing intelligence, and risk profiles about consumers, renters, and workers. Far more often than not, data aggregation helps worthy consumers gain access to financial services, employment, and housing. Data aggregation adds brainpower to our modern economy and makes it far more efficient and responsive to consumer interests. But this worldview is not dominant today, nor gaining in currency.

Data aggregators have not recognized themselves as a consumer-oriented business and they have done little to instill in the public consciousness the fact that they provide valuable services to consumers. They remain essentially mysterious to the vast majority of people—obscure and shadowy handmaidens of corporate marketers, financiers, and government investigators. They collect information from sources of which most consumers are unaware and use that information in ways that most consumers don't understand. The murk surrounding data aggregation prevents consumers from deciding straightforwardly between material well-being and privacy. Consumers are worse off for not having a clear choice.

The State Monopoly on Identification

If the welter of problems described earlier were solved, there is a strong case that data aggregation would make life tangibly better for consumers. But efficiency and tangible welfare are not the only goals. An economy is a social system that must serve all the interests of people. Those interests include privacy and control over personal information, autonomy, and the ability to choose freely. People should remain free to make choices that are unhealthful, expensive, dangerous, and ignorant. Eating greasy pizza is part of what makes being human fun.

The main point of the ACLU pizza video—and a point well made—is that too extensive tracking of people tends to convert them into the pawns or peons of institutions—of pizza companies, insurers, governments, phone companies, payment systems, and employers. The use of uniform identification and databases to track people is wrong—after a certain point. The problem is determining where that point is.

The video is premised on the existence of a national identification number. (In chapter 22, we will discuss precisely how ours has come to be the U.S. Social Security number, but here we will discuss that dynamic in theory.) The result is that consumers have no choice about when and how they are identified. Data aggregation systems become widely viewed as remote, indifferent, unfair, and untrustworthy.

The best way to think about a national identification number is as a protocol or standard. A protocol is a technical convention or standard set of rules. In this case, it is a set of rules about how people are named: We talked in chapter 4 about historical examples of governments' having pushed people to drop their indigenous naming systems in favor of formal ones. Identification numbers are a continuation of that process, the creation of a unique number for every person.

Obviously, anyone can establish numbers for people. Banks and credit card companies do it all the time when they open individuals' accounts. But when governments establish these identifiers, they do a couple of other things. Most importantly, they mandate the use of these protocols. They also create and maintain their systems at no direct cost to users—because citizens pay for them through taxes.

The U.S. Social Security number is not technically mandatory, but that technicality is irrelevant. People may not work, invest money, use most financial services, pay taxes, or collect most government benefits without a Social Security number. New parents may not collect the tax deduction due them for having children without getting Social Security numbers for their little ones. Likewise, states prohibit driving—a nearly essential activity in most places—without carrying a driver's license.

Because they are uniform, but much more because they are virtually mandatory and nearly universally used, protocols like the Social Security number and the driver's license have been adopted by institutions throughout the economy to identify people. Often, governments require themselves and other organizations to check "government-issued identification." Potential competing issuers of identifiers, authorizations cards, and identification cards like banks, credit card companies, employers, and Internet service providers have no chance of competing in this market because of the monopoly power exercised by governments.

The result is near universal convergence on the Social Security number and driver's license as uniform identifiers and identification cards throughout the economy and society. This creates substantial efficiencies, of course, but it also defies other interests of consumers, like privacy and choice. Those interests would be enhanced in a system with multiple competing identification systems rather than a government monopoly.

Heterogeneous Identification

Alas, this digression doesn't answer the question of how often tracking and databases should be used in our economy and society. It only shows how government involvement in identification—the enforcement of uniform identifiers and cards—unnecessarily promotes and subsidizes uniform, centralized tracking of people.

Were people able to choose identification systems like they choose banks, grocery stores, or phone companies, there would be competition among those systems to provide not only convenience but also protection—protection from excessive monitoring, from data retention, from unfair use, and so on.

In a competitive identification environment, people could use one identification system for one purpose and other identification systems for other purposes. They might use one identification system for ordinary purchases, another one for mental and physical health, one for communications, and another for finances and investing. Of course, people could use one identification system for all their social and economic needs if they were indifferent to privacy and surveillance.

To be quite clear, such heterogeneous identification systems would not just be different "account numbers" tied by the same identifiers to people. Rather, each would have to use different identifiers to glue people to their separate identities. One might use a token and password. Another might use a biometric like a thumbprint scan, whereas another might use the same thumb but different algorithms to record it. Another might use voice recognition and another might use one's e-mail access. There is no end to the variety of identification and authorization systems that would be possible if the market for identification were subject to competition and innovation from diverse providers and not dominated by a small number of tax-subsidized behemoths that require by law the use of their identification products.

Because they would not use uniform identifiers, those truly heterogeneous systems would not be naturally interoperable. Data mining might always reveal links between an identity in one system and an identity in another, but identification systems earmarked for particularly sensitive uses might, by policy, never preserve information or identifiers that could be traced or matched by other identification systems.

When it circulated around the Internet, the ACLU pizza video struck a chord with many people. All the reasons why are hard to know, of course, but commercial data use is widely distrusted—to say nothing of government data use.

With practical obscurity in decline, today's identification and data systems are increasingly antagonistic to many consumer interests. Although economic efficiency, lower prices, convenience, and selection are welcome in theory, they are no substitute for autonomy, dignity, and choice. As an industry and business practice, data aggregation does not now offer the latter to consumers.

The root of the problem is in the structure of these systems—most importantly, the monopoly control governments have over identification as an economic function. The extension of dossiers and data surveillance beyond consumers' comfort level is being aided and abetted by the government-promoted advance of uniform digital identification.

But this is a small problem compared with what governments themselves can do with data, which is the topic we turn to in the next chapter.

21. "Your Papers, Please"

> In the process of gaining our rightful place, we must not be
> guilty of wrongful deeds. Let us not seek to satisfy our thirst
> for freedom by drinking from the cup of bitterness and
> hatred. We must forever conduct our struggle on the high
> plane of dignity and discipline. We must not allow our cre-
> ative protest to degenerate into physical violence. Again and
> again, we must rise to the majestic heights of meeting physi-
> cal force with soul force.

Dr. Martin Luther King Jr. delivered those words on August 28, 1963, before a huge crowd at the Lincoln Memorial in Washington, D.C. Numbering 250,000 people, it was the largest demonstration up to that time, and Washington was braced for violence. But King's philosophy of nonviolent insistence on justice—the meeting of phys-ical force with "soul force"—carried the day. That gave immeasur-able power to the movement for civil rights in America and instilled a lasting sense that the struggle was just.

"Soul force" is a loose translation of the word *satyagraha* coined by Mohandas Karamchand Gandhi. He combined the Gujarati word *satya* (truth or love) with *agraha*, (firmness or insistence). It was 1906 when Gandhi's organization in South Africa became known as the Satyagraha Association, its members satyagrahis.

At the time, the Transvaal legislature was considering a law, called the Asiatic Law Amendment Act, or Black Act. When it passed, the Black Act required Indians to register as such and be fingerprinted within 30 days of July 1, 1907, or face penalties. Under the law, Indians could be challenged to produce their registration cards at any time and in any place. Police officers could enter Indians' homes to examine their permits. The clear thrust of the law was to prevent further migration of Indians into the province and perhaps to expel them entirely.

It took several years of protests, marches, and imprisonment, but Gandhi and his satyagrahis eventually found a compromise with

177

the government consistent with Gandhi's insistence on truth. That compromise was memorialized in a new law, the Indian Relief Act of 1914.

The act lifted several of the sanctions against Indians in South Africa but the histories are unclear as to whether it reversed the registration and identification card requirement. As a practical matter, registration may have been lifted by executive decision at the Transvaal Registrar of Asiatics in mid-1913, but chronologies discussing the Indian Relief Act refer to "Natal certificates of domicile," which may reflect a continuing, watered-down registration system.

In July 1914, Gandhi left South Africa forever. Some there criticized him for achieving more moral victories than real ones.[1] A few decades later, South Africa was using "pass laws" to implement its notorious apartheid system. The deceptively named Natives (Abolition of Passes and Co-ordination of Documents) Act of 1952, for example, required all black people to carry identification with them at all time, subject to criminal penalties. These laws and many others were repealed when that country renounced apartheid in the late 1980s.

South Africa's is only one of many governments that have sought to use registries and identification requirements to cow and manipulate a population.[2] The history of the past century is littered with examples that are far less gratifying than the fall of apartheid or the story of Gandhi's Indians, who successfully resisted the injustice aimed at them through an identification card system.

Forced collectivization brought large-scale dislocation and involuntary migration in Soviet Russia during the late 1920s and early 1930s. From 1928 to 1932, some 12 million peasants moved to the cities and towns—as many as 3.5 million to the areas around Moscow and Leningrad alone. These movements threatened to jeopardize the rationing systems that had been carefully constructed in those cities since 1929. Claimants for ration cards had increased from 26 million in 1929 to nearly 40 million in late 1932.

To combat this, the Soviet authorities introduced a series of steps, including an internal passport system. The decree of December 4, 1932, gave all adult townspeople a passport if they had not been deprived of their rights. A *propiska*, or official stamp showing legal residence, would determine whether they were entitled to a ration card, a social security card, or the right to a home. The authorities categorized towns as open or closed. Closed cities—Moscow, Leningrad, Kiev, Odessa, Minsk, Rostov, and Vladivostok—were better supplied. Family ties, marriage, or specific jobs determined whether people had the right to reside in them.

By the end of 1933, the government had issued 27 million passports. Anyone whose passport did not have a proper *propiska* could then be purged and deported. More than 3,000 people were "caught" without proper authorization in Moscow during the first week of the program. The government refused passports to nearly 385,000 people in closed cities, forcing them to vacate their homes. Recognizing that they would be denied passports, many other people simply left, forced into uncertain lives in the countryside.

In the following years, this passport system formed the basis for hundreds of thousands of arrests and purges. Spot checks at railway stations and marketplaces turned up thousands of passport law violators. In the week from late June to early July 1933, the authorities arrested thousands of Gypsies in Moscow and deported them to Siberian "work villages." They arrested and deported thousands more from Kiev. The police deported some 18,000 people from Leningrad and Moscow in April, June, and July of that year. There are countless stories of people who went out for cigarettes or got off a train at the wrong station being picked up for document violations and being "disappeared" forever by the government apparatus. Millions died during deportation, in exile camps, and in gulags administered by the Soviet state.

A much more benign system existed in Holland before World War II. There, and in most of Europe, municipal recording of births, marriages, deaths, and migration was traditional. Those records facilitated the prim community order and proper allocation of rights, duties, and benefits sought by Dutch bureaucrats at the time. Given its benign purposes, few had qualms about registering and most did so habitually, including Holland's Jews. The government considered a national identity card in 1939 but dismissed it because of the implication that every citizen was a potential criminal, a notion contrary to Dutch tradition.

When Germany occupied Holland in May 1940, the country's population registers made a trove of information available to the Nazis. They used these registers to compile lists of people for arrest and deportation. The mere existence of the registers convinced many,

179

including Jews, that there was little point in resisting later censuses or the identification card requirement that would be imposed. After all, the authorities already had in hand the information they needed to enforce such requirements.

Shortly after surrendering to the Nazis, the Dutch government did require an identity card. The card was highly resistant to forgery, using watermarked paper and special inks, and it included the bearer's photograph and fingerprint. The Nazis used the identity card system to regularly check people on public transportation or just walking in the streets. A huge card index (what would be a database today) housed details from the cards so that they could discover forgery and misuse of cards. Those details dramatically raised the risk for the Dutch resistance, of course, and made it very dangerous to live outside the system.

On January 10, 1941, the Nazis decreed the registration of Jews in Holland. Their papers were to be stamped with a *J*. The subsequent history of these souls is well known.

"It Can't Happen Here"

The link between identification and oppression is easy to overstate, but impossible to deny. The phrase "Your papers, please" conjures the worst images of totalitarianism and genocide that embroiled continents and threatened to sweep across the world just a few generations ago.

Opponents of national identification systems can overplay their arguments by invoking Nazi Germany and Soviet Russia. Doing so opens an easy rejoinder to proponents of a uniform identification scheme in the United States: Those dreadful crimes against humanity, many decades ago, "can't happen here."

Well, it was not just decades ago. In the 1994 Rwandan genocide, an identification card with the designation "Tutsi" brought maiming and death by machete to thousands and thousands of people.[3] That leaves only the defense that it can't happen in the United States.

It is true that America has a remarkable tradition of freedom and the rule of law and, in historic terms, democratic and liberal government is advancing worldwide. But even the United States has made some dreadfully serious errors in its history.

From the founding period until the Civil War, our national charter indulged the practice of human slavery. Many states' laws supported its remnants for the century that followed. During World War II, the U.S. government incarcerated Japanese Americans as a prophylactic against the subversion they supposedly threatened, using information from the Census Bureau to guide its efforts.

In the early 1970s, the president of the United States, Richard M. Nixon, sought to undermine the electoral process using government agencies and institutions. In 1975, the Select Committee to Study Governmental Operations with Respect to Intelligence Activities, also known as the Church Commission,[4] found that the Central Intelligence Agency and the Federal Bureau of Investigation had directed break-ins, thefts, and misinformation campaigns designed to undermine and threaten people engaged in lawful dissent, including Martin Luther King Jr. In addition, it found that the Central Intelligence Agency had opened postal mail and the National Security Agency's Project Minaret had spied on peace groups.

Each generation sees threats to the rule of law, even in an admirably stable and free nation like the United States. The American response to the terror attacks of September 11, 2001, was to reverse many of the limits on the power and activities of intelligence agencies that had been established in the Church Commission era. The country's military and security agencies held terror suspects—including a U.S. citizen on American soil—incommunicado and without filing charges. The practice of "extraordinary rendition"—transporting people to countries without American rules against torture—gained currency during this period. Shortly after the attacks, the National Security Agency began conducting secret wiretaps of U.S. citizens' communications without getting authority from any court, under a dangerously expansive claim to executive authority.

These practices are not comparable to the Nazi and Soviet horrors, and history will determine whether they were merited or successful at curtailing terrorism, but they remind us that even the best governments pose risks to liberty and life in every era.

Government misuse of identification does not need to be a budding pogrom to be objectionable. Many U.S. jurisdictions already use identification as a tool of social control.

In this large country, mobility—and thus a driver's license—is practically required for many, many things: working, visiting friends, grocery shopping, and traveling outside of metropolitan areas are just examples. Yet a wide array of offenses carries suspension of driving privileges as the punishment.

Oregon reportedly has more than 100 different offenses that can result in suspension of a driver's license—50 of them having nothing to do with driving.[5] In Wisconsin, license suspension is a penalty for unpaid library fines, failing to shovel snow off one's sidewalk, and failing to trim a tree that overhangs another's property, to name a few. With the driver's license acting as the de facto identification card used to control access to so many goods, services, and locations, the punishment of losing one's license is substantial indeed.

Any society that relies on government identification systems for access to goods, services, and infrastructure empowers authorities to deny people those things by confiscating identification documents. Deprivation of identity documents is a law enforcement method that should be very carefully circumscribed if not eliminated entirely.

Going forward, identification systems will increasingly use networks and databases rather than tokens and cards. In near-future scenarios, a notation in a database identification system could disqualify someone from access to the essentials and conveniences of life. That would compound confiscation with the difficulty of learning which government authority or employee had withdrawn a person's government-sanctioned existence.

But as noted earlier, there is an argument that such things cannot happen here. It appeals to the many rightly proud, but incautious, believers in American exceptionalism. Proponents of a national identification card for the United States point out that the country has well-functioning protection of civil liberties. Resisting a national identification on the basis of historical or comparative experience is unwarranted, they argue. Amitai Etzioni, for example, notes in *The Limits of Privacy* that identification cards have been used in European democracies for quite some time. "There is no evidence or reason to assume that their implementation will set in motion a steady descent into ever-greater restrictions on privacy and autonomy," he says.[6]

It is true that the adoption of a national identification system is not in itself a catalyst for despotism. Rather, national identification systems are tools that can be used to administer it. Etzioni's argument too cutely misses the point and fails to meet the argument for resisting national identification schemes.

Fail-safe Design

A fail-safe is a system or mechanism designed to ensure that its failure will not create worse damage than necessary. Circuit breakers are a classic fail-safe built into all modern electrical systems. If a short circuit occurs, they burn out or trip before any other part of the system does, without creating excessive heat. This minimizes the risk of fire. In other words, they allow electrical systems to fail safely. The owner of a house may lose the files on his or her computer or return home to darkness—perhaps lots of blinking digital clocks—but at least he or she will have a home to return to.

All new construction in the United States uses circuit breakers in the electrical systems. Yet all new construction in the United States also incorporates fire-retardant materials, smoke alarms, fire extinguishers, and fire exits, as appropriate to each. These safety features represent another layer of fail-safe design. The electrical circuits designed to suppress fire may fail or fire may start another way. If it does, these additional fail-safe measures are in place to slow the movement of fire and to protect lives and property.

These measures might seem to be enough, but they are not. All but the most remote U.S. communities have fire departments, either professional or volunteer. Most cities and municipalities also have fire hydrants placed throughout their territory so that their fire departments have ready access to water in the event of a blaze. These features represent yet more layers of fail-safe design—at the community level. Although their buildings have circuit breakers, fire-retardant materials, easy escape routes, fire-detection equipment, and fire-suppression equipment, most communities determine that it is worthwhile to have firefighters and water close at hand.

Nazi-occupied Holland illustrates how national population registries and identification systems operate when democracies go into failure mode. The country had no fail-safe in its administrative system against the threat of despotism—the decent Dutch people must have believed "it can't happen here." A cruel regime quickly and easily took control of that credulous population, and thousands upon thousands of people died.

It is odd that societies would dedicate so much effort to fail-safe designs in machines, structures, and processes—doing so much to protect life and property—but dedicate almost no effort to fail-safe designs that protect liberty and, in turn, life and property. The toll of despotic governments in carnage, death, tragedy, and suffering during just the past century would seem to demand some effort toward better design of social systems.

183

In a variety of ways, monolithic identification systems harm consumers' and citizens' interests. Our risk of living in a despotic society may be low, but the consequences would be profound, so it is worth some effort and cost to prevent. As practical obscurity declines, the risk of living in a society with centralized power, arbitrary exercise of power, and routine violations of rights will grow.

Indeed, this is the system into which Martin Luther King Jr. was born. The struggle for civil rights that he led and inspired did not fight against national identification, of course. But the concept of "soul force" that he used so powerfully was born in the fight against an identification system designed for injustice. The risk of uniform identification systems being used to administer injustice and oppression cannot be counted out by thoughtful people.

The remote threat of tyranny aided by uniform identification is matched by the present and very prominent problem of identity fraud. We turn to this in the next chapter.

22. Insecurity

Ken Hickman knows the Internet and he knows what happened. That is why he was so annoyed when he reported fraudulent use of his identity to the local police department and the officer taking the report said, "It's the Internet."

Ken worked for giant Internet portal Yahoo! for several years. Before that, he worked for Netscape, the company that popularized the Mosaic Web browser. It was the first easy-to-use program for navigating the World Wide Web and it brought floods of ordinary people online. Ken knows how the Internet works. His identity fraud was not caused by the Internet.

It started in 1988, when he graduated from the University of California. Ken took a job with an electronics firm and moved to a new house in the bedroom community that abutted the campus. The house he lived in had three rooms that were commonly rented to students and postgrads with jobs. The landlord was a guy named Rob whose parents supposedly owned the house. Ken never dealt with them, paying his monthly rent directly to Rob.

Rob worked at a local body shop or garage but he was into all sorts of schemes. Ken remembers that Rob was not beneath dishonesty to gain an advantage, and he would often brag about that. After a year, Ken moved to a different house with friends. He never saw Rob again. In 1995, he moved to the Silicon Valley area to pursue high-tech jobs.

In 2002, Ken received a call from a credit card company wanting to verify some information before it issued him a new card. But Ken had not applied for a new credit card. He discovered through that phone call that his financial identity was in use by another person.

Pulling his credit reports, Ken learned that since 1999 no fewer than 12 credit cards had been taken out in his name with a variety of major credit card issuers. Over the years, his old landlord Rob had made the minimum payments on each card month after month until he built up a portfolio of credit worth more than $100,000.

Rob appears to have used Ken's identity to open bank accounts for receiving fund transfers as well. At any time, Rob might have stopped making payments entirely, sending a phalanx of bill collectors after the real Ken Hickman.

Ken immediately started the long process of canceling the fraudulent cards, putting fraud alerts on his credit reports, and removing the false credit information from his files with the credit bureaus and credit card companies. Ken filed a report with his local police department. He reported the aliases that Rob apparently had used, as well as street addresses, post office boxes, and phone numbers.

Ken's face still puckers like he has bitten into a lemon when he talks about the ignorance and indifference of the police officer who thought this was some kind of Internet crime. Ken has no idea whether anyone—police agency or credit issuer—has ever even looked for Rob. He has been lucky enough not to need new lines of credit but knows that he may face real problems if and when he does.

Confusion about Identity Fraud

It is plainly wrong to identify the Internet as a significant cause of identity fraud. The Internet is simply a medium over which people conduct transactions and communications, for good or for bad. When crimes like identity fraud happen, it is because a dishonest person has taken advantage of systems like credit reporting, the U.S. Postal Service, banking, credit card issuance, and sometimes the Internet to defraud other people and institutions out of money, goods, and services. The taproot of identity fraud is criminality.

Part of the confusion about identity fraud has been perpetuated by the growth of a different crime online and in other remote-commerce environments. Credit card fraud, which is distinct from identity fraud, occurs when a criminal uses another person's credit card or credit card number to procure goods and services for him- or herself. The charge appears on the account of the credit card holder who must, of course, dispute it. This forces the merchant to prove the transaction, typically by showing a signed receipt.

Remote transactions, also called "card-not-present" transactions, are more susceptible to credit card fraud because the criminal does not have to appear in person or produce a card. He or she can falsely claim to be a credit card holder more easily. There are higher rates of credit card fraud online than when cards are used in person. Merchants suffer the most financial losses from credit card fraud, and many efforts are under way to suppress fraud in card-not-present transactions. People who don't check their credit card statements suffer losses too, if they fail to report fraudulent use of their cards and card numbers. Credit card fraud is a simple but substantial crime problem that is too often confused with identity fraud.

Much of that confusion has been sown by the U.S. Congress. In 1998, Congress passed the Identity Theft and Assumption Deterrence Act,[1] a law designed to make even more criminal the fraud crimes that were already punishable in all 50 states. Creating a federal offense redundant to state law, the act referred to identity fraud by its popular but inaccurate name, "identity theft," and defined it so broadly that all kinds of different frauds were captured within the one definition.

A theft is the taking of something with the intent of permanently depriving the true owner of it. When someone grabs a 12-pack of beer from a convenience store refrigerator and runs outside to a waiting getaway car, the thief's intent is obvious: to keep the beer. That means the store owner cannot get the benefit of selling it to a real customer. The beer is gone, and the store will never get it back. This is theft—specifically, a theft of beer.

When one person lies to another about his or her intent, associations, authority, identity, or plans and uses the lie to abscond with money, goods, or the benefit of services, that is fraud. Through trickery, a fraudster may steal something for good, which is a theft, but it is not a theft of the subject lied about. So when an identity fraudster uses someone else's name and Social Security number, he or she is not stealing an identity. The person whose name and financial information is used still has an identity, even if his or her financial reputation may be wrongly tarnished.

Imagine for a moment that your car has been stolen. You have called the police and the officer taking the report says to you, "Yep, we've seen a lot more auto fraud this year." You might point out that your car was *stolen*, not used to trick someone. If the officer wrote "auto fraud" on the police report, you might insist he call it a theft because of the confusion sure to come from that. If the officer gave you a pamphlet called "Recovering from Auto Fraud," you might want to punch that officer in the jaw. Perhaps you could defend yourself against a battery charge by insisting on calling what you did "jaywalking."

The use of the term "identity theft" for the crime of identity fraud is incorrect. It is also needlessly provocative, and it has created undue fear of victimization among the populace. It connotes some science-fictional future where a person deprived of identity cannot be recognized by friends and family members, computer systems, or businesses. That does not happen in "identity theft."

Understanding "Identity Theft"

Silence of the Lambs was a 1991 movie starring Jodie Foster as FBI Special Agent Clarice Starling and Anthony Hopkins as the notorious and devious supercriminal Hannibal Lecter. At the end of the movie, Lecter overpowers and kills two guards in order to escape from a special prison that has been constructed for him on the upper floors of a building. He changes into the uniform of one of the guards, hides the guard's body, and poses as that guard, badly injured but clinging to life. To complete the deception, Lecter tears the guard's face off and places it over his own. The police wheel Lecter out of his prison on a gurney, underneath that gruesome mask. *This* is identity theft. Lecter has taken a key identifier from the dead and mutilated guard, who will never get it back.

In the Identity Theft and Assumption Deterrence Act, Congress made it a federal crime to knowingly transfer or use a "means of identification" of another person with the intent of committing any federal crime or state felony.[2] As we saw in the first part of this book, thousands of different identifiers distinguish people from one another and combine to identify people. The law conceivably makes it a crime to use any identifying name or number falsely in the course of a significant crime, and it treats all such uses as "identity theft." A court would probably avoid this absurd result, but the 1992 Quentin Tarantino movie *Reservoir Dogs* depicts multiple cases of federal "identity theft" because the characters adopt fake names like "Mr. White" and "Mr. Brown" (as well as "Mr. Pink" and "Mr. Blond") for use in a diamond heist.

Using Congress's exploded definition of "identity theft," a report issued by the Federal Trade Commission in September 2003 found that 4.6 percent of Americans had been victimized by identity fraud in the previous year, 12.7 percent in the previous five years.[3] Using a closer definition that excludes credit card fraud and other simple frauds, those numbers dropped to 1.5 percent and 4.7 percent, respectively. They are much smaller numbers of identity fraud cases, though still significant. All those results were self-reported, raising the possibility of error in either direction.

Interestingly, more than a third of individuals who had been impersonated in a true identity fraud knew, like Ken Hickman, who the perpetrator was. And in more than half of those cases, the perpetrator was a family member or other relative. Other prominent perpetrators of identity frauds are people in companies or financial institutions with access to personal financial information, as well as friends, neighbors, or in-home employees of impersonation victims. So much for the Internet being the cause of identity fraud, though it certainly plays a role in some cases.

The Roots of Identity Fraud

Victims like Ken Hickman don't care very much what it is called, of course. He, like other collateral victims of identity fraud, would like to know why it happens and how it can be prevented. There are many answers but one of the most important sources of the identity fraud problem is the widespread—indeed nearly universal—use of a single identification system in the United States.

Imagine if someone told you to throw away your keychain because he was going to give you a single key to control access to everything: your home, your car, your safe deposit box, your office building, your office, your filing cabinets, your desk, your bike lock, and your gym locker. You would probably tell that idiot to get lost.

Under a single-key system, you could never be sure about leaving a key with a neighbor when you left on vacation, or about loaning your car to a friend or relative. They might use your house or car key to snoop around your office. They could lose your all-access key. Or they could copy it just in case they wanted to access your things later. If you gave your office key to a coworker because she needed to retrieve a file from your desk, you could not be certain that she wouldn't go into your filing cabinet to look at her personnel file. You could not be sure that she wouldn't copy it, anticipating your vacation, so she could burglarize your house. The risks from sharing your universal key with anyone would be very high because that one key would provide so much access.

Now imagine that everyone would have the same kind of lock-and-key system. Each person's key would be different, of course, but the same kind of key and the same kind of lock would secure everyone's houses, offices, cars, and other possessions. What a boon that would be for thieves. They would have only to learn how to pick one kind of lock and reverse-engineer its keys before they could access the material lives of everyone. That kind of system would be terribly, terribly insecure.

Alas, that is precisely the kind of system that is used for identification in the U.S. financial services system and, indeed, by most large institutions in the United States. With few exceptions, the Social Security number is the key identifier—each of our financial "names," if you will. It is used with a small, predictable combination of other identifiers. By breaking this simple system, identity fraudsters can access people's financial lives and perpetrate the crimes that have caused people like Ken Hickman so much annoyance and wasted time.

There should be no doubt that this system is efficient. Institutions can communicate more easily about individuals with this uniform identification protocol. Credit issuers can furnish information to credit bureaus and buy information products with sufficient confidence (for them) that they are talking about the same person. Tax collectors and law enforcement have a neat system for organizing their records about taxpayers, scofflaws, and crooks. People don't have to remember a variety of different account numbers, codes, and facts or prove themselves using complicated and intimidating biometrics.

But this same efficiency benefits identity fraudsters mightily. Our identification system is designed with too much efficiency and not enough security, one of the key roots of the identity fraud problem.

The susceptibility of uniform identification to financial fraud is just the most obvious form of insecurity that it creates. As we saw in previous chapters, uniform identification systems are insecure against despotic governments: they have been used by totalitarianism to administer horrors on a massive scale even in very recent world history. Uniform identification systems are insecure against the encroachments of institutions into our private lives: many people seek and enjoy a sense of solitude and self-dominion that is eroded or destroyed by the knowledge that marketers in the corporate world and social engineers in government have whirring banks of computers fixated on their lives and lifestyles.

With all this insecurity, steps should be taken to reinvent identification so that it better serves individuals' interests. But satisfactory solutions are not obvious. One proposal is to ban or limit many uses of Social Security numbers.

Social Security Number Regulation

For some advocates, it seems natural to ban or otherwise limit the use of Social Security numbers. That would force needed diversity in identification, of course—or even better, in the eyes of some advocates, just flummox data collection and use entirely.

There have been persistent proposals in Congress to control Social Security number use. In the 109th Congress, for example, several bills sought to criminalize the display, sale, or purchase of Social Security numbers without the affirmatively expressed consent of the individual.[4] Others sought to prohibit requiring Social Security numbers in commercial transactions[5] or disclosing Social Security numbers on the Internet without the individual's prior informed written consent.[6]

But these remedies might be as "natural" as having your nose rebroken to set it straight. The pain can be far greater, and the experience far more disconcerting, than the original injury.

At first blush, arguments in favor of banning certain uses of the Social Security number seem strong. The Social Security number is at the heart of many of the ills, discomforts, and threats described earlier and in the preceding chapters. Indeed, criminal rings apparently trade Social Security numbers and other financial information specifically for use in identity fraud. A ban on trade in this identifier would suppress crime, would it not?—and it would rein the ability of marketers and other organizations to track consumers.

Alas, a Social Security number ban would not reduce criminal use of Social Security numbers very much, for the same reason that the Identity Theft and Assumption Deterrence Act did not suppress identity fraud very much. By definition, the people committing the crime are already lawbreakers. They are also experts at masking their own identities. Adding a new, derivative offense to the litany of crimes they already commit would not significantly increase their risk of punishment. Statutory limits on Social Security number use would only affect law abiders, doing almost nothing about the law-breakers that are causing the problems.

The way to deter a crime like identity fraud is to unmask identity fraudsters, showing other fraudsters and those considering the pursuit that they cannot rely on hiding behind false identities. That is precisely what Ken Hickman's local police department did not do. Enforcement, not banning uses of any identifier, is the key to suppressing identity fraud.

Most mature proposals to restrict Social Security number use have numerous exceptions in them for existing and "preferred" uses, such as law enforcement, credit reporting, public health, research, tax collection, and so on. That means that well-lobbied interests like governments and existing industries will not be hurt by them. But it also means that new, innovative information practices that might use the Social Security number will not emerge. The benefits we have received so far from the Internet and the Information Age are not the last in store for us—unless legislation locks out further competition and innovation in the world of information business.

The arguments against banning Social Security numbers are stronger than arguments in favor. On the theoretical level, it seems odd that the government should have the power to restrict the use of an entire identifier—indeed, the identifier that currently serves as most people's financial name. Imagine the government banning certain uses of people's given names and surnames. This restriction on speech could be defended as content neutral and, if limited to corporations, as suppressing only commercial speech, which enjoys a lower level of First Amendment protection under current Supreme Court doctrine. But it is startling to imagine that the government could ban the use of an entire protocol. Consider how that might apply to other protocols, like languages: imagine an English-only rule for all commerce.

Defenders would argue that, unlike social names and language, the government created Social Security numbers, giving it unique power to control their use. But this argument proves too much. Governments have created many naming systems and protocols, like state, city, and street names, census tracts, political boundaries, and the Zip-plus-four postal code. The TCP/IP protocol on which the Internet runs was developed with federal government funding, yet few would argue that the government could now ban its use.

Ultimately, statutory limits on Social Security number use amount to rules that certain entities cannot communicate true information about real people for lawful purposes. Although they would also ban communication for unlawful purposes, the bulk of their incidence would fall on the lawful and beneficial ones. Their effectiveness for crime control would be minimal.

This is to say nothing of the fact that Social Security number use benefits consumers massively—the efficiency benefits that we talked about in the previous section. Businesses that use Social Security numbers heavily provide easy payment methods with fraud and anti-theft protections far superior to cash. They amass reputation information that allows consumers fast access to credit at favorable rates. They shave prices and buff up the quality of products to win consumer favor. And they constantly study how they can please consumers more, using personal information as an essential tool. Many proponents of limits on Social Security number use tend to ignore those benefits, neglecting dimensions of consumer welfare that compete with privacy and obscurity.

Legislatures cannot find, and statutory rules cannot set, the correct balance between unified and diversified identification systems, nor can they reveal the different types of identification systems that best serve us as consumers and citizens in all the different circumstances that might require identification. A more subtle and carefully directed technique is needed.

No proposal yet has addressed the problem of Social Security numbers at its source. What Congress can do is take the federal government's thumb off the unified-identification side of the scale, where it has been ever since the Social Security system was created.

Government Promotion of Uniform Identification

When President Franklin D. Roosevelt signed the Social Security Act on August 14, 1935, the Social Security Board (predecessor of the Social Security Administration) was tasked with registering over 2 million employers and 26 million workers in short order. The law did not require a numerical scheme or a card, but the board selected a number to be issued on a card with the worker's name. Treasury Department regulations in 1936 established that workers covered by Social Security had to apply for a Social Security number.

The Social Security number is a nine-digit number. The first three numbers are an "area number." Issued before 1972, the area number indicates which local Social Security office issued it; after 1972, it indicates where the Social Security card was mailed. The second two numbers are a "group number." Group numbers are issued within each area in a prescribed, nonconsecutive order: odd numbers from 01 to 09, even numbers from 10 to 98, even numbers from 02 to 08, and odd numbers from 11 to 99. The last four numbers are a "serial number." These are issued consecutively within areas and groups, from 0001 to 9999.

Because of the short time-frame for commencing the Social Security program, the Social Security Board opted to accept without verification a person's assertions about personal identifying information (such as name, date and place of birth, sex, parents' names, address, etc.). That was a rational choice: Employers were to collect and remit the tax, giving workers no incentive to lie. Indeed, by lying or omitting information, workers stood only to deny themselves benefits. The choice was important historically, too, because the Social Security card has never become an identification document, despite consideration of that option. The Social Security card only asserts that the person named on the card has been issued the Social Security number printed there with it.

Shortly after the Social Security program began operations, use of the Social Security number was extended beyond the purposes of the program—by the Social Security Board itself. The board decided that the Social Security number should be used for all workers insured under state unemployment insurance programs, rather than have each state agency develop its own identification system. Many workers not covered by the Social Security program received Social Security numbers for this purpose, and broadened use of the Social Security number was under way. The federal government's promotion of the Social Security number as an identifier has never relented.[7]

In 1943, Executive Order 9397 required federal agencies to use the Social Security number in any new system of records to identify persons. Few did. The expense of changing record systems was prohibitive relative to the benefit from doing so. According to the Social Security Administration, use of the Social Security number did not take off until the computer "revolution" of the 1960s when the efficiency gains of giving each person a unique number became clear.

In 1961, the Civil Service Commission adopted the Social Security number as the official identifier for federal employees. In 1962, based on Internal Revenue Code amendments requiring each taxpayer to furnish an identifying number, the Internal Revenue Service began using the Social Security number as its official taxpayer identification number. In April 1964, the commissioner of social security approved the issuance of Social Security numbers to pupils in the ninth grade and above. Also in 1964, the Treasury Department, via internal policy, began to require that buyers of Series H savings bonds provide their Social Security numbers. With the enactment of Medicare in 1965, it became necessary for most people 65 and older to have a Social Security number. In 1966, the Veterans Administration began to use the Social Security number for admissions and patient record keeping. In 1967, the Department of Defense adopted the Social Security number in lieu of the military service number for identifying armed forces personnel. Expanded use of the Social Security number was in full swing.

In the early 1970s, Congress was concerned about welfare fraud and illegal employment. It amended the Social Security Act, authorizing the Social Security Administration to assign Social Security numbers to all legally admitted noncitizens at entry and to anyone receiving or applying for a federal benefit. Subsequently, Congress required a Social Security number as a condition of eligibility for federal programs, such as Aid to Families with Dependent Children (now Temporary Assistance for Needy Families), Medicaid, food stamps, school lunch programs, and any federal loan program. Additional legislation authorized states to use the Social Security number in the administration of any tax, general public assistance, driver's license, or motor vehicle registration law within its jurisdiction. The legislation allowed the states to require people affected by such laws to furnish their Social Security numbers to the states.

During this period, private institutions such as banks, credit bureaus, hospitals, and educational institutions also began to identify citizens and consumers by the Social Security number. There was no general prohibition on private use of the Social Security number. Nor, of course, was there any general obligation to use it. But a series of requirements nestled into federal law promoted Social Security number use in the private sector.

The Currency and Foreign Transactions Reporting Act (Bank Secrecy Act), passed in 1970, required all banks, savings and loan associations, credit unions, and brokers/dealers in securities to obtain the Social Security numbers of their customers. Also, financial institutions were required to file a report with the Internal Revenue Service, including the Social Security number of the customer, for each deposit, withdrawal, exchange of currency, or other payment or transfer involving more than $10,000. That combined with tax reporting requirements keyed to the Social Security number, ensured that private financial institutions collected and used Social Security numbers.

During this period, the credit reporting industry was consolidating and making greater use of computerization and database technology. Credit reporting had begun in the late 1800s as a service to local merchants who needed to track what customers failed to pay on credit accounts.[8] In the 1970s, there were 2,250 credit bureaus, but the inefficiency of operating separately in an increasingly mobile society was becoming clear. By affiliating and nesting their data systems, credit bureaus could develop economies of scale. Undoubtedly, use of the Social Security number helped them do that.

The private sector adopted Social Security numbers for a variety of reasons, but government-mandated issuance of Social Security numbers to all workers laid the groundwork. The efficiency available from uniform record keeping moved private use of Social Security numbers forward. And mandates on some sectors of the private economy to use Social Security numbers undoubtedly advanced their use further still. In other words, Social Security number use as a form of identification was the path of least resistance—down which the private sector was pushed.

Today, the Social Security number is required in an unending variety of interactions with public and private entities. Congress has obliged the ever-expanding identification and regimentation of citizens, including its reach into the province of the family. The Family Support Act of 1988 required states to require parents to give their Social Security numbers to get a birth certificate issued for a newborn.[9] The Small Business Job Protection Act of 1996 required taxpayers to report a tax identification number of dependents (for all intents and purposes, the Social Security number) when claiming them as deductions.[10] The Social Security number is rapidly becoming a cradle-to-grave tracking number, rather than a simple administrative device for a single retirement security program.

Rather than ban the use of Social Security numbers in the private sector, the federal government should simply stop promoting the use of Social Security numbers. Foremost, it should repeal the requirement that parents register their children to receive a tax benefit. The federal government should also wean its agencies off the Social Security number rather than force the private sector to lead the way through this needed transition.[11]

Full, unmitigated retirement policy reform—in which workers contribute directly to their own retirement accounts and assistance goes only to retirees whose personal funds fall short—would dispense with the need for federal numbering of citizens. Under the right reform, privately issued accounts and account numbers, rather than a uniform national identifier, would track funds that workers deposit, as with today's individual retirement accounts and 401(k) plans. Within a few generations, American society would then be forced to transition from the Social Security numbering system into something much better designed for the security and interests of the people. Such fundamental reforms are the keys to solving problems like identity fraud.

If you were to design an identification system that most benefited and served institutions—big governments and corporations—you might choose the one we have now in the United States, where a single number is used almost uniformly to distinguish among people. You would also inadvertently serve the criminal class of identity fraudsters. Were you to design an identification system that served the interests of people—all of their interests—it would be somewhat less efficient, less homogenous, and less easy to penetrate.

The insecurity of our current identification system grows as we continue treading the path into the digital age. It is insecure against fraud. Witness the experience of Ken Hickman. It is insecure against despotism. Millions of destroyed lives make this plain. And it is insecure against the prying computers of institutions, both government and corporate.

We have arrived at this situation through a series of ad hoc and improvised policy steps. The time is ripe to replace the absence of policy we currently suffer with thought-through identification policies—specific policies like the adoption of some system that balances the interests of individuals with the needs of the institutions that are supposed to serve them. The need for change is growing: The advance of digital identification and database technology continues to increase the negative consequences of identification. Each day without thoughtful protections and policies, identification is growing more overused.

Everyone has a role in achieving the fundamental changes that are needed. Governments, businesses, and individuals alike should begin taking steps to change the identification policy landscape. The steps each should take are outlined in the following chapters.

PART V

THE WAY FORWARD

23. Use Identification Less

By 9:57 a.m. on the morning of September 11, 2001, the risk profile of passenger air transportation worldwide had changed forever. It had gotten safer.

Three minutes before 10:00 a.m. was when the passengers on United Flight 93 stormed the cockpit of their plane, attempting to overcome the Al Qaeda operatives who had commandeered it.[1]

The airline security system had failed them. In contact with friends and loved ones on the ground, those passengers knew that hijackers were flying planes into buildings, and they knew that cooperating with the hijackers would not save them. Indeed, it would take the lives of others and multiply the damage many times.

The new appropriate response to hijacking—determined in minutes, under extreme stress, and without the help of government security experts—was counterattack. The passengers on Flight 93 could not save their own lives but at least they could ensure that their flight would not become a giant bomb.

Since that day, airlines have hardened cockpit doors, they have instituted procedures to prevent commandeering, and every air passenger knows that the old conventional wisdom about cooperating with hijackers was wrong. Accordingly, the risk that a commercial passenger airplane will be "weaponized" has fallen dramatically. Passenger air transportation got *safer* on September 11, 2001.

But the nation's approach to air security did not reflect this new risk profile. Indeed, it treated the risk of commandeering as having gotten higher.[2]

Based on the old risk profile—or perhaps just collective panic—one of the most prominent reactions to the 9/11 attacks was to require not only identification of air travelers but of people entering buildings, checking into hotels, parking cars in garages, and doing many other ordinary things.

A couple of factors probably caused this reaction to "make sense" in the absence of analysis: First, it is natural and appropriate, after the fact, to determine who has committed criminal and terrorist acts. Only identification of terrorists and criminals can bring them appropriate punishments, expose their abettors, and disrupt their future plans. Second, video stills of 9/11 ringleader Mohammed Atta passing through airport security were repeatedly shown on television in the days and months following the attack. That suggested that the entrances to airport concourses were the "weak link" that allowed the attacks to occur. It seems to follow from these inputs that identifying people at entrances to facilities could suppress attacks.

The Weak Case for Broad Identification

Little analysis supports this notion. The few advocates of uniform identification or national identification schemes have not met their burden of showing how identification systems would actually deliver security, much less do so cost-effectively and consistently with the Constitution and American values.

One of few full expositions on identification requirements is a book called *The Privacy Card*,[3] authored by now Professor Emeritus Joseph Eaton at the University of Pittsburgh. Originally published as *Card-Carrying Americans* in 1986, the book argues that a national identification system would make immigration control easier and help prevent fraud in private transactions, as well as in the disbursement of public benefits. It would limit the mobility of fugitives and turn up deadbeat parents. And it would make it harder for identified terrorists to operate using false names (forcing them to stay unidentified until they strike).

Those points beg the question of how a fraud-, corruption-, and forgery-proof card system can actually be created. But Eaton does not have a hard-headed, real-world plan. He says nothing of the checkpoints and government monitoring that would actually deliver the alleged benefits of national identification. The book is full of "woulds" and "coulds"—an exercise in imagination with no grounding in identification theory, no vision for security or risk management, and few tethers to real-world practicalities.

In *The Limits of Privacy*,[4] "communitarian" George Washington University professor Amitai Etzioni cites Eaton's thinking favorably. The book is a series of case studies on contemporary privacy issues viewed through a confusing analytic lens that Etzioni has devised for the purpose.

⌈Like Eaton, Etzioni tallies up the costs of *not* having a national identification system: the numerousness of criminal fugitives, child sex abuse, income tax fraud, nonpayment of child support, illegal gun sales, illegal immigration, welfare fraud, identity theft, and credit card fraud are all laid at the doorstep of lacking national identification.⌋ Like Eaton, Etzioni deals only in passing with the problems of resisting fraud, corruption, and forgery in the identification system he would have. He says nothing about the pervasive checkpoints and surveillance needed to actually cure society's ills with a national identification system.

After reviewing polling data on public acceptance of identification requirements, Etzioni reviews many "libertarian" objections to such requirements—including objections from notable "libertarian" Phyllis Schlafly. He does not so much answer them as dismiss them, trumped by his notion of "the common good."

Conservatives David Frum and Richard Perle share Etzioni's view of the common good. They call even more glibly for national identification in their book *An End to Evil: How to Win the War on Terrorism.* Focusing only on foreign terrorism, and citing the fact that some terrorists have sometimes stayed in the United States illegally, the authors demand, ⌈"We need an identification system that makes it clear who is entitled to be in the United States and who is not and that expedites the removal of people who are not so entitled.⌋"[5]

The Frum-Perle proposal is embarrassingly rickety: Americans should accept comprehensive identification requirements, checkpoints, and surveillance so that foreign terrorist groups are forced to find attackers who can legally enter the United States, as Al Qaeda did for the 9/11 plot. America's enemies must shudder at the thought of being so ruthlessly . . . inconvenienced. Incoherently, in a December 2005 issue, *National Review* printed Frum's appeal for a national identification card as one of 10 suggestions for increasing American liberty.[6]

More thoughtful, but no more compelling, advocacy of a national identification system has been put forth in a series of papers published by the Progressive Policy Institute, a nonprofit think tank affiliated with the Democratic Leadership Council.[7] Like the others, these papers gloss over the difficulty of controlling fraud, corruption, and forgery in a uniform identification system. They omit the check-points and surveillance needed to administer such a system. And they pooh-pooh the consequences for liberty and civil rights.[8]

Again, the proponents of national identification systems and the use of identification as a significant tool in the fight against terrorism have not made their case. Yet the new reality, in the "age of terrorism," seems to be that people will have to show identification more often.

Perhaps people should have to be identified in order to access sensitive areas like airline concourses, train stations, shopping malls, and subway systems. Refusing to show identification seems like an overly individualistic thing to do when we are in a collective "war on terror," doesn't it?

It is not. Identification requirements at government checkpoints are little more than a security-themed ritual. Ending the practice would be a small but important part of steering the nation toward security methods that actually work.

Broad identification requirements are not an important part of terrorism prevention. Although identification encourages people with a stake in society to conform their behavior to law and custom, it has no similar influence on terrorists. It only plays a role in security against terrorism when particular wrongdoers are already known. When terrorists are known, they should be pursued wherever they are. Watch listing—the practice of identifying all entrants to a partic-ular area in hopes that terrorists will appear there and identify themselves accurately—is a weak, but costly, substitute. Identifica-tion requirements and broad surveillance do not expose terrorism planning. A final argument for identification is the assistance it provides investigators after an attack or attempt, but information about terrorists is not difficult to come by after they have struck.

Although security and anti-terrorism are the primary justification for it, most identification checking is unneeded and unhelpful to that end. Identifying all travelers as a routine undermines the liberty of law-abiding consumers and citizens without reducing the risk of terrorism in anything but the slightest degree. Identification is overused and misunderstood. It should be used less.

Alas, showing all the reasons why a national identification system won't help in the war on terror requires proving a negative: the absence of a substantial role for identification in terrorism preven-tion. It is important, though, so let us take a little time to walk through airline security, the focus of current debates and a case study for security in other areas. Let us carefully consider where identification fits into securing air transportation.

Promoting Good Behavior

In general, identification promotes good behavior. Aware of being identified and anticipating the accountability we discussed in chapter 11, most people control their behavior to avoid the pressure and punishments that visit them when they do wrong. When they lack an internal compass that keeps them honest, the fact that they are identified may persuade people to do right.

Posit a woman who walks her cocker spaniel in front of your house twice each day. You don't know her name, though you greet each other regularly. One of the reasons why she doesn't curb her dog in your yard is because she knows you have enough information about her—enough identifiers in her appearance—to visit consequences on her. If she let her dog defecate in your yard, you might yell at her the next time you saw her. Even your low-quality identification of her is an important deterrent.

Similar dynamics are at play in commerce. In the world of credit card payments, there is a wide disparity between fraud rates in card-present transactions and in card-not-present transactions, such as sales over the Internet or through 800 numbers. The reason is not because the Internet, mail order, or telephone order are dangerous channels of commerce but because they are the only channels to use if a fraudster has some stolen card information but no card or insufficient card information to counterfeit a card.

There is another reason: A person using a credit card in person is much easier to identify than a person using a credit card remotely, and people know that. The relatively better identification of people that occurs in person deters wrongdoing.

People know that in most situations they are watched, assessed, and commented on in some small degree. Even a modicum of identification is often enough to visit consequences on people who do wrong. This knowledge helps convince people to control their behavior and act conventionally and lawfully.

This common understanding of how social, economic, and legal pressure works is probably what leads most people to conclude that identification has a role in securing society against terrorism. But identification does not have this effect on committed terrorists in action.

People who have no stake in society, committed opponents of society—the *jihadists* who would die for their cause—and even people who just lack impulse control, are not controlled by identification. They are at least indifferent to the consequences should they be apprehended. The usual pressures to conform and obey law, brought to bear through identification, do not pertain.

Merely identifying people does not reveal anything about their will or capacity to do harm. It does not change their outlook if they are committed to wrongdoing. Against serious risks like terrorist attacks on planes, identifying people at airport concourses and other locations has essentially no effect. A person who is subject to social, economic, and legal pressure may behave better if identified, but it decidedly does not follow that a person who is identified is honest, well behaved, or harboring good intentions.

Identification and Terrorism

False identification is widely regarded as a tool of terrorists, though. In the run-up to the Oklahoma City bombing of April 19, 1995, Timothy McVeigh and Terry Nichols sometimes used false names. But they were playing cat and mouse against a cat that was not even paying attention. As soon as it did, their plot was unraveled. McVeigh and Nichols were caught quickly after the attack, their use of false identification notwithstanding.

According to notes prepared by McVeigh's defense team,[9] "Ted Parker" was the name used to rent a storage shed in Council Grove, Kansas, and also to rent a room at a Traveler's Motel in nearby Manhattan. "Shawn Rivers" rented storage at Clark Lumber in Herington. "Terry Haven" rented a room at the Starlight Motel in Salina. The list of names goes on: Joe Havens, Joe Kyle, Tim Johnson, Joe Rivers. "Mike Havens" bought ammonium nitrate in McPherson, Kansas. Most of this information is from hotel registration forms and receipts in which proof of identification was not asked for.

Timothy McVeigh had a student identification card with the name "Tim Tuttle," an alias he used at a Michigan gun show. He disposed of this card by putting it in among the explosives he would discharge in Oklahoma City. With a typewriter he borrowed from Mike and

Lori Fortier, he made a fake identification card with the name "Robert Kling." This was the card he used when he rented the infamous Ryder truck from Elliott's Body Shop in Junction City, Kansas, to fill with explosives. He destroyed this identification card, burning it and throwing it in a motel toilet before he bombed the Murrah Building.

Based on all that intrigue, it would seem that false identification has a clear relationship to terrorist acts like the Oklahoma City bombing. But the full picture is a little less clear: McVeigh was not a master impostor by any stretch. He and Terry Nichols used all those false names inconsistently and for little purpose or effect. In fact, McVeigh used his own name to register at a motel for the nights directly preceding the bombing. The defense team notes, reportedly coming directly from McVeigh, say, "Tim went into the Dreamland Motel and registered under the name Bob Kling. 'Something hit [his] mind that he did not want that there.' He reached over and took back the registration card, crumbled [sic] it up and filled out a new card with the name Tim McVeigh." This is a time when false identification would have been essential to escaping responsibility for his deeds.

The full range of his motivations will never be perfectly clear, but Timothy McVeigh may have had just as much desire for notoriety as for a clean escape after Oklahoma City.

Much has also been made of the fact that the 9/11 terrorists carried and used government-issued identification cards.[10] In doing that, they did not defeat the identification system. State drivers' licenses and identification cards were not designed to protect against terrorists and, accordingly, did not work for that purpose. The changes to identification policy found in the REAL ID Act and discussed in chapter 18 are not so much reforms to fix a broken system as an attempt to devise a new security purpose for identification.

The 9/11 terrorists did little to mask their true identities. They entered the country on tourist visas; they used the banking system in their own names; they used valid identification documents and passports; and they did not use falsified Social Security numbers.[11] Terrorist groups have used falsified and modified documents, particularly passports for international travel,[12] but identification, false or otherwise, was not integral to the planning or execution of the September 11 attacks.

There are examples of terrorist's having made anonymity central to their modus operandi. The Unabomber, Ted Kaczynski, remained anonymous while carrying out attacks on symbols of modernity sporadically across three decades. He lived in a 10-by-12-foot plywood shack on a scrap of land near Lincoln, Montana, with no electricity or plumbing. Kaczynski was scrupulous about constructing and delivering his bombs so that they could not be traced to him.

Though he tried, Eric Rudolph, who bombed an abortion clinic and the 1996 Atlanta Olympics, did not manage to remain anonymous. Once he was known, to avoid capture, he lived in the North Carolina wilderness for five years, steeling into towns at night to forage for vegetables from gardens and discarded food from behind stores and restaurants.

There is a rough inverse correlation between the effect that a terrorist can have and his use of anonymity: Timothy McVeigh was at best haphazard and inconsistent in his use of anonymity and false identification. The 9/11 attackers used little false identification. Their open and notorious attacks stunned the nation. Ted Kaczynski and Eric Rudolph were, respectively, meticulous about maintaining anonymity or avoiding accountability after being identified. They surely damaged people's lives but represent fascinating and intriguing crime stories much more than any challenge to the viability or direction of American society and institutions.

In this admittedly small sample, the terrorists who are indifferent to consequences are the terrorists who have had the greatest effect. This characteristic is also central to the current predominant means of terrorist attack in the Middle East: suicide bombing. Indeed, the suicidal commitment of the bomber is part of what makes those attacks so fascinating, horrifying, and thus terror-inspiring. As terrorism expert Robert Pape has written:

> What made the September 11 attack possible—and so unexpected and terrifying—was that willingness to die to accomplish the mission. . . . The hijackers' suicide was essential to the lethality of the attack, making it possible to crash airplanes into populated buildings. It also created an element of surprise, allowing the hijackers to exploit the counterterrorism measures and mind-set that had evolved to deal with ordinary terrorist threats. Perhaps most jarring, the readiness of the terrorists to die in order to kill Americans amplified our sense of vulnerability.[13]

Think a little bit about any terrorist attack. In the weeks, days, and moments before it occurs, is the attack itself known but the attacker unknown? No, the attack itself is unknown. Terrorist acts are most facilitated by *surprise.* The element of surprise makes the attacker metaphysically anonymous up to the moment of action, but anonymity is not the tool that gives the terrorist his or her power.

As with any crime or misdeed, the terrorist who preserves his anonymity can avoid consequences and possibly act again. But preserving anonymity requires extreme caution that limits the effect a terrorist can have. The features that are central to effective terrorism are surprise and indifference to consequences—not anonymity. Requiring better identification of all Americans—or stripping Americans of anonymity, if you prefer—does not significantly deter or inhibit terrorists.

Yet a prominent policy advanced since September 11, 2001, has been the strengthening and centralizing of identification systems in the United States. Immediately after the 9/11 attacks, better checking of identification cards became a subject of intense interest among policymakers. The Aviation and Transportation Security Act, passed shortly after September 11, established the Transportation Security Administration to take over airport security that for years had been implemented, if not directed, by airlines and their contractors.[14] Federal workers would allegedly do a better job of checking identification and screening baggage.

The REAL ID Act, discussed at some length in chapter 18, followed a recommendation of the National Commission on Terrorist Attacks upon the United States, which was created by Congress to provide recommendations designed to guard against future attacks. The 9/11 Commission's September 2004 report briefly suggested standardizing driver's licensing and identification.[15] It uncritically adopted the idea from a report issued by a New York nonprofit foundation discussing technological approaches to the threat of terror.[16]

Strengthened and centralized identification systems are not a calibrated response to terrorism. As we have seen, terrorists in the United States have made spare use of false identification or anonymity and, when they have, it has minimized their effectiveness. Research published by the UK advocacy group Privacy International in 2004 found little correlation between national identification requirements and security against terrorism.

209

Of the 25 countries that have been most adversely affected by terrorism since 1986, eighty percent have national identity cards, one third of which incorporate biometrics. This research was unable to uncover any instance where the presence of an identity card system in those countries was seen as a significant deterrent to terrorist activity.[17]

Nevertheless, the idea of strengthening identification systems in response to terrorism retains a lot of currency, probably because of many people's intuitive belief that identification harnesses people to our laws, rules, and customs. When applied to terrorists, that intuition is false and dangerous. No general, integral terrorism protection comes from having everyone identified.

The inquiry is not complete, however. There is obviously some role for identification in terrorism prevention. Let us now look into what uses of identification might help prevent terrorism.

Terrorism Risk Management

In chapter 8, we considered how Trevor Hughes managed the risks to a football pool he organized from the happy, remote hamlet of York, Maine. One of few threats to a football pool is that an impostor or scammer will join and abscond with winnings, or welsh on his bet. In Trevor's pool, the likelihood of that happening was low, as were the consequences if it did. Based on this risk assessment, Trevor allowed a simple e-mail address to serve as sufficient identification for a new participant. A similar assessment of threats to passenger air travel can reveal whether identification might control air transportation risks.

Because of the 9/11 attacks, and because planes in flight are isolated and enclosed, the threats to air travel are relatively well articulated and limited. An entire book would be required to fully address them all in detail, of course, but the most prominent threats include detonating explosives brought or placed aboard, shooting a plane out of the sky, and commandeering a flight to take passengers hostage or to use the plane as a weapon.

Now, the risks: Each of the threats discussed previously is relatively unlikely to materialize but the consequences would be large if it does. If a plane is blown out of the sky, it will kill the passengers and crew, destroy the plane, and potentially cause death and property damage on the ground. Those consequences roughly compare with the death toll from car accidents in the United States from anywhere between a single day and a long weekend.[18]

As alluded to at the beginning of this chapter, the threat that a commandeered plane would be "weaponized" and flown into buildings or other infrastructure was essentially unaccounted for before September 11, 2001. The weaponization of planes—a destructive technique not seen since the kamikaze attacks by Japanese forces in World War II—was not incorporated into federal air security calculations. A federal commission convened in 1996 had canvassed available expertise in and outside of government and did not mention suicide hijacking.[19] The Federal Aviation Administration's "Common Strategy" called for cooperation with terrorists and its regulations required that cockpit doors permit ready access into and out of the cockpit in the event of an emergency.[20] This was still policy, even though popular author Tom Clancy had written the attack into a 1997 novel called *Debt of Honor* and the intelligence community had received information from several sources about plans to use it.[21]

The harms caused by weaponizing a plane are an order of magnitude higher than knocking a plane out of the sky, as we learned so painfully on September 11, 2001. Al Qaeda's use of planes to strike strategically selected targets increased the loss of human life about tenfold and the damage to property far more. Sufficient precautions against this threat obviously had not been taken. That oversight in risk assessment was a key reason why the attack succeeded so well.

Risk-reducing measures address threats. The hardening of cockpit doors, new procedures at the fronts of planes, and newfound resolve of passengers and crew against commandeering have deeply reduced the likelihood that a plane will ever be weaponized again. To the extent it remains, the threat probably comes from infiltration or recruitment of flight crews because of crew members' special access to the flight deck. Ensuring their emotional stability and nonalignment with terrorists seems the most natural measure for reducing even further this now small risk.

The other threats listed earlier remain: A bomb may be sneaked on board a plane and used to knock it from the sky. A shoulder-fired missile could be used to shoot a plane out of the air.

Notice that the listing in the paragraph above uses the passive voice. The passive voice hides the actor in a sentence. Authors use

211

it when they don't know who the actor is, when they want to be obscure ("mistakes were made"), and sometimes just when they are poor writers. The use of passive voice in the previous paragraph reveals a key point: *Nobody knows who might do these things next.*

Good risk management addresses threats and risks without regard to who might cause them, long before any bad actor has been identified. The reduced risk of commandeering since 9/11 illustrates this well. Hardened cockpit doors stop anyone who might enter the flight deck without permission. The resolve of crew and passengers to attack hijackers does not turn on who they are but extends to any and every hijacker. This entire method of attack has largely been cut off.

These techniques to reduce risk do not rely on identification. They meet threat vectors head-on. The same is true of security against other tools and methods of attack. Magnetometers screen for all weapons. X-ray machines scan for all guns and bombs. Sensors sniff for bomb residues and chemical or biological agents no matter whom or what they are on. Identification of people plays no role in the most direct and substantial methods for managing the risks to passenger air travel.

Let us visit more familiar territory to pursue this important point further: If your house had been burglarized twice, you would know you have a problem. In pursuit of your possessions and justice for the burglars, you and the police would rightly ask, "Who did this?"

To protect yourself from future burglary, you could follow the same line of inquiry, asking, "Who will do this next?" You could seek out all the individuals in your county or state who might be predisposed to burglary in your area. Learning everyone's motivations and capabilities would be an enormous problem with fascinating intellectual challenges.

But real people with real houses and valuables to protect take a different course. Learning from experience that the threat of burglary is substantial, they harden their houses against future attacks with alarm systems, stronger doors and windows, better-secured valuables, and mean-looking dogs. Perhaps they move.

This does not exclude a role for police in tracking down criminal gangs, fences, and all the other cogs in the burglary enterprise, which analogizes to terrorism planners, financiers, and supporters. (We will turn to this next.) Nowhere in the anti-burglary arsenal, though, is general investigation of all members of American communities.

212

That is not to say that there is no role for identification. There is. Indeed, in this section we talked about the special precautions that might be taken regarding people that have access to the flight deck. Identification is an essential part of such precautions. Identification is also essential when suspects have been located.

Interdicting Attackers

Earlier, we addressed "threat"—the vector along which harm may come to infrastructure, people, or processes—and "risk," the combined likelihood of a threat manifesting itself and the consequences if it does. Abstract calculations using these concepts help determine the appropriate measures to ensure the safety and security of infrastructure ahead of time.

An attacker, on the other hand, is a real, identified person or entity who is animated to do harm. When an attacker is known, identification has a role. Counterattacking someone who is trying to commandeer a plane, for example, is a form of interdiction that comes into play once the attacker has been identified by fellow fliers.

When intelligence turns up information about an individual or group that is planning an attack on an airline, those attackers, including their associates, suppliers, and financiers, should be brought to justice. They should be prevented from acting further, and they should be punished.

Here, identification has a role. Authorities should use whatever identifiers are available to direct their actions against the correct person, group, or thing. When a particular suspect is in mind, identification is the glue that allows interdiction to happen. With known suspects, identification is essential.

The limiting factor on capturing terrorists, though, is not finding them after they are known. It is learning who they are and what they plan. It is defeating the element of surprise, not anonymity.

Once enough information about active terrorists is known, finding and apprehending them is relatively easy. That is truer than ever because modern commerce creates traces of people's transactions and interactions in the records of merchants, banks, payment processors, Internet service providers, and other communications providers.

The 9/11 attacks help prove this point. The U.S. national security apparatus failed to look for the few 9/11 attackers it knew about, including Nawaf al Hazmi, who was listed in the San Diego phone

213

book.[22] As we discussed above, a terrorist that practices anonymity cannot enjoy the access to society that allows him to be effective, and he becomes at best just a bizarre crime story like the Unabomber, Ted Kaczynski.

Watch Listing and Checkpoints

So perhaps compiling lists of suspects and comparing them with travelers in the United States is an appropriate form of interdiction. In fact, the practice of "watch listing" and stopping people at checkpoints for domestic terrorism prevention is almost certainly ineffective and, in fact, absurd.

In September 2003, Homeland Security Presidential Directive 6 created the Terrorist Screening Center and charged it with consolidating the government's approach to terrorist screening.[23] The center maintains the Terrorist Screening Database, which consolidates other terrorist lists and takes nominations for new list members from the National Counterterrorism Center and the Federal Bureau of Investigation.

According to the directive, the database is to contain people "known or appropriately suspected to be or have been engaged in conduct constituting, in preparation for, in aid of, or related to terrorism." Agencies like the Transportation Security Administration use the Terrorist Screening Database to populate their lists, such as the "no-fly" and "selectee" lists based on additional threat criteria. To administer a watch list, of course, each person must carry accurate identification and show it at key places such as airline security checkpoints.

The United States has limited ability to reach terrorists on foreign soil, and foreigners have no basic right to enter the United States, so watch listing at the borders to prevent undesirables from entering the country is an acceptable practice. Comparing people who have been detained on suspicion of wrongdoing to terrorist lists may also be acceptable and create a margin of security.

But the equation is different when watch listing is used wholesale at domestic checkpoints. Domestic watch listing and checkpoints work according to this theory: if you know who the terrorists are, making a list of them and comparing each American with the list as they pass through key bottlenecks in society will probably eventually round them up. Given the tiny increment of security the practice provides, it does not overcome the United States' traditional distaste for seizure of citizens by government officials in the absence of suspicion.

If terrorists are known—and this big "if" is the nub of the problem—watch listing is like posting a most-wanted list at a post office *and then waiting for criminals to come to the post office*. It is a singularly lazy way to "pursue" terrorists. Real suspects should be actively sought wherever they go rather than awaited at the airport. The latter, lackadaisical approach only works if terrorists present themselves for inspection using the identities under which they raised suspicions.

Moreover, watch listing and identification checking can reveal to terrorist cells which of its members are current suspects. A 2002 study called "Carnival Booth: An Algorithm for Defeating the Computer-Assisted Passenger Screening System,"[24] showed that terrorist cells can defeat screening programs more easily than they can defeat random searches. By traveling multiple times in advance of an attack, they can determine whether they are subject to different treatment. Those who are not subject to screening can be assigned to act. This brittle identification-based security policy provides a road map to terrorists.

Considering the small number of attackers needed and the possibility of developing operatives from any of the billions of people in the world, terrorist groups like Al Qaeda should have little concern with watch lists. The evidence shows that the 9/11 terrorists were already operating in a mode to defeat watch lists when they hit the United States. Although one terrorist leader claims not to have been so selective, Khalid Sheikh Mohammed and another leader told investigators that they selected operatives for the 9/11 attacks who had no known records of involvement in terrorism.[25] This practice, in effect even before 9/11, renders watch listing, checkpoints, and identification requirements essentially impotent.

In the end, using watch listing domestically to prevent attacks is an odd half measure that protects the national security bureaucracy from hard choices and hard work. At the border, watch listing is needed because the authorities cannot pursue terrorists everywhere in the world and some may try to enter the United States using their true names. Once they are in the country, they should be either brought to justice immediately or actively monitored while cases against them are painstakingly built and brought—as is done with

Mafiosi. Enough resources to do this could come from the approximately $5 billion budget of the Transportation Security Administration.

People who are not real terror suspects should be free to partake unfettered in all the benefits of society without having to identify themselves to federal authorities. The deeply flawed practice of domestic "watch listing" does not justify broad identification requirements. The checkpoints Americans traverse at airports today are not set up to catch terrorists so much as to create the appearance that the government is actively looking for them. Checking the identification of all passengers is a ruse designed to make air travelers feel like they are better protected than they are.

Security Theater

There are arguments that "security theater"[26] of this kind is merited because it makes people feel safe and acting as if they are safe—that is, flying and spending and doing all the things that keep the economy moving. Its treatment of the American people like children is basis enough to reject this approach, but if that is not enough, security theater should be recognized as a needlessly risky counterterrorism strategy.

Remember that the goal of terrorist groups like Al Qaeda is to undermine Western institutions. By using security theater instead of real security, politicians are placing their own authority and leadership on the betting line. With only the small corresponding benefit of public calm (which could be gotten with accurate and informed communication of risks to the public), they are putting the legitimacy of their political leadership in play. If terrorists hit infrastructure or populations protected by security theater, that may truly strike a blow against our institutions. The public's confidence in the authorities' ability to protect—a basic role of government—could evaporate.

So far, we know that identification is useful only when there is a known suspect. Identification must be used to locate that person. The wholesale identification of air passengers is a superfluous and unnecessary overuse of identification. But perhaps there are other theories for using wholesale identification as a security tool. Let us explore those questions now.

Prediction

Another theory behind using identification in the effort to thwart terrorism is that widespread surveillance can ferret out incipient acts of terrorism and the people who would perpetrate them. Identification itself lacks any substance of its own but, as a framework for comprehensive surveillance, the argument goes, it can turn up leads that reveal terrorist acts in the planning stages. This theory is mistaken.

Let us begin by looking more carefully at what is known about a person when he or she has been accurately identified. To do so, we return to the identification card as a communications device.

Assume that a card has been properly issued and that the many weaknesses in the card identification process have been overcome. The facts conveyed are still quite limited. The average card tells little more than the information printed on it. A typical driver's license might include name, address, date of birth, biometric information (physiological: picture, height, weight, gender, eye color—behavioral: signature), standard identifier (i.e., license number), issuance date, qualification to drive, and organ donor status.

As we discussed in chapters 10 and 11, in ordinary life, identification cements and smoothes relationships, whether they be commercial, work, or family relationships. It facilitates accountability. That is, it ties people to their acts so that others can appropriately reward or punish them.

And, as we discussed earlier, the knowledge of identification's use in accountability promotes conformity to law and custom. But it does not create conformity among those who are suicidal or indifferent to consequences.

Identification facilitates surveillance. It allows people and institutions to collect, organize, and know more information about one another. The consumer data industry, for example, uses surveillance to better understand the consuming public: what people want, what influences them to buy, and whether they pay their bills.

Perhaps the surveillance function of identification could be extended into use for terrorism prevention. If the government knew enough information about all the people in the United States, through careful study it could find which of them were planning terrorist activity.

Perhaps psychographic profiles and algorithms would turn up terrorists before they acted, based on the intentions they revealed in their myriad purchases, movements, medical treatments, and communications—information that can be captured, stored, sorted, and sifted by modern database technologies and by future technologies to be pursued. Identification-based surveillance could facilitate prediction of terrorist acts and provide the essential link among activities, predicted bad behavior, and intervention against the wrongdoer-to-be.

The foremost manifestation of this theory was the Total Information Awareness program, created in the Information Awareness Office of the Defense Advanced Research Projects Agency at the U.S. Department of Defense.[27] Coming to light in early 2002, elements of this project would have captured a vast swath of data about the behavior of all Americans and applied algorithms designed to turn up threats. It would have used data from every conceivable commercial, health, financial, and communication activity of Americans. The public strongly rejected Total Information Awareness because of privacy concerns, and Congress denied the program funding in July 2003.[28] Nonetheless, many different programs premised more or less on this theory continue forward. They seek to use "data mining" as a predictive tool.[29]

The problem of finding terrorists has been analogized to finding a needle in a haystack. A theory behind Total Information Awareness was that massive computing power and well-designed algorithms would create the ability to effectively "x-ray" the haystack of information in which terrorist planning data lay. More data would make more clear which behavior was anomalous. Abnormal activities and communications would stand out like a shard of metal in a pile of cellulose. This ability to see through information would lead to the discovery of terrorists.

Data mining can be a predictive tool in some cases—or more accurately, a probabilistic tool. Marketers mine data to learn the characteristics of their most likely customers, for example. Knowing that current users of a product or service are in a certain age bracket, income level, Zip code, and so on helps them determine where to troll for new customers and how to design and market their products better for existing customers. When they do this well, they raise the results of their marketing programs by a few percentage points and make a few more dollars.

Studying group characteristics and attitudes to determine probable interests is quite different from attempting to learn the specific intentions of particular individuals. Consumer behavior is habitual, patterned, common, and easy to study. Corporations that study consumer behavior have millions of patterns that they can average into profiles of their typical or ideal consumers. Even data mining aimed at turning up the (relatively) rare instances of identity and credit card fraud relies on many thousands of examples a year on which to model searches.

Effective terrorism is sporadic and unpredictable. Indeed, a discrete goal of terrorists is to be unpredictable—not just because it makes them harder to catch, but because uncertainty increases the fear they can generate. Terrorism provides no store of indicia similar to commerce. With only one or two major terrorist incidents or attempts every few years—each one being distinct in terms of planning, parties, and execution—there are no meaningful patterns that would show what behavior indicates terrorism planning or preparation.

With no pattern of behavior to look for, national security authorities "x-raying" the "haystack" of American society through its stores of data would not learn anything useful. They would not know whether they were looking for a needle, a rubber band, or two pieces of hay arranged a particular way. In other words, the theory behind predictive data mining for terrorism planning is fundamentally flawed.

Though they may have hundreds of thousands of patterns to study, marketers may be more than 90 percent wrong in their predictions—sending unwanted mail to millions—yet still make money because they find enough new customers to make the mailing worthwhile. Predictive data mining for the purpose of turning up terrorist planning would result in false positives even higher than the 90 percent plus error rates in the highly sophisticated commercial data mining done today. Law enforcement and national security officials who might attempt to use data mining for prediction would waste incredible amounts of money and cut Americans' civil liberties to ribbons if they accepted error rates even approaching 1 percent.

The one thing predictable about predictive data mining for terrorism is that it would be consistently wrong. Data mining cannot be used for terrorism control the same way it is used in marketing.

Forensics

There is one final theory supporting the use of identification: the idea that identification and surveillance assist with forensics.

Observing the entire population will reveal who was responsible in the aftermath of a terrorist attack. The 2005 London bombings produced images of the suspects in fairly short order, given the cameras that bristle from thousands of ceilings and standards throughout that city.

Using identification in forensics is not a preventive measure at all, of course. Proponents of mandatory identification who make an argument based on mopping up after terror attacks are lowering the bar dramatically.

Less obvious but just as important, there has been no problem with identifying terrorists or their methods after they act. There is no forensics deficit.

Within days of the 9/11 attacks, the perpetrators were well known. Within a few weeks, the *Washington Post* had assembled a detailed account of their actions for the years leading up to the attack, including the relationships among them, hotels where they stayed, identification cards they had acquired, cars they had registered, and so on. Ordinary business records, created without reference to surveillance or crime control, are perfectly satisfactory to uncover the preparatory actions of terrorists after the fact.

Again, there have been cases where nominal "terrorists" have avoided detection. As we discussed, Unabomber Ted Kaczynski and Eric Rudolph, who bombed the 1996 Atlanta Olympics, both avoided detection for several years. The steps required of them to avoid detection greatly reduced their effectiveness as terrorists, of course. For terrorists to make the dramatic statements they seek, they must be engaged with the society. Their actions must leave footprints that make forensics relatively easy.

There have been instances where terrorist plots failed and camera surveillance helped reveal who the terrorists were. In that case, identification of those terrorist failures may help. It seems a rather obvious waste, though, to set up a surveillance system monitoring all of society to improve by a small margin the chance of capturing the rare terrorist who fails. The techniques and levels of surveillance that are appropriate for general crime control are a subject of ongoing debate. Terrorism adds essentially no weight to arguments in favor of general surveillance, which must be balanced against the threats from identification and surveillance to the human interests we discussed in earlier chapters of this book.

Identification is a powerful influence on willing participants in our economy and society. It has little influence over those who do not seek the benefits of our society, however. It does not reveal their one-time attacks before they happen. An overweening identification system going to all actions of all people might turn up more ordinary crime, but still not reach terrorists before they act.

What to Do: Advice to Individuals

The attacks of September 11, 2001, were shocking and gut-wrenching to people in the United States and around the world. In the years that followed, the nation and its leaders hurried to secure the country against terrorism any way they could think of. During that period, many policies were instituted based on knee-jerk reaction rather than study and analysis.

Widespread use of identification is one such policy. Not just federal authorities at airports, but institutions of all types and sizes began checking identification because of the security benefits it supposedly holds.

With nearly five years since the attacks, and no repeat attack of anything even close to the consequences of 9/11, the time is right to bring analysis, logic, and balance back into security policy. Steps that manage significant risks of terrorism should be taken if they are cost justified. Steps that do not manage the most substantial risks, steps that only create the appearance of security without the reality, and steps that have costs out of proportion to the benefits should be resisted and eliminated.

There is a case for multilayered security. We discussed the most important layer: directly addressing threats, the tools and methods of attack that terrorists may use. Human intelligence to develop leads and track down terrorists, their accomplices, and supporters is another direct interdiction against terror. Identification-based security is an additional layer, but it is costly in both dollars and lost liberty, provides little additional security, and is risky in and of itself.

Identification has little role in suppressing terrorism. It only really comes into play when terrorists and terrorism planning have been discovered. Turning up leads about terrorist activity is the hard part of the anti-terror job. Requiring identification from everyone who accesses goods, services, or infrastructure does not help with that job.

Identification-based security is "security theater." It gives much of the populace the impression of security but it does not effectively foreclose terror attacks. Government officials are taking a dangerous gamble when they stake their authority and credibility on security theater.

The major costs of today's heavy use of identification are not paid by the political and business leaders who have decided on this course, however. In fact, they benefit because the institutions they lead get natural access to more information about consumers and citizens. A hotel may require a driver's license on check-in as a claimed security measure, then use the data from it to learn the demographics of its customers or market to them. A government may use identification information collected as a security measure to conduct a later investigation of a traveler. The old saying is true: Information is power.

The costs are paid by every citizen and consumer who must wait in security lines that are longer than necessary—or not necessary at all. Those costs are paid in higher taxes and higher prices on goods and services to fund security appearances. Most importantly, consumers and citizens pay those costs in lost and threatened liberty. Each increased demand for identification, and the concomitant expansion of surveillance, is part of a constant nibbling encroachment on our ability to do the things we want to do free of the encumbrances authorities would put on us.

Identification, and the surveillance that inevitably accompanies it, can have a role in crime control by making it easier for authorities to track and find criminals. There will always be a cat-and-mouse game between law enforcement and criminals, and law enforcement will always push for more crime-control tools, including broader surveillance and identification. However, the costs of this kind of crime control fall primarily on the innocent. When you are next asked for identification, ask yourself whether you became a criminal on 9/11.

Because the costs of overidentification are diffuse, and paid by individuals, no civic or business leader will step up and lead institutions out of the security wilderness. Only a small but insistent band of individuals, perhaps inspired by this book and others like it, can push back against the increasing mistaken and wrongful use of identification.

As we saw in the early chapters of this book, identification is primarily about relationships and accountability. In other words, someone asking for your identification is asking to begin a relationship with you. When they do this, you should ask yourself three questions about their proposal:

- "Who is trying to start or continue a relationship with me?" Learn what institution is making the demand for identification. Is it a government entity or a business? Is it one you trust? Will it safeguard information about you consistent with your interests and values?
- "Am I getting something from this relationship to which I was not already entitled?" What benefit are you getting in return for being identified? When a business collects identity information, treat it as a surcharge. Rather than dollars, it is denominated in facts. Do you want to pay it? When a government collects identity information, treat it as an information tax. Do you want to pay it? Are you being taxed for something that is already your right or already owed you?
- "Do I want to have this relationship?" Make your decision about whether to be identified.

Finally, be prepared to decline being identified. Politely tell the requester—who is rarely responsible for the policy—that you would prefer not to be identified. It may sometimes require getting a manager or supervisor and having some discussion to determine whether the transaction can go forward. Plan ahead so you can be relaxed and patient with people who do not understand your vigilance in protecting privacy and liberty, a struggle that benefits even them.

When you agree to be identified, consider controlling the depth of the relationship by withholding certain identifiers. Depending on the circumstances, you may want to resist giving your Social Security number, address, photo, fingerprints, or other pieces of information that serve as identifiers. Share the identifiers needed to serve you, and no more.

In many cases, you may appear to be acting foolishly. If you are making payment by credit card and are asked to show a license, refusing will seem senseless because your name is on the credit card. If you refuse to give your Social Security number, an organization might be able to find it through research. There is a difference between making a payment authorization that reveals your name and revealing all the data on your identification card. There is a difference between using a privately issued card and using a government-issued card. And there is a difference between revealing your Social Security number and forcing an organization to spend extra time and money to find it out.

You may be derided, talked about, and stared at. You may slow down a line, causing other people distress or delay, and they may resent it. Government authorities may try to intimidate you. Decide how insistent you want to be. Take the opportunity to educate others about your concerns with identification, surveillance, and its consequences for our society. Think of yourself as being a little bit like one of Gandhi's satyagrahis. Leave your driver's license in your car. It is for administering driving laws.

It is not easy to refuse the many conveniences that are conditioned on identification today. But refusing them is essential for Americans desiring to live the freer life that is available. Only if enough people complain about being identified too much, or if they refuse to be identified entirely, will government and corporate policies about identification change.

24. Use Authorization Instead

Mary Rathbun was voted Volunteer of the Year three times at San Francisco General Hospital's Ward 86. That was only a modest acknowledgment of her community work. Every Thursday for more than 16 years, this petite older woman with curly white hair showed up to visit patients, feed them treats she had baked herself, carry specimens to the lab, and perform other errands and chores.

Her consistent service won her accolades. In addition to Volunteer of the Year at the hospital, the San Francisco Board of Supervisors dedicated a day to her: August 25, 1992. In 1994, she received a Saints Alive award from the Metropolitan Community Church of San Francisco. In 1996, she served as grand marshal of a San Francisco parade.

In the 1970s, Mary's daughter had died in a car accident. To fill the void, Mary made friends with the young people in her adopted city. In the mid-1980s, when her friends began falling ill in disturbing numbers, she began working in San Francisco General's AIDS ward, to comfort her "kids." Many of Mary's kids died, of course. This was during the dramatic onset of the AIDS epidemic, before any therapies had been found.

The police arrested Mary three times for her community service because, among other things, Mary delivered marijuana-laced brownies to AIDS patients. Consuming the drug eased their pain and bolstered their appetites, thus combating the "wasting" syndrome that accompanied AIDS. "Brownie Mary" Rathbun outspokenly defied the marijuana laws because obedience to them would have kept her from easing the suffering of dying people in the best way she knew. Mary died in 1999 at the age of 77, a hero to both the gay community and the marijuana decriminalization movement.

The medical marijuana debate is a subject of great passion for many people, but it is also a fascinating study in American governance. For one thing, it illustrates well how the federal system puts levels of government—local, state, and federal—in tension and competition with one another. That leaves room for challenges to the status quo and for change.

San Francisco is a special place, with a history of openness and tolerance perhaps unmatched in the United States. It has always been an immigrant city, with new cultural waves regularly coming through. Babylon by the Bay, as it is sometimes known, was the West Coast epicenter of the countercultural movement in the late 1960s and early 1970s. The Haight-Ashbury district saw more than its share of drug use and experimentation with lifestyles outside the American mainstream. Then there is the gay community. Beginning nominally with the 1969 Stonewall Riots in New York, this group has fought hard for decades to reverse cultural prejudices. San Francisco's gay community has long been overtly political and well organized.

The confluence of a tolerant culture, a politicized gay community, and the AIDS epidemic set San Francisco in stark opposition to the national consensus. While the bulk of the nation was dead set against marijuana possession and use under any circumstance, in 1991, San Francisco voters passed a medical marijuana law called Proposition P by a wide margin. Use and possession of marijuana for any purpose remained a violation of state and federal law, but a San Francisco Board of Supervisors resolution passed after Proposition P made medical marijuana the lowest enforcement priority of the San Francisco Police Department.

In 1992, the first marijuana buyers club opened in San Francisco. It was modeled on the buyers clubs that had emerged in the late 1980s to distribute alternative AIDS therapies and treatments smuggled from overseas because the federal Food and Drug Administration was not approving drugs fast enough for a desperate, dying population.

The Cannabis Buyer's Club issued cards to its members based on an interview with a doctor. It sold marijuana in sealed baggies with an "Rx" sticker and the notation "Not for Resale." By 1996, the club had moved into a five-story building and had over 11,000 members.

The activist community was still working to bolster legal immunity for medical marijuana, of course. Proposition 215, a statewide ballot measure passed by California voters in 1996, extended protection for medical marijuana possession and use statewide.

Proposition 215 was not a product of unanimous acclamation, of course. It was bitterly contested. In August 1996, a few months before the passage of Proposition 215, agents of the California Bureau of Narcotic Enforcement raided the Cannabis Buyer's Club in San Francisco, seizing cash, marijuana, and clients' records. This was one of many raids on cannabis clubs and arrests of key individuals that punctuated that election season. With the authority of local law, however, a hardy challenge to the status quo survived and even flourished.

Federal authorities have also raided medical marijuana clubs, homes, and businesses because marijuana possession remains illegal under federal law, which overrules contrary state law. The Supreme Court's 2005 decision in *Raich v. Gonzales** found that the Controlled Substances Act was a proper exercise of federal power under the Commerce Clause in the face of strenuous arguments that possession and use of medical marijuana is noncommercial, noneconomic behavior that should be regulated only by states, localities, and individuals.

The tension between state and federal law persists and a strenuous battle over the country's policies continues, in no small part because there are different levels of government that vie with one another to serve the people's interests.

Going back to the 1996 California raids: Authorities claimed that they were not going after medical marijuana users. They knew how impolitic it would be to arrest and jail people suffering from sometimes deadly illnesses. But there was widespread recognition that the community of medical marijuana users was at risk. Cannabis club operators and local officials recognized that records about users could be used by state and federal authorities for large-scale enforcement actions. They devised a protective system to prevent that.

In early 2000, the San Francisco Board of Supervisors authorized a card system that would help protect legitimate local users of medical marijuana from arrest for possession or use of marijuana. Because of the risk of federal enforcement efforts, the system was designed specifically to protect users from exposure or surveillance.

To get a card, users of medical marijuana in San Francisco bring to the department of Public Health a physician's statement recommending use of medical cannabis, a medical release form, proof of

*545 U.S. _____ (2005).

identity, and proof of residence. The department uses this information to confirm with the physician that the recommendation is authentic. It uses the identification card to confirm that the recommendation is for the right person. And it uses the proof of residence to confirm that the person lives in the city. Then it gives all the documents back to the individual. The department keeps no copies of the documents and makes no record of the patient's name or other identifiers.

The card itself has dates of issue and expiration printed on it, as well as a serial number. The serial number (which is 16 digits long and randomized to resist forgery) allows law enforcement to call and confirm that the Department of Public Health issued the card. Finally, a photograph printed on the card shows to whom it was issued. This biometric is easily used for in-person identification but not easily converted to computerized tracking.

Thanks to the design of this card system, if the San Francisco Department of Public Health were raided by federal authorities, it would not reveal information about who in the city was using medical marijuana. If the department itself wanted to know who was using medical marijuana, it would not have the information. Cannabis clubs that accept the card do not have records about who uses medical marijuana. In the crucible of the medical marijuana debate, the city of San Francisco has taken a remarkable step that puts the interests of its residents ahead of its own administrative interests and the enforcement interests of other governments.

The separation and tension among federal, state, and local government authority created the space in which a dedicated movement has sought to give American adults the authority to decide for themselves what substances they ingest for palliative care. Even those who would not themselves use medical marijuana should see the advance for liberty it represents.

Perhaps, also, the crucible of the medical marijuana debate has produced an exemplar for other institutions to emulate: the use of authorization in place of identification.

What Is Authorization?

Throughout this book, we have been studying identification, truly a fascinating, essential process. We use it all the time, so much so that it is second nature—or perhaps first nature. But we have also seen that it is not always needed.

In many transactions, it is not a known identity but a set of qualities or characteristics that determines whether the transaction can or should go forward: The characteristic that qualifies a person to legally possess medical marijuana in San Francisco is a doctor's recommendation.

Although it is called the "Medical Cannabis Voluntary Identification Card," San Francisco's unique government-issued card is not for identification at all. Rather, it is an authorization card. It provides for administration of medical marijuana, but it is so weakly identifying that it is essentially useless as a surveillance device.

The characteristic needed of a person who is going to buy something is possession of sufficient money or proof of ability to pay. The characteristic needed of someone entering a building is a lawful purpose. In some buildings and public forums the only necessary characteristic is the absence of an unlawful purpose. The characteristic needed to rent a hotel room is willingness to pay and the ability to assure that the room will be returned in good order. The characteristic needed for entry into a movie theater is possession of a valid ticket. The list goes on and on. Authorization is what happens when a transaction goes forward based on relevant characteristics rather than identification.

Sometimes the relevant characteristic is one's identity, as when a certain person is entitled to receive a particular benefit. But the true instances of this are relatively rare. When an employer bars access to a secure facility from all but certain employees, one might assume that identity is the key characteristic, but the relevant characteristic is the fact of having permission, not the identity of the person. A system for securing a facility can be designed so that entrants are not identified but, rather, are authorized without their identification information being collected. That system parallels what the San Francisco Department of Public Health did with its medical marijuana authorization card.

Chapters 19 through 22 discussed the many negative consequences of identification, which are increasing in intensity with our advance into digital identification and record keeping. Those increasing negative consequences make it important—and increasingly important over time—to use authorization when it will suffice and identification only when it is truly necessary.

It is easy to understand why identification is used so often for, or in place of, authorization. Since the beginning of human society, people who engaged in transactions knew each other already so the possession of authorizing characteristics and the communication of identification went hand in hand.

Identification also serves institutional interests because it helps develop and maintain relationships that many institutions want. A marketer that knows more about a particular consumer can offer him or her better refined products and services, reaching out for a sale at the best possible time and in the best possible way. A government that knows more about a particular citizen can provide more social welfare programs, regulate and tax more efficiently, and be more certain to arrest the right body more quickly when a crime has occurred.

It is counterintuitive to think that the practice of identification should be purposefully restrained. But increasingly, the practice threatens individuals' interests so it requires reconsideration.

The city of San Francisco created a program that accords specific benefits to specific people without identification. This system is not amenable to tracking and surveillance, and it serves the privacy interests of San Franciscans very well, along with their self-directed health needs. If the public health department of a major American city can administer a program without identification and tracking, just about anyone can. Businesses and institutions of all kinds should reassess the role of identification in their practices and be prepared to minimize the use of identification in favor of authorization.

What to Do: Advice to Businesses

Chapter 23 advised individuals to be more skeptical of demands for identification. When asked for identification, individuals should seek to know who wants a relationship with them. They should consider whether the relationship would benefit them and whether they want to have that relationship.

Businesses, in turn, should prepare to encounter individuals who are considering those questions. They should ask themselves a similar set of questions. Before they ask for identification, institutions should know the answers to the following questions:

- "What characteristics do I need to go forward with this transaction?" As noted, many transactions require only payment. Identification is built into many business processes merely out of habit, a product of historical accident. Businesses should decide precisely what information is needed to go forward with transactions.

- "Can I transact with this person not knowing his or her identity?" Envision a transaction that does not make use of identification. Are new risks created by dealing with people anonymously? Is the risk prohibitive, or can it be addressed by other risk-reducing measures or by raising the price to cover the costs created by the added risk? Does an anonymous transaction prevent monetizing customer information? If so, can raising the price make anonymity an equally viable option?
- "Am I prepared to decline a transaction with someone who declines to be identified?" Be prepared to interact with customers who have read this book. They may ask you to refrain from identification demands. Can you explain why you must have their identity to sell them a product or give them access to a location or service?

These interrelated questions require careful, thoughtful assessment. A great deal of effort will be necessary to overcome the natural assumption that identification is integral to transacting. In general, businesses that serve all comers, such as hotels, airlines, office buildings, and restaurants do not need identification to transact. Faced with turning away, say, 5 percent of customers, managers of businesses should quickly recognize that they can do almost all of their business without identifying customers.

There are many examples, and unfortunately the list is growing, where businesses are required by law to capture the identities of customers. But in a surprising number of instances, they will find that they do not need identification. This, again, is counterintuitive because the use of identification is so habitual in business practices, just like it is interpersonally. With other changes in the economy and society, like the growth of a credentialing industry discussed in the next two chapters, it may become easier for institutions to base transactions on characteristics rather than identities.

There are many cases where consumers enjoy a relationship with an institution. In those cases, the institution should consider how well it is protecting the customers' interests. The substantive concern underlying routine identification is surveillance, so institutions should consider whether, or how broadly, their relationship with a customer is contributing to surveillance by other entities, such as data aggregators or government investigators.

It is easiest to think of customer protection in human terms: How good a friend is the institution being to the individual? Is it digitally "staring" at the customer? Is it gossiping about the customer to others? Or using gossip to judge the customer? Is it snitching on the customer to authorities?

Business leaders should know why they need identification and whether they can do without it. If customers choose a relationship with an institution, the institution should treat that relationship tactfully by resisting excessive tracking and overuse of personal information, by resisting the sharing of information, and by asserting the customer's interest in privacy as against government authorities.

Businesspeople must realize that they play an integral part in shaping the society of the future. They should consider whether they personally want to live in a society of heavy surveillance and design their information systems with the answer in mind. Most businesspeople believe in freedom. There is important work to be done designing protections for freedom even into private business practices.

25. Use Diverse Identification Systems

Take out your wallet.

Seriously, take out your wallet.

Many people feel that a government-issued identification card is what provides them entrée to all the goods, services, and infrastructure that society has to offer. But when they actually remove their wallets from their pockets or purses and open them to look, they discover a wide array of documents and devices, each with its own distinct design and purpose.

Along with cash and receipts, people carry all kinds of cards and documents to identify themselves and to authorize various transactions. Some of those cards are issued based on in-depth examination of the person. Others carry no information about the person at all, providing authorization to whoever is the bearer. Some cards are made difficult to forge with holograms, embedded computer chips, special laminates, and forgery-resistant printing. Others are simple black printing on heavy paper. Some cards are tied to a person by biometrics—a picture, signature, or description of the person. Others are designed for use in combination with a biometric card. Some support back-end networks and databases that collect usage information for billing and payment purposes. Others have no utility for collecting and tracking information at all.

Each card in your wallet was created with a particular design for a particular use. Collectively, they represent healthy diversity in identification and authorization systems.

You might think that the simple laminated paper card in your wallet has almost nothing to do with modern identification, because modern cards must be highly technical and secure. But that is not true. When a card or token has one use, it is not rewarding to use in crime and has little value to a fraudster or forger, so the likelihood of misuse drops. Accordingly, the need for card security is low.

The recent drive to put increasingly more uses on single cards like the driver's license has made these tokens profitable to forge and corruptly procure. The battle over card security is not inherent to modernity. It is the result of choices about the design of identification systems.

Discussions about identification in both public policy and technology circles often assume that a unified identification system would be better. In some cases, that may be true, but further unification of identification systems along the current, government-dominated trajectory is very likely to exacerbate the concerns discussed in chapters 19 through 22. The better approach is probably to reinforce and extend diversity in identification and authorization systems.

Modern identification and authorization—among remote parties and with institutions—should be recognized as an important economic process. Just like payments, communications, and reputation gathering (i.e., credit scoring), credentials allow institutions and people to interact and transact with greater ease, efficiency, and confidence. Providers of these services bring parties together on mutually beneficial terms, and they should get a cut of the action for providing that service.

Identification services should be opened to competition. Identification should not be unified unless consumers demand that in the natural course of their market decisionmaking. The current monopoly enjoyed by governments, which issue drivers' licenses and passports, should not be extended; it should be canceled, allowing private providers to compete over the identification forms and processes that serve consumers best. Getting there will be a long journey, but the first steps are already being taken.

Identification in the Clear

While policies like the REAL ID Act, passed in early 2005, promote further centralization and uniformity of identification, the federal government has also opened a small window on a preferable identification future. Something called the "Clear" Card being used at the airport in Orlando, Florida, provides hints at where identification policy should be going.

Secure Flight is the name of the U.S. government's most prominent passenger air security program in early 2006. The program compares passenger name records from domestic flights with names in the Terrorist Screening Database as used in a "no-fly" list—people barred from air travel—and "selectee" lists of individuals known to be or suspected of being engaged in terrorist activity. As we discussed in chapter 23, comparing boarding passes with identification cards at entrances to airport concourses across the country completes the Secure Flight process by allegedly stopping or slowing the terrorists who apparently will present themselves at airports using their true identities.

The advisability and actual utility of the program is subject to doubt. It also presents a planeload of privacy and civil liberties concerns. But an obvious practical concern is the amount of time American travelers spend standing in line, and the amount of time they waste because they come to the airport early, uncertain of security delays.

The Transportation Security Administration instituted a program called Registered Traveler to address this logistical issue to at least some degree. In Registered Traveler, the TSA collects personal information from travelers, including name, address, phone number, and date of birth, along with biometric data: a fingerprint and iris scan. A background check then determines whether the traveler qualifies for accelerated access to the concourse area through a special line. Registered Travelers are still subject to primary screening, but more extensive secondary screening is largely eliminated for them.

A "subpilot" of the Registered Traveler pilot is called the Private Sector Known Traveler Program. In this program, a private-sector "partner" has responsibility for procurement, operational, and marketing functions.

The Greater Orlando Aviation Authority is the first participant in the Private Sector Known Traveler Program. Orlando chose a company called Verified Identity Pass to operate its pass-card system. Verified ID's card is trademarked "Clear." This is a welcome innovation: the use of a privately issued identification card.

Clear collects information from applicants for Registered Traveler, including fingerprints and iris images, high-quality, machine-readable biometric identifiers. It forwards applicants' personal information to the TSA so that the TSA can investigate the applicants. (Conditioning travel on government investigation is unacceptable, but the card process is our focus here.) Once the TSA has approved the applicant, the Clear Card can be used to access airport concourses.

At the airport, the Clear member places the card in a reader and allows his or her finger or iris to be scanned. The scan is compared with the biometric information embedded in the card using an algorithm (mathematical description) of the biometric presented. If the card information matches the person carrying it, the system compares a unique identifier on the card with a database of members' identifiers kept at the airport. If the card identifier is on the list of approved cards, the Clear member will continue through the expedited Registered Traveler line.

The Merits of Privately Issued Identification

The cutting-edge technologies the Clear system uses are well and good, but its most interesting and important characteristic is that it is not operated by the government. Verified ID is a private company headquartered in New York City.

Because it is a nongovernment entity, Verified ID's Clear website has a privacy policy that acts as a contract with users. It gives Clear members enforceable legal rights and potential applicants information that they can rely on when deciding whether to use it.

In other words, a private identification service like Clear submits itself to enforceable contractual terms, and it commits itself to future actions consistent with its contract. Neither is true of government privacy policies or the Privacy Act notices routinely published by U.S. national government entities in the *Federal Register*. Privacy Act notices can be changed merely by a new publication, undoing whatever "promises" may have appeared in previous notices.[1] Congress, federal agencies, and state governments can change the privacy commitments they have made because they are lawmakers, not law subjects.

The Clear system is designed for resistance to surveillance of travelers' movements. That is an attractive feature, laid out in the privacy policy as a firm contract with members. Specifically, Verified ID tells us:

> For purposes of real-time maintenance and customer support (e.g., if your card doesn't work, we need to be able to run tests to understand why), we will maintain "log files" of entrances to local venues. However, we keep such records only at that location, we purge these records automatically every 24–48 hours, and we have designed our network so that neither Verified ID nor its subcontractors, including Lockheed Martin Corporation, can track and record Members' activities from location to location.[2]

Assuming the Clear system works as stated—and, if it does not, Verified ID is on the hook for deceiving its customers—this is a tremendous anti-surveillance feature that has never been seen in government-operated programs.

To the extent they reveal the government's plans, the Privacy Act notices and privacy impact assessments issued for federal government–run identification-based security programs like Secure Flight have been ambiguous about how long they would maintain information about Americans' travels in their records. Indeed, at the time that the Clear Card was introduced, the Privacy Act notice for the Registered Traveler pilot covering TSA's portion of the program said that data will be retained "in accordance with a schedule to be approved by the National Archives and Records Administration."[3] This is both perfectly ambiguous and subject to change by a subsequent *Federal Register* notice, regardless of whether participants in Registered Traveler might object.

A program like the Orlando Registered Traveler pilot, operated as it is by a private identification card issuer, can be much more protective of privacy than a government-operated program, about which future privacy consequences cannot be predicted. Clear's contractual promise to use a surveillance-resistant data destruction policy is a major improvement over the alternatives we have seen so far.

Verified ID was started by entrepreneur Steven Brill, who earlier founded American Legal Media and Court TV. When writing a book called *After*[4] that cataloged America's response to the 9/11 attacks, Brill was inspired to create an identity system that would aid government security efforts without destroying civil liberties.

Focus groups and study directed him to three major points on which he believes competition for cards will turn: price, customer service, and privacy. Hence, he incorporated the anti-surveillance feature: a Clear user is identified to the system and permitted through a government checkpoint but is not identified to the government. Users' travels are not cataloged in a database. The fact that airlines have traveler data and might share it with government does not make this irrelevant. The anti-surveillance design of this system is its key feature, which should be applied elsewhere.

The Clear Card also comes with an "identity theft warranty." If a Clear user is the victim of identity fraud that results from unauthorized dissemination or theft of data from Verified ID or its subcontractors, Verified ID will reimburse unpaid losses from the fraud and help the user restore the integrity of his or her financial or other accounts.

To make a viable business, Brill knows he needs a larger market than just Orlando and there needs to be more than just his company offering credentialing services. When the Private Sector Known Traveler Program expands, Brill wants the cards and kiosks used at other airports to be interoperable with the ones in Orlando so that multiple providers can compete in a large market for identification card customers.

Identification Standards

Brill is onto something with his advocacy of standards and interoperability among privately issued identification cards. Identification is an economic service that could be just as subject to competition as, say, hauling freight. The existence of standards can make that happen.

Consider the use of standards for train tracks and the railway cars that run on them: If a continent had railroads that operated on different gauges in each country, only the trains of one country could ride on the tracks of that country. Goods would have to be unloaded and transferred at each border and the trains of one country could not provide service in another. If all tracks were built to one standard, however, the trains of all countries could run throughout the continent, wringing out the inefficiency of multiple standards and improving service overall through price and quality competition among train lines.

Standards will do the same with the cards issued in the Private Sector Known Traveler Program. Adoption of a uniform standard for taking biometric measurements of people, for recording them on the smart card, and for comparing the biometrics on the card with people at checkpoints will allow any and all comers to seek customers for those services. Multiple providers in competition with one another will drive costs down while they press one another to improve quality along all the vectors that consumers prefer, including customer service and surveillance resistance.

In chapter 14, we observed the three parts of the identification card communication chain: The first was communication of data from the data subject to the card issuer, and the question was the veracity of the information. The second was the communication from the card issuer to the verifier, and the question was the security of the card. Finally, there was the verifier check, which confirms that the card is about the person who presents it. The standards that Brill talks about for the Private Sector Known Traveler Program have to do with the verifier check link in the identification card chain.

A standard procedure for the verifier check certainly may allow multiple entrants into the market for government-approved security checkpoints, but the array of uses for cards and tokens is much bigger. The identification and authorization needs of individuals and institutions range widely. The privacy and anti-surveillance desires of consumers range widely as well.

Competition and diversity along other links in the communication chain is a step that the Clear Card points to, but that it does not yet take. Standards should be developed for card security and for the quality or provenance of the information that a card imparts.

Diversity along the Data Axis

With standards for biometric cards and readers in place, producers of cards can compete for the nation's Registered Travelers, and incremental security business beyond that. But the communication of identity is not terribly important for many transactions, and it is something that consumers should actively resist, as we discussed in previous chapters. Standards should be put in place so that cards like Clear can be used for multiple purposes that serve all the interests of consumers and citizens.

In many cases, as we have seen, authorization—not identification—is more relevant to a transaction. Cards should be able to communicate facts about the bearer independent of his or her identity. The employee of a company may be entitled to access company buildings, parking lots, vendors' facilities, commissaries, or other facilities merely by virtue of his or her employment. Standards should exist for communicating the fact of employment without the employee's identity.

Payment cards need not convey identity information, though they must create a record of the transaction with the financial services provider. A standard lexicon should allow any card to serve as a payment card that is anonymous to all but the bank or credit issuer. A standard lexicon, or protocol, should be able to tell bartenders and bouncers that a person is of legal age to drink without telling them the name, address, and birth date of the customer.

Standards should also allow for conveying the provenance or certainty of facts about people. There could be a standard protocol for conveying creditworthiness as established by credit bureaus or other institutions, so that a person could use a credential to buy on credit without a credit card. There could be a standard protocol for conveying the quality of a person's driving so that rental car companies could price their services accurately to the risk of loss. The list of possibilities goes on and on. A card protocol could communicate the certainty of facts going into it and automatically apportion the risk of loss from fraud in the card or in the transaction.

Cards should be versatile along all vectors. There is no reason why one card should not be an anonymous payment card for some purposes, a secure access authorization card for other purposes, and an identification card for other purposes.

Because the dominant providers of identification are governments, the emerging standards for identification cards being worked on by the International Standards Organization, the American National Standards Institute, the International Civil Aviation Organization, and the National Institute of Standards and Technology may fail to encompass the full range of consumer interests, including card standards that provide full support to anonymous authorization.

The standards issues are too detailed and the standards themselves not yet developed enough to discuss here but, just like there should be competition on the card-issuance level, there should be competition at the standards level so that the most relevant, useful, and consumer-friendly card standards emerge.

Although it is not essential—indeed, it is potentially risky—people may ultimately use a single card or token to access most goods, services, and infrastructure, yet preserve their anonymity and related interests. Systems that do this are called "identity management." If identity management takes hold, it should be because it emerged from a competitive market for credentialing services that rides atop competitively adopted standards. It should not be forced on consumers and citizens by law.

A Credentialing Protocol

In computer science, a standard for regulating data transmissions is often called a protocol. The widespread adoption of the Transmission Control Protocol/Internet Protocol underlay the growth of the Internet. It is basically a settled language that computers use to share information with one another.

Extensible Markup Language (XML) is another such protocol. It is a simple, flexible syntax for describing information so that it can be shared across widely varied systems. Because it uses ASCII characters, XML is easy to understand with a little study. Characters or phrases bracketed by the less-than and greater-than symbols begin and end every description of data, and the ending phrase is identical except for starting with a forward slash (/). The English phrase "My name is Gene" might be written "⟨name⟩Gene⟨/name⟩" in an XML syntax.

Let's take a look at how the recipe for bread might be written in XML. In the following example, the line at the top tells the computer what protocol to use (XML version 1.0) and the rest of the brackets describe bread making in a format that could be adopted by all bakers across the world no matter what kind of computer systems they used:

```
⟨?xml version = "1.0"⟩

⟨Recipe name = "bread" prep_time = "5 mins" cook_time = "3 hours"⟩
   ⟨title⟩Basic bread⟨/title⟩
   ⟨ingredient amount = "3" unit = "cups"⟩Flour⟨/ingredient⟩
   ⟨ingredient amount = "0.25" unit = "ounce"⟩Yeast⟨/ingredient⟩
   ⟨ingredient amount = "1.5" unit = "cups"⟩Warm Water⟨/ingredient⟩
   ⟨ingredient amount = "1" unit = "teaspoon"⟩Salt⟨/ingredient⟩
   ⟨Instructions⟩
      ⟨step⟩Mix all ingredients together, and knead thoroughly.⟨/step⟩
      ⟨step⟩Cover with a cloth, and leave for one hour in warm room.⟨/step⟩
      ⟨step⟩Knead again, place in a tin, and then bake in the oven.⟨/step⟩
   ⟨/Instructions⟩
⟨/Recipe⟩
```
[Source: Wikipedia XML page ⟨http://en.wikipedia.org/wiki/XML⟩.]

(continued next page)

A Credentialing Protocol (cont.)

The same kind of descriptive scheme can be used to indicate the identification or authorization information provided in a card credential scheme. Used at a government-regulated checkpoint to allow anonymous access, the card might transmit the following information in "Credential Markup Language":

⟨?cml version = "1.0"⟩

⟨credential⟩
 ⟨TSAauth⟩yes⟨/TSAauth⟩
⟨/credential⟩

This communicates the sole piece of information relevant to the transaction: the person is authorized by the TSA to access a certain area.

Let's try a more complicated transaction. A user presents a card at an entrance to a secure part of her employer's facility. The card communicates information about her access status as follows:

⟨?cml version = "1.0"⟩

⟨credential⟩
 ⟨employment⟩
  ⟨employer⟩Acme Roller Skate⟨/employer⟩
  ⟨authlevel⟩3⟨authlevel⟩
 ⟨/employment⟩
⟨/credential⟩

If her level 3 authorization allows it, she can go into the secret testing facility at her roller skate manufacturer employer.

(continued next page)

A Credentialing Protocol (cont.)

This kind of data structure can be extended in any direction. If a system wants to use a card to convey identifiers, aliases, and other information, as well as the source and level of assurance about these facts, the data might look like this:

```
⟨?cml version = "1.0"⟩

⟨credential⟩
    ⟨identity source = "Phillsbury National Bank" assurance = "medium"
guarantee = "no"⟩
        ⟨name⟩
            ⟨firstname⟩Margaret⟨/firstname⟩
                ⟨alias type = "firstname" reason = "custom"⟩Maggie⟨/alias⟩
            ⟨middlename⟩Adele⟨/middlename⟩
                ⟨alias type = "middlename" reason = "custom"⟩A.⟨/alias⟩
            ⟨lastname⟩Mancini⟨/lastname⟩
                ⟨alias type = "lastname" reason = "marriage"⟩Croup⟨/alias⟩
        ⟨/name⟩
        ⟨account type = "bank checking" routing = "073000345" owner = "Margaret A. Mancini" guarantee = "yes"⟩44172345⟨/account⟩
    ⟨/identity⟩
⟨/credential⟩
```

Here, Phillsbury National Bank provides the provenance for information with medium assurance of its veracity, but no guarantee. The bank knows a Margaret Adele Mancini, who sometimes uses Maggie for her first name and the initial *A* in place of her middle name. She used to go by Croup but changed that because of marriage. The bank associates a checking account with her and guarantees to others that it has an account in the name Margaret A. Mancini.

This protocol would be useful to a public relations firm verifier who is considering hiring a Maggie Mancini for some freelance writing. It would have the same level of assurance about her identifiers as Phillsbury Bank, though no guarantee of her identity from the bank, which is probably good enough for this transaction. The firm could also trust writing samples she gave with the name Margaret Croup on them. And the firm would know for certain where to send the money when the project is finished so that Maggie gets properly paid for her work.

Steven Brill's Clear Card may be a first step toward identity management. It allows people to enter airport concourses without identifying themselves to the federal government.

What to Do: Advice to Governments

Elsewhere in this book, we have laid at the doorstep of governments the flaws with current identification systems. The federal government in particular has promoted the use of a single identifier, the Social Security number, and mandated surveillance of Americans with it. With the REAL ID Act, the federal government is now a chief promoter of the state-issued driver's license as the nation's master identification card and surveillance tool. As we discussed in chapter 22, the government has had its thumb on the uniform-identification side of the scale for decades. The negative consequences of that policy are growing.

"Path dependence" is the term used in the economics literature to describe how widespread use of a standard or technology tends to lock in its use. A technology may have been adopted for serendipitous reasons, or for no reason, but it persists even though it may not be the best option. The costs of switching make it prohibitively difficult for users to change to another technology or standard.

Because of government involvement, the identification world is highly subject to path dependence. Governments have been creating and promoting identifiers for generations. Indeed, to the extent they require "government-issued identification" or require others to use it, governments have given themselves a monopoly on identification and credentialing services. That should change.

To help us escape from the morass they have created, governments should cease promoting uniform identifiers and identification cards. Instead, they should promote a diverse, competitive market for credentialing services. The Private Sector Known Traveler Program holds the seeds of what could be a very dynamic economic sector: credentialing. It may become a very important and very large Information Age service akin to payments and communications.

Governments are regular demanders of identification and authorization. They require those things routinely for administering taxation, controlling borders and secure facilities, and regulating driving, various professions, hobbies, and businesses.

Rather than specifying the particular identification cards they will accept, though, and issuing cards themselves for the purpose, governments should promote a private credentialing market. They should issue specifications for the credentials they need, based on uniform standards, and let those specifications be satisfied in any way that credential issuers and credential users can.

As this book is being written in early 2006, it is too soon to tell what will happen. The Private Sector Known Traveler Program may establish a uniform standard for the verifier check step, the third in the identification card communication chain. The algorithm used there for fingerprint and iris measurement may become the standard, and the method of communicating that information from a card to a kiosk may be the template on which the market for biometric cards converges.

Card security standards are the second step in the card communication chain. Card security is fairly straightforward and various technical card standards are already seeing adoption. Various encryption techniques can almost guarantee against forgery, at least by outsiders to the card production system.

The first step in the card communication chain is the most important and will undoubtedly be the most difficult to subject to standards, but doing so is essential. The information, veracity of information, and other data communicated by cards and tokens should also be standards based, using a variable, extensible standard.

Standardization will allow the fullest array of cards and tokens to be used for the broadest array of purposes. It will allow a market to develop that might allow a credit card company to create a key fob that is both a payment card and a driver's license. A piece of jewelry might prove that a person is entitled to check out a book without revealing her name. A watch or phone might contain the data that permits a person into a secure government facility or across a national border without exposing her movements to surveillance. Those things are beginning to happen in different parts of the world—unfortunately, on systems that use different communication and data-structure standards.

An important issue is liability: what happens if one of the links in the identification card communication chain is broken and harm comes to someone or something as a result? If an identification card meets the standards required by the verifier for veracity, security, and verifiability, there can be no liability to the card issuer. But there may be instances where a card issuer claims to meet the standards and does not.

Say, for example, that the verifier demands in-person collection of a biometric, but the card issuer has allowed the cardholder to submit the biometric by mail, as Jerry Iannacci did with the photograph on his credit card in chapter 17. For the most part, this is a subject for card issuers and verifiers to work out among themselves, by contract. Sophisticated commercial entities in every industry use contracts to apportion the risk of loss. Identification services are no different from any other commercial service: Things can go wrong— and wise parties prepare for the possibility.

The price a verifier pays for identification services might be determined in part by the liability regime the parties choose. If a verifier wants perfectly accurate identification and no risk of error, it may be expected to pay a very high price. If, on the other hand, it is willing to bear some risk of misidentification, it will probably pay a lower price for identification.

It is worth noting that government issuers of identification bear no risk of their systems failing users. When a state's department of motor vehicles is defrauded or corrupted, the state pays nothing to collateral victims, who might suffer from financial frauds perpetrated with false identification. Indeed, as we saw in chapter 15, motor vehicle departments fail upward, getting more tax money and more employees when their systems do not work.

Government card issuers, particularly state motor vehicle bureaucrats, are currently the entrenched monopoly provider of credentialing services. As is typical of governments and government-protected monopolists, their services are homogeneous, low quality, and too expensive.

The homogeneity of government credentialing is best illustrated by the fact that identification is about the only credential available today. If you need to prove your age, you show identification. If you need to prove that you are qualified and permitted to drive a car, you show identification. If you need to prove that you are not a risk to air travel, you show identification. In most of these processes, individuals share more information than they should, and often verifiers get less information than they need. The credentialing services available from government providers poorly suit the needs of both individuals and institutions.

The costs of this market structure for credentialing are high and growing. Chapters 19 through 22 warned of the losses to autonomy, privacy, and security that are accruing as the practical obscurity we have traditionally enjoyed falls away. They are all costs of the government credentialing system that uses only identification cards. More concrete costs are paid through the taxes and fees that everyone pays to motor vehicle departments for the privilege of using their subpar product.

With mild changes to their systems, many of which are already under way or on the near horizon, many different card issuers could meet the credentialing demands of all institutions and governments—if those demands were communicated in standardized formats. Governments should promote a credentialing system in which they specify the information they need to know and the level of assurance at which they need to know it, along with their security and verification needs, in standardized formats. Then they should accept whatever credentials provide those facts and assurances satisfactorily.

Such a system would jump-start a market for identification and credentialing services that is innovative and efficient. That market would protect consumers and citizens from the ills of centralized and unified identification systems that we examined in this book, ills that are now looming large on our horizon.

26. Conclusion

The day before the formal opening of the 2005 Computers Freedom and Privacy Conference in Seattle, Washington, there was an all-day workshop on "vanishing anonymity." CFP is an annual meeting that explores cutting-edge issues in privacy and technology. It is not the best organized conference—the panels never seem to happen on time—and it underweights intellectual depth in favor of privacy activism and dire prediction. But CFP makes up for these drawbacks by exposing and publicizing some of the most interesting social problems generated by the newest technologies and business methods.

On the morning of the workshop day, Dr. Stefan Brands gave a talk with the unassuming title "User Identification." Brands is a renowned cryptographer, a soft-spoken Dutchman who lives in Canada. He is affiliated with Credentica, a software company that focuses on identity and access management; he is also an adjunct professor at McGill University in Montreal. Dr. Brands was better dressed than most of the folks who come to CFP.

Brands's talk dealt with many of the topics in the early chapters of this book: identifiers, verifiers, the contextual nature of identification, its purposes, and so on. Although he addressed them from his own perspective as a cryptographer working on digital identification, he raised many of the same concerns found in this book: the trend toward increased surveillance, which is reinforced by increased reliance on the same identifiers—what we have called here "uniform identification systems."

Insightfully, Dr. Brands divided identifiers into two different categories: "self-generated" identifiers and "certified" identifiers. An online username is an example of a self-generated identifier. These identifiers protect the interests of individuals by putting them in a position to prevent the tracing and linking of their activities. But self-generated identifiers provide almost no protection to institutions, which have little assurance about the user of a self-generated

249

identifier. Institutions are unlikely to engage in transactions of high value that rely on self-generated identifiers.

A certified identifier is created for the protection of institutions—such as a multifactor identification card with a good strong biometric. Such identifiers have all the elements of identifier "quality" that we talked about in chapter 7: fixity, distinctiveness, and permanence. This kind of identifier serves the interests of institutions by allowing highly accurate surveillance and confident use of the identifier to control the rights and entitlements of the individual.

Between the two types of identifiers is a wide empty space. A self-generated identifier leaves institutions in dire straits because they cannot be certain if a transaction will be safe. Using a certified identifier puts the individual in an equally bad position—subject to surveillance and control.

Clearly, Brands pointed out, we need a next-generation identifier—an identifier that serves the versatile purposes of identification and that benefits both parties to an interaction. Such an identifier would prove that a person is entitled to access goods, services, or infrastructure without creating a record that the person had accessed them. It would prove unalterably that a person agreed to a contract or other commitment. Or it could be used once anonymously, like a movie ticket, stamp, or coin.

Brands said that he has created this next-generation identifier using highly advanced cryptographic communication and transaction techniques. If adopted, an identifier like this could open a whole new world of possibilities for online communication, commerce, and collaboration—with hardy protection for individuals' interests in privacy, anonymity, and personal power.

And then he stopped. Dr. Brands's time concluded, he finished his talk and alighted from the stage.

Later that day, I caught up with him. I expressed my combined delight and dismay at being "teased" with his next-generation identifier—showing a corner of it to the CFP audience and then not letting us see the whole thing. If there was something to this identifier, I wanted to know about it.

With only a short time on the agenda, with a relatively nontechnical audience, and with the identifier still in development, it was inappropriate to go through the whole thing at the conference. But Dr. Brands and I spent the better part of an hour talking through his   credentialing system and identification in general.

I do not know whether Brands's identifier could or will revolution-ize identification. Time will tell whether his identity management system, or another like it, works as advertised and whether it will gain the acceptance among all the parties it must. With governments now monopolizing the identification business, and using it to increase their power, it will take quite a struggle to institute a widely used identification system that truly empowers individuals.

A Snapshot in Review

I do not know what the future holds for Brands's identifier and, obviously, I do not know the future of identification policy as a whole. As I noted in the introduction, this book is a group of snap-shots, pictures of identification from many angles.

I have attempted to capture and advance human identification theory. The theory may change, but if we know better the minutia of identification, each of us can understand its dynamics and better decide when and how to use it.

We all use the suite of four identifiers—expanded from three in the literature to date—to identify ourselves and others. These identifiers—something you are, something you are assigned, some-thing you know, and something you have—represent a progression of sorts through human history. In prehistoric times, humans, like all beings, used the physical characteristics of one another to distinguish friend from foe and family from food. With the development of primitive language and social concepts like time and place, we started assigning identifiers to one another and ourselves: things like personal names, descriptions, place names, and so on.

A further step was to use knowledge as an additional identifier. Shared knowledge—of histories, cultural traditions, and so on—allowed humans to engage in a broader array of relationships across a broader physical expanse, based not just on personal familiarity, but on reputation, family history, cultural affinity, and the like.

The final identifier is something you have. They are identifiers constructed by the hand of man for the purpose of identifying people, as well as for other social necessities and functions like security and adornment. These "identifiers with ingenuity" represent the highest order of identifier, in a sense, and they are at the center of identifica-tion policy debates today.

251

These advances in identifiers correlate roughly to advances in remote commerce—among villages, then across regions, countries, and even continents. Today, we are embarked upon an explosion of remote commerce, communication, and interaction through the medium of the Internet. In just the past few hundred years, we have also witnessed growth in the size and scope of institutions, along with the intensity of their demands for identification. We are at a crossroads for identification. This essential social process should be better understood.

As we saw, identifiers vary in quality. The identifiers that are attached to or inherent in a person are obviously high-quality along the "fixity" vector because they resist being removed or transferred. Identifiers that are distinctive are obviously higher quality because there is a lower probability that they will appear twice in a given population. Finally, the permanence of identifiers affects their quality. Identifiers may last an instant or a lifetime. A variety of techniques go into reducing the risk of misidentification while identifying people efficiently.

Because we use near perfect biometrics to identify one another every day, it may be habitual to choose the highest-quality identification in every circumstance. But as we conduct more and more transactions remotely and with institutions, the better approach is to use only the level and quality of identification that are necessary. Very often, identification is not needed at all. Rather, nonidentifying authorization or low-quality identification is most appropriate.

My hope is that my extension and refinement of human identification theory and practices will be valuable or at least provocative. Perhaps the discussion of identification theory you have read will meet with widespread acceptance and deepen the general understanding of identification. Perhaps it will elicit greater study of identification theory and all its facets. Once again, this is a snapshot of identification theory and practice as it stands in what are probably its early stages.

Understanding the uses of identification and the benefits of anonymity is essential. Foremost, identification is used to commence and continue relationships. Identification ties people to information about them, so that when two people encounter each other again (or when an institution encounters a person again) the relationship can pick up where it left off. Identification is a sort of social and economic glue.

Just as identification allows relationships to begin and go forward when all is well, it binds people together (and people to institutions) when things go badly. Identification is the tool that ensures that accountability for bad behavior falls on the correct actor.

We all start our lives with a clean slate of personal, emotional, economical, and political relationships. By selective identification and selective sharing of information, we craft our lives and the versions of ourselves that we exhibit to whomever we encounter in the world. This anonymity default should not be abandoned lightly. In fact, it should not be abandoned at all. Life and personality are shaped just as much by what or whom we avoid as by what or whom we engage with.

For good and important reasons, our public policy limits identification to limit accountability. Free speech, dissent, and other cherished activities flourish in the shelter of anonymity. Anonymity prevents accountability from being brought to bear on people for engaging in specially protected types of activity.

The identification card and similar tokens are at the center of identification policy debates today, and we have looked at a snapshot of those debates, centered on the REAL ID Act. By parsing the operation of the identification card as a communications device, I hope I have made it easier to understand the many weaknesses of this device. Each of the three steps in the identification card communication chain exposes it to error or fraud. The veracity of card information may be compromised when the card is based on forged documents or produced by corrupted issuers. The security of the card may be disrupted by alteration or forgery. And the verification step may fail if verifiers lack care or proper security themselves.

The ultimate fix, which would steel each link in the chain against all its weaknesses, is repugnant: biometric surveillance of all people beginning at birth. A card identification system could be perfected, but only if the interests of individuals in privacy, anonymity, and other social goods are subsumed entirely to the surveillance needs of institutions.

The better goal is not perfection in identification systems but selective use of identification in situations where it holds mutual benefits for individuals and verifiers alike. Identification should be a risk-reducing strategy in a social system, not a rivet used for pegging humans onto government or economic machinery.

The battles over identification card accuracy and security are battles we do not need to fight. The choice to regulate many high-value functions and activities through one identification system has created these battles. Choosing a diverse identification system would allow us to avoid this fight almost entirely, which is the ultimate victory.

The least we could do is to recognize that there is such a thing as identification policy. As a nation, as businesspeople, and as individuals, we have all been backing into the current state of identification methods and practices. It is time to turn around and address identification as a discrete set of public and social policy choices.

The heart of the matter is this: With the advancing digital age, the consequences of identification are changing. The stakes involved in identification policy are rising.

The decline of practical obscurity is the dominant motif of the Information Age. In the past, records about us were collected only intermittently, and they were quite difficult to make use of. Today, personal information is captured, stored, transferred, and used more often than it ever has been before. Information storage and processing techniques are only getting better. Identification means something different now.

Dossiers and surveillance are a greater threat to more people than they have been before. And data collection fundamentally changes the power relationship between individuals and institutions. Although identification schemes are not a catalyst for oppressive government, oppressive governments have used identification time and time again, even in recent history, to administer evil. Uniform and centralized identification systems provide no fail-safe in the event a democracy fails, or fails to protect liberty. A diverse identification system is more difficult to navigate. That makes it a bulwark of liberty.

Today, identity fraudsters are successfully navigating the homogenous identification system used by the government and financial services sector. That is good evidence of just how insecure uniform identification systems are. Their very uniformity is a design flaw.

Three general prescriptions, found in the final three chapters of this book, show the way forward.

Overuse of Identification

We have relied too long on instinct in formulating both public and private identification policies. The result is that identification is overused.

People generally believe—and it is *generally* true—that identifying someone helps ensure that they are not a threat. The accountability role of identification creates conforming incentives for people with a stake in society, meaning that identified people are less of a threat than unidentified people.

But massive increases in the use of identification after the September 11, 2001, terror attacks apply this general rule precisely where the exception pertains. Terrorists, willing to die as they are, do not fall within that large category of people whose behavior is controlled by identification and the threat of accountability.

Identifying people at checkpoints is security theater. Surveying the general population to make people feel safer does not actually make them so.

The slender remaining reed supporting identification checkpoints is that identifying people at airports may interdict a known terrorist. That is akin to placing wanted posters in the post office and waiting for criminals to present themselves there.

Security theater is a dangerous gamble for public officials to take. When their bluff is called, they may lose all their authority and ability to lead.

Risk management techniques show that passenger air transportation is protected by safeguarding planes against the tools and methods of attack that terrorists might use, not by identifying all the people who get on planes.

All institutions, public and private, must do more careful assessments of the risks to their operations and their need for identification of the people with whom they interact. More often than not, identification is not needed. Yet it is a condition of access to an increasing array of economic and social transactions today. People are giving up something for nothing.

And that raises an important point: Institutions will not voluntarily cede ground on identification. Individuals will have to demand it. Every person who cares about the shape of our economy and society should demand to know who is asking them for identification and why. Then, they should consider carefully whether they are willing to have a relationship with the requesting institution. If the minority of people willing to act on this priority is large enough, institutions can and will change their practices.

Institutions should prepare themselves to hear from consumers who are reconsidering how well they want to be identified. Businesses should consider whether they can structure and price transactions in a way so that consumers who want to can go unidentified. With care, businesses will find ways to do so. If they lack care, they may find themselves turning away a certain amount of revenue and profit.

Several times in this book, I declined to state the optimal level of use of identification in society. I declined to say what level of database use by private companies would properly balance consumers' interests in low prices, convenience, customer service, privacy, and other dimensions of their welfare. Rather, I alluded to some other system for determining these things. That system is the marketplace.

As we saw in the previous chapter and in this conclusion, systems are emerging that may provide credentialed access to goods, services, and infrastructure while maintaining anonymity on the terms consumers want and need it. These systems have the potential to deliver all the bounty of large-scale remote commerce while preserving the human freedoms and protections that are so essential.

If you and the people you know see fit to refuse the uniform identification system we have today and demand something better, you will get it. Governments must stop promoting uniform identifiers, identification requirements, and data collection. Then, each of us pursuing our own interests can guide the private sector toward serving our identification and information interests in the best possible way.

In the future, identification policy will move our society in one of two directions: toward greater uniformity, surveillance, and conformity or toward diversity, competition, and protection for individual rights and liberties. It will be a challenge to make individuals, businesses, and governments understand the importance of well-crafted personal and institutional identification policies.

With no final outcome to predict or report, this book is a bit like Dr. Brands's talk at the Computers, Freedom, and Privacy Conference. It does not have an ending. It just stops. You must decide where identification policy goes from here.

Notes

Chapter 2

1. The seminal document laying out this approach to identification theory is Roger Clarke, "Human Identification in Information Systems: Management Challenges and Public Policy Issues," *Information Technology and People* 7, no. 46–57 (December 1994): 6, http://www.anu.edu.au/people/Roger.Clarke/DV/HumanID.html. Clarke's framework has been adopted and used by nearly all subsequent authors.

Chapter 3

1. See, for example, James V. Haxby et al., "Human Neural Systems for Face Recognition and Social Communication," *Biological Psychiatry* 51 (2002): 59–67, http://www.paed.uni-muenchen.de/allg1/ lehrveranstaltungen/akt_arb/Haxby2002.pdf.

2. Human Genome Project, "DNA Forensics," webpage, http://www.ornl.gov/sci/techresources/Human_Genome/elsi/forensics.shtml.

Chapter 4

1. This and other examples of regularized naming in this chapter come from James C. Scott, "The Production of Legal Identities Proper to States: The Case of the Permanent Family Surname," *Comp. Stud. Soc. & Hist.* 44 (January 2002) excerpted in Carl Watner with Wendy McElroy, eds., *National Identification Systems: Essays in Opposition* (Jefferson, NC: McFarland & Co., 2004).

2. Pat Gelsinger, vice president and general manager, RSA Data Security Conference and Expo '99, Intel Corporation (Keynote speech, January 20, 1999) http://www.intel.com/pressroom/archive/speeches/pg012099.htm.

Chapter 5

1. *Episteme* (knowledge) and *metron* (measure or degree).

2. Frank W. Abagnale, *Catch Me If You Can: The True Story of a Real Fake* (New York: Grosset & Dunlap, 1980).

3. Demara's life was fictionalized in the 1960 movie *The Great Impostor*, starring Tony Curtis.

4. The creation and maintenance of trust in the modern economy are fascinatingly described in Daniel B. Klein, *Reputation: Studies in the Voluntary Elicitation of Good Conduct* (Ann Arbor: University of Michigan Press, 1997).

5. See Bruce Schneier, *Applied Cryptography* (New York: John Wiley & Sons, 1996), pp. 4–5.

Chapter 6

1. Daniel 6:1–28.

Chapter 10

1. *In re Owens-Corning Fiberglas Corporation*, 774 F.2d 1116 (Fed. Cir. 1985).
2. Likely influences on the development and deployment of RFID are discussed in Jim Harper, "RFID Tags and Privacy," *BNA International's World Data Protection Report* 4 (July 2004): 19, http://www.cei.org/pdf/4217.pdf.

Chapter 11

1. 252 Ill. 534 (1911).
2. Pub. L. No. 106–229.

Chapter 12

1. Jane Jacobs, *The Death and Life of Great American Cities* (New York: Random House, 1961).
2. Hillel Schocken, "Intimate Anonymity: Breaking the Code of the Urban Genome,"*INTBAU Essays* 1, no. 5 (2003), http://www.intbau.org/essay5.htm.
3. See Tom G. Palmer, "Classical Liberalism and Civil Society: Definitions, History, and Relations," in *Civil Society and Government*, ed. Nancy Rosenblum and Robert Post (Princeton, NJ: Princeton University Press, 2002), pp. 48–78.

Chapter 13

1. *NAACP v. Alabama*, 357 U.S. 449 (1958).
2. *Id.*, p. 460.
3. *Id.*, pp. 460–63.
4. See Jonathan D. Wallace, "Nameless in Cyberspace: Anonymity on the Internet," Cato Institute Briefing Papers no. 54, December 8, 1999, p. 2, http://www.cato.org/pubs/briefs/bp54.pdf. *Cato's Letters* are the inspiration for the Cato Institute's name.
5. See Jonathan Turley, "Registering Publius: The Supreme Court and the Right to Anonymity," in *Cato Supreme Court Review*, 2001–2002, ed. James L. Swanson (Washington, DC: Cato Institute, 2002), pp. 57–83, http://www.cato.org/pubs/scr/docs/2002/turley.pdf.
6. Wallace, "Nameless in Cyberspace," p. 2.
7. *McIntyre v. Ohio Elections Comm'n*, 514 U.S. 334, 357 (1995).
8. See, e.g., *Talley v. California*, 362 U.S. 60 (1960).
9. 124 S. Ct. 2451 (2004).
10. *Id.*, p. 2459.
11. *Id.*, p. 2458.

Chapter 14

1. John H. Reese, *The Legal Nature of a Driver's License* (Washington, DC: Automotive Safety Foundation, 1965), pp. 35–36.
2. *Wignall v. Fletcher*, 303 N.Y. 435 (1952) ("A license to operate a motor vehicle is of tremendous value to the individual and may not be taken away except by due process").
3. James J. Flink, *America Adopts the Automobile, 1895–1910* (Cambridge, MA: MIT Press, 1970), p. 174.

4. U.S. Department of Transportation, Federal Highway Administration, Office of Highway Information Management, *Highway Statistics Summary to 1995*, Table DL-230, http://www.fhwa.dot.gov/ohim/summary95/.

5. James J. Flink, *America Adopts the Automobile*, pp. 174–75.

6. See *Highway Statistics Summary to 1995*, Table DL-230.

7. American Association of Motor Vehicle Administrators, *Minimum Driver License Examination Standards* (Washington, DC: AAMVA, 1939), p. 11.

8. American Association of Motor Vehicle Administrators, *Driver Improvement through Licensing Procedures* (Washington, DC: AAMVA, 1956), p. 18.

9. Department of Health, Education, and Welfare, *Report of the Secretary's Advisory Committee on Traffic Safety* (Washington, DC: DHEW, 1968).

10. See American Association of Motor Vehicle Administrators, *Personal Identification—AAMVA International Specification—DL/ID Card Design* (September 25, 2003), http://aamva.net/Documents/stdAAMVADLIDCardSpecs_092003.pdf.

Chapter 15

1. State of Connecticut, Executive Chambers, "Governor Rell Announces Findings of Audit of DMV Licensing Procedures: Efforts Already Under Way to Address Numerous Issues," news release, May 6, 2005, http://www.ct.gov/governorrell/cwp/view.asp?A = 1761&Q = 292550.

2. Auditors of Public Accounts, State of Connecticut, *Performance Audit of the Department of Motor Vehicles' Internal Controls over Drivers' Licenses and Identity Cards*, May 5, 2005, http://www.state.ct.us/apa/pdf2005/962006.pdf.

3. WTNH Television News, "News Channel 8 Investigation Results in Massive DMV Probe," November 7, 2004, http://www.wtnh.com/Global/story.asp?S = 2533237.

4. WSET.com, "DMV Fraud Prompts Va. to Suspend Hundreds of Licenses," December 21, 2004, http://www.wset.com/news/stories/1204/195751.html.

5. "DMV's Mass License Fraud Persists," *Orange County Register*, October 1, 2000, http://www.ocregister.com/features/dmv/dmv01001cci.shtml.

6. Center for Democracy and Technology, *Tracking Security at State Motor Vehicle Offices*, December 9, 2004, http://www.cdt.org/privacy/030131motorvehicle.shtml.

7. National Immigration Law Center, "State Driver's License Requirements," December 5, 2004, http://www.nilc.org/immspbs/DLs/state_dl_rqrmts_120504.pdf. Current resources and tables are maintained at http://www.nilc.org/immspbs/DLs/index.htm.

8. U.S. General Accounting Office, *Security: Vulnerabilities Found in Driver's License Applications Process*, GAO-03-989RNI, September 9, 2003.

9. U.S. General Accounting Office, *Social Security Numbers: Improved SSN Verification and Exchange of States' Driver Records Would Enhance Identity Verification*, GAO-03-920, September 2003, http://www.gao.gov/new.items/d03920.pdf.

10. See U.S. General Accounting Office, *Security: Counterfeit Identification and Identification Fraud Raise Security Concerns*, GAO-03-1147T, September 9, 2003, p. 6, http://www.gao.gov/new.items/d031147t.pdf.

11. U.S. General Accounting Office, *Social Security Numbers: Ensuring the Integrity of the SSN*, GAO-03-941T, July 10, 2003, http://www.gao.gov/new.items/d03941t.pdf.

12. "FY2006–FY2007 Biennium, Governor's Budget," Summary B-51, C-18, D-5, http://www.opm.state.ct.us/budget/2006-2007Books/2006-2007SummaryHome.htm.

13. "Swiping Back at Credit-Card Fraud," *BusinessWeek*, July 11, 2005, http://www.businessweek.com/magazine/content/05_28/b3942095_mz020.htm.

Chapter 16

1. Department of Motor Vehicles Director Ginny Lewis, "Statement on Donovan DMV Break-In," March 11, 2005, http://www.dmvnv.com/donovan_statement.htm.

Chapter 17

1. Merchants seem rarely to insist that their staffs check credit card signatures against the signatures of the people bearing them. Sometimes they do, though, and sometimes they also ask for a piece of identification. In most transactions, merchants bear the risk of loss if they do not have a matching signed receipt. That is their choice to make. Given the relatively low levels of credit card fraud, it is generally a time-wasting customer annoyance to compare card signatures against receipts too intensely, especially in small transactions, and the average store clerk is probably not very good at ferreting out forged signatures anyway. The credit card associations no longer require signatures for small-value transactions, typically of less than $25.

2. Notice that we call it an "authenticator" rather than an identifier. A credit card can be used to identify, the credit card systems identify users, and a credit card sale leaves behind identifiers, but the transaction itself is an authorization of payment to the merchant, not an identification of the credit card user to the merchant. Within the electronic payment system itself, there is no way to know who actually used the card—the cardholder, someone the cardholder permitted to use the card, or a fraudster using a stolen or counterfeit card.

3. Professor John C. Brigham was one of the most prolific researchers of this effect. See C. A. Meissner and J. C. Brigham, "Thirty Years of Investigating the Own-Race Bias in Memory for Faces: A Meta-Analytic Review," *Psychology, Public Policy, and the Law* 7 (2001): 3–35; A. E. Slone, J. C. Brigham, and C. A. Meissner, "Social and Cognitive Factors Affecting the Own-Race Bias in Whites," *Basic and Applied Social Psychology* 22 (2000): 71–84; R. K. Bothwell, J. C. Brigham, and R. S. Malpass, "Cross-Racial Identifications," *Personality and Social Psychology Bulletin* 15 (1989): 19–25.

Chapter 18

1. H.R. 151, 109th Cong. (2005).
2. H.R. 418, 109th Cong. (2005).
3. See John J. Miller and Stephen Moore, *A National ID System: Big Brother's Solution to Illegal Immigration* (Washington, DC: Cato Institute, September 7, 1995), http://www.cato.org/pubs/pas/pa237.html.
4. Pub. L. No. 109-13, § 202.
5. *Id.* at § 202(c).
6. *Id.* at § 202(c)(2)(B).
7. *Id.* at § 202(c)(2)(C).
8. *Id.* at § 202(d)(1), (2).
9. *Id.* at § 202(d)(3).
10. *Id.* at § 202(c)(3).
11. *Id.* at §202(d)(9).

12. *Id.* at § 202(c)(3)(C).
13. *Id.* at § 202(d)(5).
14. See Transportation Security Administration, Department of Homeland Security, "Privacy Act of 1974; Systems of Records: Secure Flight Test Records; Privacy Impact Assessment; Secure Flight Test Phase; Notice," *Federal Register* 70 (June 22, 2005): 36,319, http://a257.g.akamaitech.net/7/257/2422/01jan20051800/edocket. access.gpo.gov/2005/05-12405.htm.
15. Pub. L. No. 109-13, § 202(d)(13).
16. *Id.* at § 202(d)(8).
17. *Id.* at § 202(b)(8).
18. *Id.* at § 202(d)(7).
19. *Id.* at § 202(b)(9).

Chapter 19

1. See Intel Corporation, "A Prediction Made Real Improves Billions of Lives," http://www.intel.com/technology/silicon/mooreslaw/index.htm.
2. This is known as Kryder's law. See http://en.wikipedia.org/wiki/Kryder percent27s_law.
3. Progressive Insurance, "TripSense," webpage, https://tripsense.progressive. com/home.aspx.
4. Some people go to extraordinary lengths to avoid identification and information sharing. See J. J. Luna, *How to Be Invisible* (New York: Thomas Dunne Books, 2004).

Chapter 20

1. http://www.aclu.org/pizza/.
2. 15 U.S.C., § 1681 *et seq.*
3. Pub. L. No. 107-56, §§ 358(g), 505(c).
4. See, for example, Farhad Manjoo, "Acxiom Is Watching You," *Salon.com*, February 10, 2004, http://www.salon.com/tech/feature/2004/02/10/acxiom/index_np. html.

Chapter 21

1. Essop Pahad, "The Development of Indian Political Movements in South Africa, 1924–1946" (PhD diss., University of Sussex, July 1972) chap. 1, sec. 3, http:// www.sahistory.org.za/pages/sources/pahad_thesis/chapter1c.htm.
2. This illustration comes from Calvin Kytle, *Gandhi: Soldier of Nonviolence: An Introduction* (Santa Ana, CA: Seven Lock Press, 1982) excerpted in Carl Watner with Wendy McElroy, eds., *National Identification Systems: Essays in Opposition* (Jefferson, NC: McFarand & Co., 2004). The latter book also provided the examples that follow, of the Soviet *propiska* system, from Stephane Courtois et al., *The Black Book of Communism* (Cambridge, MA: Harvard University Press, 1999), and Holland's population register system, from Bob Moore, *Victims and Survivors: The Nazi Persecution of the Jews in the Netherlands 1940–1945* (London: Arnold, 1997).
3. See Jim Fussell, "Indangamuntu 1994: Ten Years Ago in Rwanda This Identity Card Cost a Woman Her Life," http://www.preventgenocide.org/edu/pastgenocides/ rwanda/indangamuntu.htm; Jim Fussell, "Group Classification on National ID Cards as a Factor in Genocide and Ethnic Cleansing," November 15, 2001, http://www. preventgenocide.org/prevent/removing-facilitating-factors/IDcards/.

4. Assassination Archives and Research Center, "Church Committee Reports," http://www.aarclibrary.org/publib/church/reports/contents.htm.

5. Simson Garfinkel, "Nobody Fucks with the DMV," *Wired Magazine*, February 1994, http://www.wired.com/wired/archive/2.02/dmv.html.

6. Amitai Etzioni, *The Limits of Privacy* (New York: Basic Books, 1999), p. 126.

Chapter 22

1. Pub. L. No. 105-318.

2. See 18 U.S.C., § 1028(a)(7).

3. Synovate, "Federal Trade Commission—Identity Theft Survey Report," September 2003, http://www.ftc.gov/os/2003/09/synovatereport.pdf.

4. S. 116 (109th Cong.) (2005); H.R. 1745 (109th Cong.) (2005); H.R. 1078 (109th Cong.) (2005); S. 29 (109th Cong.).

5. S. 116 (109th Cong.); S. 29 (109th Cong.) (2005).

6. H.R. 82 (109th Cong.) (2005).

7. See generally Social Security Administration, "Social Security Numbers: Social Security Number Chronology," http://www.ssa.gov/history/ssn/ssnchron.html.

8. See Evan Hendricks, *Credit Scores and Credit Reports: How the System Really Works, What You Can Do* (Cabin John, MD: Privacy Times, 2004), pp. 157 *et seq.*

9. Pub. L. No. 100-485, § 125.

10. Pub. L. No. 104-188, § 1615.

11. Modest proposals to begin this process have been introduced in Congress. H.R. 92 (Frelinghuysen) in the 109th Congress would have permitted people to use an alternative to the Social Security number for administration of their Medicare benefits. H.R. 220 (Paul) would have done a number of things to prevent uniform federal numbering of citizens.

Chapter 23

1. The National Commission on Terrorist Attacks upon the United States, *The 9/11 Commission Report* (2004), p. 13, http://www.9-11commission.gov/report/911Report.pdf.

2. More than four years after 9/11, the Transportation Security Administration finally eased restrictions on carrying small tools and scissors onboard aircraft, items that were useful only for the essentially defunct commandeering threat. See Transportation Security Administration, Department of Homeland Security, "TSA Unveils Enhanced Security Screening Procedures and Changes to the Prohibited Items List," December 2, 2005, news release, http://www.tsa.gov/public/display?theme=44&content=090005198018c27e.

3. Joseph W. Eaton, *The Privacy Card: A Low-Cost Strategy to Combat Terrorism* (Lanham, MD: Rowman & Littlefield, 2003).

4. Amitai Etzioni, *The Limits of Privacy* (New York: Basic Books, 1999), pp. 103–37.

5. David Frum and Richard Perle, *An End to Evil: How to Win the War on Terrorism* (New York: Ballantine Books, 2003), p. 58.

6. "How to Increase Liberty in America: Ten Suggestions," *National Review*, December 19, 2005.

7. See Shane Ham and Robert D. Atkinson, "Using Technology to Detect and Prevent Terrorism," January 2002, http://www.ppionline.org/ppi_ci.cfm?knlgAreaID=140&subsecID=900017&contentID=250070; Shane Ham and Robert D.

Atkinson, "Modernizing the State Identification System: An Action Agenda," February 2002, http://www.ppionline.org/ppi_ci.cfm?knlgAreaID=140&subsecid=290&contentid=250175.

8. PPI has at once advocated for a national identity card and denied that it is doing so. Compare Shane Ham, "Winning with Technology," *Blueprint Magazine*, January 16, 2002, http://www.ppionline.org/ppi_ci.cfm?knlgAreaID=140&subsecID=900017&contentID=250070 ("We need a national identity card. . . .") with Shane Ham and Robert D. Atkinson, "Frequently Asked Questions About Smart ID Cards," http://www.ppionline.org/ppi_ci.cfm?knlgAreaID=140&subsecID=900017&contentID=250075 ("Is PPI proposing a 'national' ID card? No.").

9. PBS *Frontline*, "McVeigh Chronology," undated, http://www.pbs.org/wgbh/pages/frontline/documents/mcveigh/.

10. Of the 19 hijackers, 18 acquired state-issued identification documents. *The 9/11 Commission Report* says that "some" cards were acquired by fraud, but does not say how many, which ones, or by what method. *The 9/11 Commission Report*, p. 390.

11. *Id.*, p. 237.

12. See, for example, *id.*, p. 169.

13. Robert Pape, *Dying to Win: The Strategic Logic of Suicide Terrorism* (New York: Random House, 2005), p. 5.

14. Pub. L. No. 107-71, § 101.

15. *The 9/11 Commission Report*, p. 390.

16. Markle Foundation Task Force on National Security in the Information Age, *Creating a Trusted Information Network for Homeland Security* (New York: Markle Foundation, 2003), p. 42.

17. Privacy International, *Mistaken Identity; Exploring the Relationship between National Identity Cards and the Prevention of Terrorism*, April 2004, http://www.privacyinternational.org/issues/idcard/uk/id-terrorism.pdf.

18. According to the National Highway Transportation Safety Administration, 42,636 people lost their lives in car accidents in 2004, an average of about 117 a day. Department of Transportation, National Highway Transportation Safety Administration, *Traffic Safety Facts 2004*, early ed., p. 85, http://wwwnrd.nhtsa.dot.gov/pdf/nrd-30/NCSA/TSFAnn/TSF2004EE.pdf.

19. *The 9/11 Commission Report*, p. 344.

20. *Id.*, p. 85.

21. *Id.*, pp. 344–45.

22. *Id.*, p. 539, fn. 85.

23. See "Homeland Security Presidential Directive/Hspd-6," September 16, 2003, http://www.whitehouse.gov/news/releases/2003/09/20030916-5.html.

24. Samidh Chakrabarti and Aaron Strauss, "Carnival Booth: An Algorithm for Defeating the Computer-Assisted Passenger Screening System," May 16, 2002, http://www.swiss.ai.mit.edu/6805/student-papers/spring02-papers/caps.htm.

25. *The 9/11 Commission Report*, p. 234.

26. The term "security theater" comes from Bruce Schneier, *Beyond Fear* (New York: Copernicus Books, 2003), pp. 38–40.

27. An archived version of the Total Information Awareness website, including a description of the program can be found at http://web.archive.org/web/20020921161341/www.darpa.mil/iao/TIASystems.htm.

28. Pub. L. No. 108-87, § 8131.

29. Government Accountability Office, *Data Mining: Federal Efforts Cover a Wide Range of Uses* (Washington, DC: GAO, 2004).

Chapter 25

1. 5 U.S.C., § 552a(e)(4).
2. Verified Identity Pass, "Clear privacy policy," http://www.flyclear.com/privacy_fairinfo.html.
3. "Privacy Act Notice," *Federal Register* 69 (June 1, 2004): 30,948.
4. Steven Brill, *After* (New York: Simon and Schuster, 2003).

Index

Page references followed by f or b denote figures or boxed text, respectively.

265

About the Author

Jim Harper is director of information policy studies at the Cato Institute. He focuses on adapting law and policy to the unique problems of the information age. Harper is also a member of the Department of Homeland Security's Data Privacy and Integrity Advisory Committee. His work has been cited by *USA Today*, the Associated Press, and Reuters, and he has appeared on Fox News Channel, CBS, and MSNBC. His scholarly articles have appeared in the *Administrative Law Review*, the *Minnesota Law Review*, and the *Hastings Constitutional Law Quarterly*. Harper is the editor of *Privacilla.org*, a Web-based think tank devoted exclusively to privacy, and he maintains federal spending website *WashingtonWatch.com*. He holds a J.D. from Hastings College of the Law.